ENDORSEMENT PAGE

From interviews and reviews of the book neutralizing the power of Fear that has emerged this book. Here is what was said:

"Dr. Henry's work is extensive and excellent. I know of no other book that so clearly and completely communicates such a necessary body of knowledge on the subject of fear—a relevant issue with appropriate solutions that individuals and institutions need for today."

—Dr. John Beeson, Ph.D.,
Former President of Southwest Bible College & Seminary

"A very thought-provoking book with insightful applications for the human spirit. A must-read for every person as they all struggle with life's issues."

—Sheila K. Horsley', M.D., M.PH.,
Family Practitioner, Ft. Worth, Texas

"Dr. Henry presents a unique way of understanding fear from both a spiritual and psychological perspective."

—Jesse C. Ingram, Ph.D.,
Licensed Psychologist,
Diplomate of the American Academy of Pain Management

"This is solid stuff. I've read several books on health, including alternative and traditional medicine guides, and most agree these are key elements to a healthful life. Dr. Henry goes a step further and argues these steps also will help produce a fear-free life."

—Emory Daniels, author

"From spiders to intimacy, blood to toads and tombstones, there is an official name for the phobia. [Avoiding the Fear Trap] is quite thorough and full of valuable information. It is meant to show readers how to subdue your fears and make them harmless. Squash that spider fear and put your mind at ease."

—Heather Froeschl,
BookIdeas.com, Callaway, Virginia

"Dr. Henry was certainly a breath of fresh air, as he of knows how to translate his message into a form any audience can understand."

—Dr. Rus D. Jeffrey, News Director/
I dye dine Talk Show Host, 1420 WACK—
www.142owack.com, Newark, New York

"The book has groundbreaking information."

—The Late Dr. L. Alex Swan, Ph.D., CCS, Dpl. Psych.,
Former Sociology Professor and Chairman of the
Faculty/Senate of Texas Southern University

AVOIDING THE
FEAR
TRAP

LEARNING TO NEUTRALIZE AND
OVERCOME THE POWER OF FEAR

DR. CASALNNIE O. HENRY

To order additional copies of this book, contact:
Bookwhip
1-855-339-3589
https://www.bookwhip.com

CONTENTS

DEDICATION

To my beloved wife, Beverly, who has been so supportive and understanding, enduring the periods of separation while I spent countless hours at various libraries.

To my wonderful children—Casalnnie Henry Jr.; Lorraine and her husband, Gabriel; Jennifer, and her husband, Lester, for their encouragement and support.

Most of all, I thank God the Almighty for giving me health and the ability to achieve my goal of successfully completing this endeavor.

ACKNOWLEDGMENTS

I am deeply indebted to Dr. Jane Konditi, former academic dean at Northwood University, Cedar I Hill, Texas, for arranging the distribution and collection of my 2001 survey and for her timely suggestions; Mike Chrietzberg, former principal of Duncanville High School, who administered the survey to his students; The late Dr. Harold Reents, former academic dean at Christ for the Nations, who administered the survey to his students; and, finally, to Dr. Eunice Warfield for administering the survey at her teachers' workshop to teachers from live states in the Southwest Region Conference. I also thank the participants who made the data possible; Dr. Theodore Brown and Mrs. Yvonne Collins for their encouragement; Ms. Elaine T. Patrick, former adult services librarian at the Duncanville branch for her assistance; The late Dr. Alex Swan, psychotherapist, for the foreword; and Dr. Janice Pettis, practitioner, for her counsel and suggestions

FOREWORD

This work by Casal O. Henry attempts to address the issues related to the power of fear, the way to avoid the fear trap, and the way to neutralize it so that a path to hope and happiness may be discovered and pursued. What we must first understand is that there is nothing implicit in or endemic to situations, events, or other objects of fear that lead to our labeling them as frightening. However, we do know that people see things differently and experience them in different ways. That is the reason one discovers differentials among those involved in the observation and interpretation of any particular event. We can, therefore, make choices that lead to happiness and hope by being in the present and facing life's realities with a positive attitude, which weakens the potential for negative thoughts and emotions. Another concept that provides perspective is that the past is significant only to the extent that it is affecting one in the present. There is, however, no question that fear is a powerful emotion and, once embraced, needs to be neutralized for hope and happiness to be realized.

This book is written for Christians as well as non-Christians. You do not even have to be religious to embrace many of the concepts of this book. The principles articulated in this work are so profound and all encompassing that anyone can apply them to achieve a better quality of spiritual, psychological, and physical life. With this valuable resource, if you begin to experience fear, you can activate the concepts to overcome or neutralize the effect of that fear.

There are a variety of sources or situations that induce fear. These sources or situations should be identified and explained in order to have effective intervention. The decision to change belongs to each individual and only to that individual. Nothing external or internal, except the individual's will, can determine the thoughts and behavior of that person. Consequently, the individual has the ability to interpret situations and sources and assign meanings that do not engender fear. Interpretation and thought are intertwined. The disposition of the mind determines the thought patterns, and thoughts translate into behavior through interpretation. No thought exists without interpretation, and there can be no interpretation without thought. The fact that the functional brain and source of thought are from the Creator does not preclude the brain's functional independence to accept or reject what it thinks or interprets.

The individual's ability to make choices determines the functionality of things internal and the impact of things external to the individual, including the Creator. "Choose you this day" (Joshua 24:15). "Behold I stand at the door and knock" (Revelation 3:20); these are evidence of the independence—not absolute but functional independence—of a person's ability to think, choose, and interpret situations and sources that can induce fear. Not only can one choose to ignore or not act upon his or her generated feelings, but one can choose not to feel the expected feelings. The individual is empowered with the choice and the ability to interpret situations, events, occurrences, circumstances, and outcomes in such a way that fear is not a reality and not present. Thought is the outcome of choice, the ability to access, define, designate, and assign meaning to persons, situations, events, occurrences, and settings for the purpose of deciding how to act and behave. This is what separates human beings from animals.

We are admonished in Scripture not to be afraid because God has not given us the "spirit of fear" (2 Timothy 1:7). Many times, Jesus told his followers—those close to him and those who followed from afar—not to be afraid.

The encounter with fear is graphically depicted in the lives of men and women in the Old Testament as well. The Bible speaks of a famine in Israel and how a widow told the prophet Elijah that she and her son were preparing to eat the last drop of meal she had in her pantry and then die (I Kings 17:12). Elijah said to the woman, "Do not be afraid, do what you said you were going to do, but when you make the meal, serve me first" (I Kings 17:13). The woman had already told him that the meal would be her last because she had no more; to give it to him instead of eating it herself and sharing it with her boy meant that their deaths were still certain but would be quicker. She feared death because there was a famine in the land.

This woman's obedience was crucial to Elijah's prophetic career. In verse 14, Elijah informs the woman that what he was instructing her to do came from the God of Israel. Then he added, "The barrel of meal shall not waste [be used up] neither shall the curse of oil fail [run dry] until the day that the Lord sends rain upon the earth" (1 Kings 17:14). The woman now had a basis for not being afraid of the outcome of her obedience, and she could act as though what she hoped for was already a reality. It is evident that she overcame her fear with faith because she did what the prophet told her to do (1 Kings 17:15). If at this point she had clung to her fear, she would be embracing the acronym FEAR, which stands for "false evidence appearing real."

It has always been my position in examining and seeking to explain human occurrences and human behavior to complement my psychology and social thinking with Scripture. I trust the principles therein with more certainty than the explanatory principles of these secular disciplines. Elijah had to depend on this woman overcoming her fear because he also was affected by his own prophecy about the drought. She did not realize it at the time, but her life and that of her son rested on her overcoming her fear. Overcoming her fear was related to her obeying the instructions of the prophet. Overcoming her fear meant that she would obey the prophet's word and trusts it to come true.

The fact that the woman mentioned in this biblical narrative faithfully obeyed the instructions of Elijah and trusted in the God of Elijah is evidence that she overcame her fear and was therefore sustained through the drought that was in the land. For me, trusting and obeying God is the way to neutralize whatever fears we have, even the fear of death. Whatever he says, he will do. Whatever he promises, he will bring to pass. Reliance upon these promises is the sure "path to hope and happiness" (Henry 2007).

L. Alex Swan, Ph.D., CCS, Dpl. Psych.

INTRODUCTION

A s we approached the twenty-first century, the dawn of the third millennium AD, the world was permeated with great anxiety as to what lay in wait. Residents of the global community showed in so many ways the extent to which humankind tries to mask the tumultuous fear that has been bubbling in the deep recesses of the heart for many decades. For example, internationally concerted efforts to establish multinational coalitions and to achieve religious cooperation toward global governance show that people's fears now have a planetary context.

Even though many hoped peace and safety would result from better global governance, the reality is that much fear prevailed: fear that our world would erupt in deadly flames of tribal wars within national boundaries; fear that hunger and starvation would overtake poorer countries; fear that environmental disasters would devastate the very few pristine, idyllic land reserves left on this continent and elsewhere; and fear of the real probability that without global assistance in the Middle East, the entire region could become a raging inferno.

Christians who consider themselves students of biblical prophecies felt that the realization of those fears would indicate the imminence of Jesus's return. Others, however, felt differently about those events. I was intrigued by expressions of fear about the future made by government leaders, corporate entities, educational institutions, religious organizations, and individuals. Everyone sought solutions, but the fear of what the future held did not dissipate because no obvious panacea could be found. People appeared to resign themselves to coping with fear because it just would not or could not go away. I wrote this book to offer ideas about how to neutralize fear since it cannot be destroyed. We can do more than just cope. We have the assurance from a greater source that "perfect love casteth out fear" (I John 4:18). If fear is kept outside, it has no power over anyone.

Finally, there is at least one fear that is not debilitating. Humanity is admonished by the Bible to fear God and revere him as greater than all else. God's attributes and vastness are beyond human comprehension; there is none that can vie with him. Hence, we must realize that we should not be so foolhardy as to set ourselves in opposition to his demands.

I wrote this book after observing the tension that people experience due to fears within and around them. Many people seem to act solely out of fear. This was especially true as the year 2000 drew near. Almost everyone appeared jittery, and I saw a need for an explanation that could weaken the power that fear has over the human race. Individual fears have been discussed by some in the mental health profession and by authors of textbooks, but this book offers a way to weaken or destroy fear's power—to neutralize not a specific fear but any fear.

For example, if one is in pain, it does not matter whether the pain originates in the foot, hand, head, from an internal injury or a burn; the person in pain needs a painkiller to block the brain from sensing the pain and causing discomfort. So it is with the power of fear. The cause of our fears is less important than our need to know how to short-circuit the power those fears have over us and make them less dominant in our lives. How can this be done? This book provides an answer to that question. By applying biblical wisdom and the techniques of Christian counseling, individuals can gain peace and tranquility in their lives, and entire organizations, large groups—even society as a whole—can lessen tensions and conquer fear itself.

Throughout the book, I refer to Christian principles and Scripture. In particular, this book can be an excellent resource for Christian counselors, for laypeople seeking to lessen the grasp that fear has on them, and for businesses and organizations that see the Christian antidote to fear as a way to transform their workplaces or groups. However, people of any religious persuasion—or no religious persuasion—can find truth in the solutions offered by this book.

CHAPTER 1

HOW FEAR AND VITAMIN DEFICIENCIES AFFECT THE BRAIN

One morning in the spring of 1964, my classmates and I went on a field trip to a destination in St. Andrew, Jamaica. I believe it was called Black River. It was a beautiful morning, and the sun was in its usual form. Although it was rumored that there were alligators in that area, many of my classmates proceeded to swim in and across the river. I watched as they dove in one by one. Everything seemed okay, so when my turn came, I dove in and swam across.

On my way back, however, I dove in and came up in an almost vertical position, as opposed to a more advantageous horizontal position. The difference between those two positions in a river with undercurrent is that unless you are a very good swimmer, you could find yourself unable to swim while upright; instead, you would only be treading water, which could tire you in a short time. That is what happened to me.

When I realized my predicament, I almost panicked. My brain was telling me that my body was getting tired and that I needed help. However, my emotional response was to not let anyone know of my situation because the guys might laugh or view me as weak, which is a horrendous feeling for a teenager. My feelings dominated my better judgment and would not allow me to call for help while I was literally

1

fighting for my life. My brain was telling in, that my arms and legs were getting tired, but I would not listen. Providentially, one of the boys either saw that I was in trouble or just wandered over inadvertently. He pushed me, and I was able to swim to shore. As I regained my bearings, I wondered why I'd allowed my emotion to override what my brain was telling me to do.

In retrospect, I discovered that one fear can trump another. In other words, if a person who is fearful of heights is in a building that is on fire, he may jump out of that building and die from the fall rather than remain inside and die from the fire. In essence, the fear of falling is trumped by the fear of being burned. Our daily life decisions, while complex, are usually nowhere near that extreme. Nevertheless, some of the decisions we make could prove very costly—and even fatal.

At this moment, you may be experiencing some form of fear. This fear may be associated with certain family or social issues or employment issues, such as what the future holds for you or your company. Or you may be fearful about the direction in which your government is taking the country. Perhaps you wonder, How did I become so fearful? Am I the only one having these fearful thoughts? Where did fear originate? It is my hope that as you read through the pages of this book, you will find the answers to your questions or at least discover a new approach to resolving such issues.

Interestingly, we cannot resist fear on our own because our thoughts are aided or inspired by one of the two supernatural powers—God or Satan—that exist in the universe. We need an external force to combat the problem. The choice between these two supernatural powers must be made wisely because the problem of fear is a part of a larger problem: sin. The choice we make will lead either to everlasting joy or eternal catastrophe.

What Is Fear?

The word fear, or the concept of being fearful, deserves clarification. Everyone accepts the idea that fear exists. But understanding fear means acknowledging that evil exists. Whatever a person thinks is desirable for the self or for others is what that person considers "good." But good, whatever we may think it to be, implies the existence of evil, or that which is bad. Evil is a spoiler that denies us the good we desire; therefore, we despise evil and seek the good. We will not explore the question of the origin of evil in this book, but avoidance of evil is connected with fear.

There are three types of fears. The first type pertains to excess worrying over situations that may never occur, the second pertains to a present perceived danger, and the third pertains to future events that will occur. Regardless of the type of fear, they are caused by negative thoughts. Yet positive thoughts about certain dangerous situations, as in the following scenario, may not change the outcome, but neither will negative thoughts unless appropriate action is taken to avoid or minimize the danger.

For example, a man in the forest sees a bear. If he believed that petting the bear is a good thing and he wanted to do so, he would—without hesitating or having any negative thoughts—walk up to the bear and attempt to pet it. He would be devoured by the bear and die having thought all along that walking up to the bear and petting it was good for him. If he could then resurrect himself from the grave and obtain the foreknowledge that he would be killed by the bear—a negative thought but a true one—then that negative thought would motivate him to flee for his life, and he would be saved. In this case, a negative thought about the situation actually reflects a real fear, as opposed to anxiousness about a situation that might never occur.

A counterexample of unnecessary anxiety is an individual in his living room in New York City worrying about a mountain lion breaking into his house and mauling him to death. Let's say he imagines this scenario after having seen a similar situation in a movie on television. Needless to say, this possibility is very unlikely.

The third type of fear concerns dangers that are real but in the distant future. In Luke 21:26, Jesus speaks of "men's hearts failing them for fear, and for looking after those things which are coming on the earth." Perhaps Jesus meant that some people who would suffer from heart problems in the last days would suffer because of fearfulness about future events. This fear could include heart attacks caused not only by cholesterol-related situations due to diet or heredity, as some may suggest, but also because of the lifestyle they have chosen, which results in their anticipation of the day of eternal damnation for the wicked. These future events would not actually be witnessed by the individuals but would impact them as though they were occurring. In other words, although the events are real, they are not necessarily imminent. This gives rise to the question: Is the brain playing tricks on us, or is there more to the brain and thought process? Let us explore the brain chemistry and fear and how they play out in the individual.

Brain Chemistry and Fear

Contemporary psychologists such as Dr. Archibald Hart believe that high adrenaline output on a constant basis depletes the brain's natural tranquilizers and causes anxiety and even panic attacks. Other causes of fear could include heredity, biological conditions, or overreaction to normal bodily sensations (Hart 1999, 55, 143-44). Bipolar depression and schizophrenia may also be factors.

However, some fears are connected with the way messages are transmitted from cell to cell in the brain based on our nutritional intake, which provides vital substances. For example, Dr. Hart says that there are some substances that "aggravate anxiety" and recommends avoidance of those foods and eating of foods that provide your "entire mineral and vitamin needs naturally. [Some foods, he suggests, affect] your brain's neurotransmitters in a harmful way. [Thus, he goes on to recommend a vegetarian diet]." (Hart 1999,103-105). A 2005 News-Medica.Net report indicates that the neurotransmitters (chemicals released from one nerve cell that send an impulse to another nerve cell) in the brain move messages from one cell to another. Due to an increase or decrease of vital substances in the brain, the communication provides a condition for different emotional responses, including fear (July 18, 2005, under "Nerve cells can also release neurotransmitters outside of synapses").

According to Nancy Schimelfening on the Web site About.com: Depression, deficiencies in vitamin B (thiamine) will cause the brain to run out of energy, because the brain uses it to "convert glucose or blood sugar into energy. This can lead to fatigue, depression, irritability, anxiety and even thoughts of suicide. Deficiencies can also cause memory problems, loss of appetite, insomnia, and gastrointestinal disorders." Schimelfening also notes that deficiency in vitamin B can cause pernicious anemia. "This disorder can cause mood swings, paranoia, irritability, confusion, dementia, hallucinations, or mania, followed by appetite loss, dizziness, weakness, shortage of breath, heart palpitations, diarrhea, and tingling sensations in the extremities" (Schimelfening 2006, under "Vitamin for Depression?").

These deficiencies inhibit one's ability to think properly. Women are told by their doctors and various publications that deficiencies in the B-complex vitamins can cause birth defects, cholesterol problems, and even loss of libido, or sex drive. These situations create stresses and various kinds of fears in some women so that they are unable to function at their optimum. Proper nutrition is one of the keys to health and happiness. Other debilitating fears may come from irrational thought patterns that result from stress, prior experiences, or distorted perceptions of life. These irrational thoughts must be countered with a therapy that helps to generate rationally and morally acceptable thought patterns. Thus, fear in people who are not clinically mentally ill may be addressed psychologically, using therapy that includes lifestyle adjustment.

The human brain has the ability not only to generate thoughts but also to be aware of the nature of those thoughts and to exercise willpower to accept, reject, and act or not act upon those thoughts. This ability cannot be fathomed by human study. Why? The source of that ability is external, not internal. It was given to the brain by its designer and not produced by the brain. For example, from a biblical perspective, God initiated the brain function when he breathed life into the lump of clay and it became the living, functioning person, Adam (Genesis 2:7). God also gave humans the ability not just to think but to be able to organize thoughts, make distinctions between thoughts, and separate the good from evil (Romans 12:3).

The Brain, Conscience and Therapy

So far we have discovered that God has given the brain the capacity to think (intellect). However, we need to dig a little deeper to determine what goes on with this thought process. God does not force us to think one way or the other. He only encourages us to think the way he knows is best for us because our thoughts lead to actions and consistent and persistent thought patterns lead to habits which form character.

This ability that God gave to the brain to think, can be weakened or strengthened depending on what is fed to the brain and how we exercise the ability to think; or whether a certain degree of psychological abuse has been experienced. For example, if we injest alcohol on a continuing basis, it destroys brain cells; so does illicit use or abuse of drugs, etc. Foods that do not provide proper nutrition also weaken the ability to think properly and rationally and comprehend complex issues. This is one reason children become lethargic and are unable to function well at school. The brain also needs to be exercised to keep it alert and in good condition.

A very important part of this discussion that I do not want you to miss is the decision-making process of the mind and its responses to those decisions (resulting emotions). God does not appeal to or ask us for our hands, feet, or any other organ of our body to do anything for him. He appeals to our minds–the seat of intelligence–the cognitive aspect of our being—the ability he gave us to think and make decisions. That's what he wants to control.

Our ability to generate thoughts, categorize those thoughts, be aware of the nature of those thoughts, what kind of feelings (moods) to express relative to those thoughts, how to decide on which thoughts to entertain, how and when to decide on which thoughts to act upon and what kind of actions to take; how to feel about the actions taken, how to decide on the level of satisfaction of those actions, and finally; whether you would do things the same way you just did them; that is your conscience—whether your mind can be at peace (feeling good) with what you have done. Otherwise, you feel remorseful and uncomfortable (your conscience is bothering you). You may become moody and depressive and have to talk to God or someone about what you have done and how you feel about it. It could be said that your mind or your conscience is bothering you.

All those exercises that the mind went through were based upon the ability to receive and process information obtained through the senses (seeing, hearing, smelling, tasting, feeling) or through direct communication from a source greater than humanity–God or Satan, depending on which one you allow to control your thought process. God gave you the ability to think but he does not force you to choose him to control that ability. Nevertheless, he encourages you to allow him to control it because he knows that if you do, you will have special protection from him and help in dealing with your problems. And in the end, good things will happen to you–you will have eternal life. However, if you do not allow him to control your mind, bad things will happen to you. The sinister forces of evil will take over, fear will rule your life and in the end, eternal damnation will be the result.

The Bible further shows that God can and does increase an individual's intelligence and understanding (1 Kings 3:11-12). He can take away the intelligence or understanding (Daniel 4:31-33) if he chooses and put it in an entity of his choice (Daniel 4:34 and Numbers 22:28-30).This is a quantum leap from the physical to an abstract dimension. The concept of creating intelligence in an inanimate object so it will function as a person is of such interest that the scientific realm has been vigorously engaged in artificial intelligence research. Researchers with the use of supercomputers are trying to perfect that endeavor with the use of robots, for example, so that the object will think like a human and even simulate moods.

In the realm of humanity, however, thoughts transcend moods. A person may be in a "bad mood" because of some chemical imbalance in the brain. Nevertheless, that person can decide to ignore the way he feels by deliberately choosing to invoice certain principles that enable him to be nice to others despite a temptation to act otherwise. Thoughts can also create moods. Bad thoughts can produce bad moods; good thoughts can produce good moods. And thoughts can counteract one another. A good thought can not only override a bad mood but also can dispel or replace a bad thought. Hence, a brain's activity, though physical in nature, can be governed. Unless some significant and permanent physical damage prevents rational thinking, thoughts, not moods, rule. Many fears originate in the mind and are the result of negative thinking.

In addressing the issue of secular psychotherapeutically approach to the mental and emotional healing and wellness of humanity, I give kudos and accolades, for the most part, to the practitioners. Why? They have identified the major portion of the problem, that is, that the problem relates to the mind. This gives rise to questions such as: Why is the person thinking the way he is thinking? Why is there so much anxiety, fear, or phobia in the person's life? The clinician is aware that fear is a negative feeling about someone or something that makes people feel they will be harmed by close contact with it. If they are forced to make contact, they do so with great hesitation and stress.

However, a phobia is a fear that has taken on a more intense degree of trepidation to the extent that it affects the person's behavior or normal lifestyle. There is a psychological paralysis that makes the individual refrain from engaging in things that would normally be desirable. With this in mind, the obvious question is: How can this problem be fixed? Then the practitioners do their best to fix the situation the way they know how. The only problem is that the application of a secular solution is like a tourniquet on an arm with a severed artery. It's only a temporary fix until you get to the hospital, where a physician can properly attend to the wound.

The most reliable solution is a spiritual psychotherapy used in Christian counseling that has a biblically based foundation such as Spiritual Euphoric Therapy (SET). SET is not a pseudoscientific approach to mental healing and wellness. It is the path to real healing and permanent mental wellness. It also addresses all aspects of human life—social, physical, mental, emotional, financial, and so on—and it provides the formula for physical and emotional wellness.

Categories of Fear and the Psychology of Christian Counseling

In this book, we refer to concerns, anxieties, fears, and phobias. Concern generally means the perception that certain negative experiences will occur if certain things happen or certain issues are raised. Concern is not a constant feeling that plagues the mind. It is experienced or expressed only when a specific subject matter comes up.

Anxiety is the needless worry over future events that may or may not occur. Concerns may develop into anxieties. Anxieties can be so intense that they become fears and phobias. Therefore, these terms often overlap.

Fear is a negative emotional response to stimuli, internal or external, that cause a person to desire to be away from a situation or a place where that negative emotion can be experienced. Such a fear can become a pervasive, obsessive, and compulsive phobia. For example, one may be claustrophobic, or fearful of being in a confined place, such as a crowd. Agoraphobic people feel they may be trampled, or they have a suffocating feeling in confined spaces. The fear might relate more to the experience that results from being in the crowd rather than the crowd itself.

If not dispelled or neutralized, fear will dominate a person's life. Little distinction, if any, needs to be made between those fears and phobias because fear is the essence of a phobia. The degree of fear a person possesses is not at issue; what matters is the presence of fear.

Psychology involves the study of the mind, which is a function of the brain, and how one can affect it. Its real purpose is to understand how people think and why and to help them maintain or achieve a balance when they are off center or when things go awry in their lives. Many benefits may accrue to individuals who accept help from contemporary secular psychology (although in many cases there may be too much bonding, dependency, long-term attachments, and so on). This book's approach to neutralizing fear, however, emphasizes a holistic approach to treatment of the patient or counselee through Christian counseling psychology. The permanence of its principles is inherent in its applications. Any apparent conflicting views between secular and Christian counseling should be evaluated in context. Spiritual counseling includes certain concepts that are also used by secular psychology, although contemporary secular psychology does not always include the spiritual dimension in its therapeutic approach.

Let us discuss this distinction a bit further. Normal, natural brain function is a phenomenon that involves maintenance, depletion, and restoration of vital chemicals. The human brain, in its imperfection, produces highs and lows according to the increase, decrease, and restoration of those chemicals, which are transmitted from brain cell to brain cell. However, even if a person's brain had perfect physiological function, it would still be only a thinking entity. When French philosopher Rene Descartes wrote "I think; therefore I am," he discounted much of human spiritual experience. Thinking alone is insufficient and can solve neither the ills of the mind nor the problems of society. Without thoughts, solutions cannot be obtained; however, if one only thinks and never exercises the decision-making ability to act upon those thoughts, the thoughts, for all practical purposes, would become meaningless. One would merely be a thinking entity; that's all.

Humans, however, are not merely thinking entities. We also have the ability to distinguish between good thoughts and bad thoughts. Moreover, we have a decision-making capacity—the ability to choose between conflicting thoughts. In the Christian approach to counseling, this ability to choose is understood as a gift from God, who established a paradigm of right and wrong. This approach recognizes that some choices are so difficult that determining the right choice is beyond human ability.

For this reason, people seek solutions from outside themselves. In fact, they seek a divine connection. Christians know that truly "it is not in man that walketh to direct his steps" (Jeremiah 10:23). That is the reason people seek to worship something or someone greater than themselves. Thus, in moments of anxiety, fear, or desperation, people tend to call on God or the entity that they believe has greater power than themselves to provide the help they need or the solutions to their problems.

Fear and the Genesis of Creation

Fear has existed since the early stages of life on this planet. From a creationist perspective, the first recorded interaction of human beings found in the Bible was between Adam and Eve. In all my research, I have not seen any record of an individual who evolved and communicated the experience of the evolution process to other humans, explained what life was like as a subhuman, or produced documentation of his or her genealogical profile as progenitors of the human race. We must then start at the beginning and discover the origin and nature of the problem with which we find ourselves grappling: the problem of fear. It is interesting to note that those who espouse the theory of evolution (i.e., that life came as a result of the big bang, that man evolved from the amoeba, or that cavemen preceded Adam and Eve) have great difficulty explaining origins. Where did the first speck come from, the one that accumulated more specks until that ball of dust exploded? We could ask many other questions, but that is unnecessary.

Adam's account is that he came from the hand of the Creator; that is the information that the book of Genesis passed on to the human race. There is no proof in any other sacred writings, or even in scientific literature, that man was not created but evolved. The theories offered by science are believed by faith, just as creationists believe the biblical account by faith. The reason is that all the materials and processes that are available for scientific experiments are post-creation and cannot be used to disprove creation. In order for science to disprove the creation account, science would have to create a prematter (i.e., what existed before the formation of any matter) environment and reproduce an evolutionary process to show that evolution did occur to bring matter and living organisms and then human-kind into existence.

There is conflict in the scientific world about the origin of humans, and theories change as years go by. It is impossible to use a created substance to prove the origin of that substance or any prematter. It is also significant to note that evolution, by its very nature, cannot reach finality. It is continuous. If it stops with mankind and does not allow mankind to continue into some other entity, it becomes a planned process. A planned process can only be clone by a thinking entity. Therefore, the existence of mankind would be by the design of an architect (God) and not by evolution. The fear of the consequences of not producing viable arguments to maintain the debate or of accepting creationism and the result of such acceptance motivate evolutionists to continue exploring, changing, and refining their theories in order to maintain respectability and acceptance. Thus, fear surfaces in every facet of man's existence.

Fear did not just appear in recent times. The Bible points out clearly that after Adam and Eve sinned, they went and hid themselves (Genesis 2:8). When Adam was asked why he was hiding, he said that he heard God coming and was afraid (Genesis 2:10). Fear has been in the human family for six thousand years.

Looking at Human Fears

Individuals are confronted with various fears that Christian counseling psychology can help them deal with. Exploring many root causes of fear and the influences of thought processes and activities is part of this strategy. Fear is derived from negative thoughts about any one or combination of the following: past experiences, knowledge of other people's experiences, perceived future experiences, or present experiences. That, in essence, is the anatomy of fear. A person may say that he is afraid of dying. However, the truth of the matter is that person may not really be fearful about death but about how he may die—the process. This fear may have originated out of observation of other people's experiences. This and other subconscious thoughts embedded in the mind may only he discovered through a counseling process or self-revelation.

In 2001 I conducted an unpublished survey to determine the degree of fear resident in most people. The simple survey was administered to people from at least three institutions and a public forum in Dallas, Texas. It included people of various ages, ethnicities, social and economic strata, and geographic origins, including foreign countries.

The survey was limited to 350 individuals. All respondents lived within the United States, though some were from other countries and resided here temporarily. I found that with the exception of one group that had (92 percent) 100 percent of any selected group reported feeling a degree of fear (an overall ratio of 99 percent). The attacks of September 11, 2001, which occurred after the survey was taken, have undoubtedly intensified the degree of fear people are feeling. Today, people are still looking for relief from the additional fears that arose out of that event. Since that time, we have the government's War on Terror (a cause of societal fear) and heightened tension for the citizens when the terror alert is increased (a cause of individual fear) or when an incident is classified as an act of terrorism.

During the 2006 elections, the Republicans used a veiled message of fear to scare the public into believing that if the Democrats won the majority in the U.S. House and Senate, they would be soft on terrorism, and America would be vulnerable to the enemy. The Democrats, on the other hand, claimed that America should be fearful about the Republicans retaining the House and Senate because their party led an invasion of Iraq under the false pretense that Iraq threatened the United States with weapons of mass destruction. Democrats warned that unfavorable conditions in Iraq and the number of U.S. soldiers that have been killed were not encouraging, and the federal budget deficit and other conditions would only worsen if Republicans were returned to office. That's how fear is spread in organizations and societies: one group of influential individuals vocally expresses its fears and transfers them to the larger population.

Until this world comes to an end, fear will not be eradicated. However, it is important to recognize its existence, acknowledge its power, and apply measures that will neutralize its effect upon the mind. Fear is not a physical phenomenon but a mental experience that acts upon one's emotion. When fear is reflected outward, it can result in either a physical display of courage or cowardice and abnormal behaviors. Fear is a negative emotional state that a living creature experiences when it perceives a lack of control over self or circumstances that will result in imminent danger or death.

Fear can also be described as having knowledge of an event (immediate or future) along with an intense desire not to participate in or be present for that event. We may perceive inadequacy to deal with that event or want to avoid embarrassment, as I did as a young boy in that river when I felt more fear of being ostracized than drowning. In other words, fear results when one perceives that one will not be able to control a situation or make it a positive experience. There is fear in society in general—fear in the individual family, fear in the home, and fear in school. In the religious arena, where there should be peace and assurance, the fear factor, at times, becomes evident.

CHAPTER 2

TYPES OF FEARS

Before exploring the types of fears, we must keep in mind that all fears have one thing in common: the potential power to dominate your life. When a fear exists and is not neutralized or rendered harmless, it can become a phobia or can develop into obsessive-compulsive disorder (OCD). According to the DSM IV-TR, OCD is an anxiety disorder featuring "recurrent obsessions or compulsions that are severe enough to be time consuming or cause marked distress or significant impairment." However, for our purposes, the degree to which fear exercises dominance over an individual does not matter. What matters here is the power that fears exert over people and what can be done to neutralize them whenever they surface.

In addition to the five new fears that I have discovered—acknowlophobia, alleophobia, alliophobia, futurophobia, imperfectophobia—Dr. Alan Gray lists more than five hundred phobias (Gray 2006, under "List of Phobias" in Appendix C). However, some of those listed have several descriptions, so the actual total appears to be about 545. In an April 10, 2006, e-mail to me, he says that "the power of fear is very real, as is the power of the human imagination. Generalized anxiety/fear is one of the more frequent conditions that I see in my clients. These fears can haunt people and pose a real challenge to those who are affected by them. We may think that people who are afraid of a seemingly normal thing or situation are silly, but until one has occasion to have similar experiences, one cannot truly begin to understand, to some extent, the other person's plight.

Theodore Bernstein lists a number of fears in his dictionary and asks the reader to precede the definition of the words with "irrational fear of (Bernstein 1988, 181-182). He suggests that these fears are unfounded or are a result of irrational thought. Implicit is that if the fear were rational, it could possibly be given another name.

It must be understood that while fears are the result of negative thoughts, those negative thoughts might be related to real threats that can cause physical or psychological pain. If so, those fears are not unfounded. Many people face death, illness, embarrassment, and disappointment by remaining aware that those events are going to occur; because they are prepared for those situations, they don't entertain negative thoughts about how they will manage or feel in those circumstances. They face them as a hero would. Hence, negative thoughts do not control their mental state and impair their judgment or decisions. The unpleasant events may be probable, even inevitable, and the effects of death and illness, for example, are quite real. Even so, the mind can be conditioned to accept misfortune when the possibility of escape is nonexistent.

A good example is the case of the child who, as reported by the media, had to live in a sterile environment because of his extremely fragile immune system. If he came in contact with other humans or the air itself, he might contract any number of diseases and become fatally ill. For him, fear of contamination (mysophobia) was not irrational. It was based on reality. Death would be the probable result if the doctor's instructions were not observed.

The boy's parents could have dismissed the possibility of death for their son, conditioned him to accept his mortality, and not had to fear contravening the medical community's recommendation. If that had occurred, there might have been legal consequences, but they could have ignored that possibility. Instead, by accepting the negative thought (fear) about the consequences of their son's potential exposure to germs, they obtained the benefit of the extension of their child's life. Sometimes real fears are well founded and should not be swept aside. This example brings us to our classification of the two basic categories of fears.

First, there are fears that are physiologically based. These may involve chemical changes in the brain or other physical ailments that require medical and possibly psychological treatment. The second category of fears—and one within the scope of this discussion—includes the many kinds of fears that impact a person emotionally or psychologically. These emotional or psychological fears stem from how a person thinks about his environment, its occupants, and his relationship to them. Attached to the mental or emotional fears are those relating to religion—fears of whether there is a supreme being and how one should relate to that being. This last one includes the element of accountability and what happens when a person's life on earth ends. Consequently, I contend that there are rational fears as well as irrational fears.

Anxiety versus Fear

At this point, I would like to clarify the distinction between anxiety and fear and provide a helpful guide to overcoming your fears.

Dr. Harold Reents, an acquaintance of mine, once told me about the familiar acrostic FEAR (false evidence appearing real), adding that an instructor once told him that whatever is feared is 97 percent not likely to occur. That is where my distinction between anxiety and fear comes into play. Anxiety is false evidence appearing real, and its object may be 97 percent not likely to occur; on the contrary, real fear of an event occurring means that there is a greater probability of it occurring than not occurring.

In other words, events about which we are fearful have a greater probability of occurring because they are legitimate events about which some fear is justified. How much of that fear is appropriate to have? That question is relative. Events over which we display anxiety, on the other hand, are events that may never occur; at least, the probability of them not occurring is far greater than the probability of them occurring. A simpler way of saying it is: You are worrying for nothing. Your worry is uncalled for or ill advised. Algernon Charles Swinburne said, "Hope knows not if fear speaks truth, nor fear whether hope be blind as she" (Forbes 1997, 77). To this I would add that hope must be wary of fear, take hold of action, and travel on the wings of faith in order to meet success. Even if fear were right, hope should stick with faith because "joy cometh in the morning" (Psalm 30:5).

It would do well to remember that every person has the gift of choice and just because I chose A over B does not necessarily mean that I chose A because I am fearful of B. However, it could be that prior personal experience with B caused a fear to be developed that led me to choose A. The point I am making is that you should address any fear that you have of things that you encounter in the normal course of your everyday life.

Things that are not really relevant to living your normal life do not have to be a part of your selection of activities. Thus, any fear you have of those things can be addressed only when there is a possibility that you will have to engage them. Thus, you can select other things or other activities that fit into the genre of activities in your everyday life.

I developed aviophobia, also called aviatophobia — fear of flying, due to the sensation I felt when I rode the ferris wheel as a child and which was repeated when I first flew to the Bahamas (details on page 47). While at this point, I do not feel the need to ride the ferris wheel, the sudden drop I experience when riding in automobiles or flying in airplanes, creates the same sensation felt on the ferris wheel as a child. However, I deal with it as a normal occurrence with no fear attached to the experience. The experience on the plane for that trip to Jamaica (see page 47) was a life-changing one that led to my writing this book. I had to reach back into the recesses of my mind to access the biblical principles articulated in this book. These principles gave me the tools necessary to combat and neutralize my fears. I had finally found the answer to the fear trap—the condition of being controlled by fear and feeling helpless. I realized that there is a way to avoid it. Here are five steps I have practiced over the years. If you use these as a starting point, they will help you combat and overcome your fears:

Learn how to live, and you will not be afraid to die. Why? Because at the end, you would have had no regrets about your life and you would have been prepared to meet your Maker.

Character is the outgrowth of the condition of the mind and there are no philosophical or psychological materials that can provide a permanent foundation for character building. Therefore, I have used a biblical approach to begin that character development. You also can start by believing and acting upon St. John 3:7 and Psalm 1:1-3.

John 3:7: "Ye must be born again." This is an invitation for you to become a new person with a new mindset. Confess your inadequacy and humanness to God and ask him to take control of your life. You will be able to think better and not be so fearful of so many things. You will be a better person. Others will begin to notice the difference.

After this life-changing experience, you can begin to claim the following promises outlined in Psalm 1:1-3:

"Blessed is the man that walketh not in the counsel of the ungodly, nor standeth in the way of sinners, nor sitteth in the seat of the scornful. But his delight is in the law of the LORD; and in his law doth he meditate day and night. And he shall be like a tree planted the rivers of water, that bringeth forth his fruit in his season; his leaf also shall not wither; and whatsoever he doeth shall prosper."

Read, believe and repeat God's promises as often as possible (i.e., Psalm 34:4: "I sought the LORD, and he heard me, and delivered me from all my fears." 2 Timothy 1:7: "For God hath not given us the spirit of fear; but power, of love, and of a sound mind." And Psalm 91:11: "For he shall give his angels charge over thee, to keep thee in all thy ways").

Begin taking proper care of your body (physical aspect) as you do your soul (spiritual aspect); see the SET principles in chapter 9.

Finally, Allow some time for you to see the frill effect in your life of the above action you have taken. Psalm 27:14 says: "Wait on the LORD." After you practiced these steps for awhile, they will become second nature and your body will be in synchronization with your mind.

The Relation of Fears to Stress

Although fears cannot be destroyed, they can be conquered in the sense that they are neutralized using powerful words found in the book of mysteries—the Bible. I will elaborate on this in subsequent discussions. Powerful words cannot destroy fear's power over a person but can indeed neutralize fear so that it becomes ineffective. You are a conqueror in that sense, but don't forget that fear can resurface and become a nemesis again. John F. Milburn called fear a fire: if controlled, it will help you; if uncontrolled, it will rise up and destroy you (Forbes 1997, 67, 77).

When a fear resurfaces, it is important to remember how that fear was neutralized in the past. Past successes will help provide reassurance that returning fears can be overcome or made ineffective again. Sometimes fears resume after many years of latency. In that case, the fear did not really go away but was lurking around, as it were, waiting for the opportunity to regain its foothold. That's why it is important to begin and continue to apply the recommended Spiritual Euphoric Therapeutic prescription to build up your mental immunity. This prescription for neutralization is found in the solutions to the various problems and scenarios presented in this book. Continuous practice will help to refine the process, as well as ensure the neutralization of all categories and types of fears mentioned.

Fears are stress facilitators and should not be ignored. The more fearful a person becomes, the more stress accumulates in that person's mind and body. Soon the stress feeds on the fear, and the fear increases because of the stress. I call this syndromatic and designed a diagram to illustrate the cycle (see figure I).

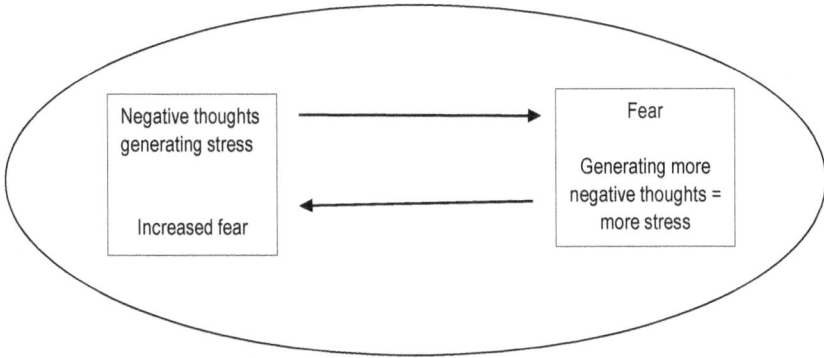

Figure I. Syndromatic Stress Diagram

When a person is trapped in this cycle, the only way out is to find something that can short-circuit the negative energy or fear power that keeps traumatizing the mind. Dr. E. M. Gherman states that "People can literally worry themselves sick" (Gherman 1981, 167). He also quotes Dr. Marvin Stein of the Mt. Sinai School of Medicine in New York who states, "There is considerable evidence that grief and stress retard the body's ability to fight disease" (Gherman 1981, 167). I find the SET principles (see chapter 12) very helpful to counteract the stresses that one faces. I also suggest that as one interrupts the fear-stress flow and is dislodged from the cycle, one profits from the experience by learning valuable lessons about the fears.

Some people's minds are so dull because they consume foods that are unwholesome or abuse the body through the misuse of drugs and other harmful substances that they cannot see the need to abandon unhealthy practices. They seem to lack the will to dislodge themselves from the hypnotic flow of the fear-stress cycle. This lethargic condition may be related to a physical condition. Indeed, Scripture exhorts us to pay attention to the physiological aspect of our being because health is important (3 John 2). No one is expected to do for you what you are to do for yourself. Optimum physical and mental condition are paramount for a healthy you.

Physiological Factors

The role that certain nutritional deficiencies play in one's physical or mental prowess should not he discounted. One's mental and physical strength could he weakened by a diet that is inferior to the recommended minimum standard set by the government. Many people in the United States go to bed hungry every night and have suffered the consequences. In fact, some of these individuals or their children have behavioral problems. Counselors, social workers, and teachers have seen firsthand the effect of nutritional deficiencies as they play out in many of our schools and communities. There have been many discussions on this well-established fact in the media and other forums.

When an individual suffers from nutritional deficiencies, the ability to think and perform at a high level could be mildly or severely impacted. In some cases, a person may develop physical ailments, maladies that may divert the concentration from studying to worrying about the illnesses. Fear of the future could ensue because the individual's hopes and dreams are jeopardized by the uncertainty of the resolution of those illnesses. Another issue regarding nutritional deficiencies is the chemical imbalance that could occur. These have their own sets of problems (medical and nutritional experts have spoken and written extensively on those issues), but the result is virtually the same: the inability to perform at the optimum. Fear of the future or other fears might be the result.

CHAPTER 3

LEARNING FROM INDIVIDUALS' FEARS

In describing psychological types, C. G. Jung, who was heavily influenced by Sigmund Freud, says that in his work with nervous patients, he identified two types of individuals: introverts and extroverts. He proposes that humanity consists of these two types of individuals. As we reflect upon human history, he notes, we see how the destiny of one individual may be conditioned more by external objects of his interest while another may be shaped more by the subject of his own inner sell Jung states that each of us is more inclined toward one side than the other. We are naturally disposed to understand things in the sense of our own types (C. Jung 1954, 183-188).

This concept that humans possess only one of these two extremes, and may even be controlled by them, leaves no room for a balanced psychological type. A possible constant conflict between types with no hope of resolve can be imagined. Jung's thought processes may have begun in his early years when he observed his parents' marriage problems, the emotional disorders and depression that his mother suffered, and the irritability of his father, with whom he had many conflicts. He became reserved, but he snapped out of that condition when studying various subjects, including philosophy, which dealt with suffering, passion, and evil. He became an extrovert but quickly retreated to his introversion when he was not accepted by his peers and his teachers (C. Jung 1954, 183-188). His experiences with the occult and the paranormal generated a curiosity that led him into the field of psychology and psychopathology (Hall and Nordby 1999, 17-21).

A third type Jung did not observe is what I call the biversional type, a blending of introversion and extroversion that brings a balance to life. The biversional type carries with it a practicality and realism that does not present an antithesis to introversion or extroversion. This third dimension can be more easily understood by those who have experienced a change from the ordinary way, of life to a Christian lifestyle.

Focusing only on the introversion and extroversion types described by Jung can result in the fear of helplessness and resignation to fate or destiny,. Such was Jung's case when he retreated to his introversion because of lack of acceptance by his peers. He was frustrated. On the other hand, the biversional type does not always face the problem of frustration because of the withdrawal of the libido (sex drive) from an object "as though ascendancy on the part of the object must be continually frustrated" (Hall and Nordby 1999, 17-21). It also does not have the attitude of the extrovert, maintaining a positive attitude toward the object but minimizing the value of the object. For biversional types, an object is not viewed as having sufficient or insufficient value. Rather, this type approaches the object with a balanced view—reality where reality is to be perceived and practicality where practicality is to be applied, always using a biblical perspective.

It should be remembered that the two psychological types addressed by Jung were observed by his interaction with nervous individuals. Although he did not necessarily characterize the condition of these individuals as being in a state of fearfulness resulting in a nervous condition, it appears evident that such was the case. Apparently, their inability to control, conquer, or neutralize fear led to the nervousness for which they sought treatment or relief.

We must not forget the multitudes who are not the nervous ones, but who have, in the ordinary course of daily life, experienced traumatic events. Even if those events were isolated, and most likely they were, the average person has nonetheless experienced the power of fear and has relived some of those episodes time and time again. Many of these individuals have been known to give testimony of a change in their value system due to the acceptance of Christian principles that empowered them to withstand the onslaught of fear.

An introvert may experience a paradigm shift due to an encounter with the Christ of the Bible, expressing responses that are as "a spring of water" that cannot be squelched (John 4:13-14). This change is visibly reflected in an attitude that departs from the psychological type originally assigned. You may have heard people say, "This is the way I am. I was born this way and I cannot change." But conversion experiences prove this is not the case. Some people hate themselves for being the way they are. They feel hopeless and fear having to discuss their shortcomings with others. Some of these psychological and sociological issues cannot be dispelled with mere adaptation or socialization. There seems to be a need for a source that is greater than that which we see around us. Consequently, the question to be addressed is how can one eliminate or neutralize one's own existing fears regarding the perceived psychological type that one has due to hereditary and environmental influences?

Examples of Individuals' Fear Experience

When I was about five or six years old, my family lived in the West Indies in an area where outhouses were common. We had one because my family could not afford indoor toilets. One day, one of my older brothers, Moses, and I went over our fence and into a neighbor's yard and began playing with some stones. We began throwing the stones into the street. This was not such a smart thing to do because we were inviting trouble from motorists who would be the recipients of the impact of the stones.

Of course, we were immature and did not realize the silliness of our activity. It is true that not many cars passed that way because few people had cars, only the fairly wealthy. We, of course, did not know the difference, did not want to know the difference, would not have fully understood the difference, and would not have cared about the difference. We were just out there throwing stones and having fun, that is, until a black car showed up. One of the stones might have hit the car because the driver jumped out and ran toward us.

We quickly made our way under the fence, into our backyard, and toward the best possible hiding place. We were sure that the man had followed us across the fence and that sooner or later he would catch up with us. We were petrified. We panicked. To compound the matter, our parents were away from home. (No, there was no child protective services department to investigate why we were left alone; every neighbor served as a parent to his neighbors' children.) Our concern was to find a safe hiding place.

We thought about hiding under the bed, but we agreed that it would be easy for the man or the police to spot us there. Yes, we were now thinking about police involvement even though we were so small. We knew we had done something wrong and that when people did wrong, the police got involved. We thought about climbing a tree, but we came to the conclusion that it would be easy for them to find us there. Fear had me licked. I was in a panic mode. I had to find a place quickly because I was sure the man was in hot pursuit and time was running out.

A sure hiding place came to my mind. I remember it as vividly as if it were a few months ago. Yes, this would be the perfect hiding place. It would be dark and out of sight. They would never suspect that I was there. That place of refuge was the outhouse. Yes! The latrine was the solution. I started toward it and was about to begin my descent when my brother—thank God for him—stopped me. I really don't remember the words he used, but subsequently I understood that my choice might have led to a most unpleasant death. The driver of the car, it turned out, was only trying to scare us away and had not pursued us. But on that day, fear could have cost me my life. Only a willingness to accept wise counsel from someone I trusted, my brother, and the assurance that the driver was not following us helped allay my fears and saved my life.

Another simple but fearful situation happened to me when I was in my early teens. My brothers and I and some of our friends went to a fair at one of the schools I attended. Like all the other young people, we went to have fun, and we did. However, as was customary; there was a Ferris wheel on which all the young people were riding. I decided to ride with the other fellows. I had not ridden a Ferris wheel before. Even though it was my first time, I was just as relaxed as I could be. I saw no cause for alarm. Others had ridden it before, and other people would be riding it with me. I did not think there would be a problem.

The Ferris wheel began to turn slowly; and then it picked up speed. On the descent, I felt as if my stomach was left up in the air. The sudden drop caught me by surprise. After that, I just could not regain my composure. There was no time to regroup because the thing kept going, and I was as scared as I could be. That feeling of leaving my stomach in the air has never left my mind. Since that day, I have not been on another Ferris wheel. I have, however, performed many feats that could be considered more dangerous than riding the Ferris wheel without being fearful.

About six years after the Ferris wheel incident, I boarded an airplane for the first time to go to the Bahamas. I was very excited about the possibility of taking up residence there. My focus was not on the plane ride but on my destination.

I arrived at the airport as scheduled and boarded the plane. At takeoff; I felt a funny sensation, but I tensed my stomach and psyched myself up, telling myself that in a little while everything would be all right. As the plane took off; it proceeded at what I perceived to be about a fifty-degree trajectory; then it dropped fifty feet or more before climbing again to gain the desired altitude. That drop gave me the same sensation I had had six years earlier on the Ferris wheel. Instantly, that same fear was resurrected. As I recall, some air pockets caused the plane to rise and fall during the trip, compounding the problem. Every bump and lurch was a very unpleasant experience for me.

My trip was no longer exciting; I was tense all the way to Grand Bahama. On my return trip, I had the same fear and tension. I feared that at any time, without warning, the plane might hit air pockets again. Since that trip, I have been uncomfortable with airplane travel. Even though I took my next plane ride the following year, I did so only out of necessity. Fifteen years would pass before I flew again, and that flight was also taken reluctantly. Since that time-1985—I have flown only a couple of times, primarily for my wife's sake. It is important to note, however, that the fear was motivated not by the prospect of death but by the unpleasant rising and falling sensation while in flight.

I experienced that fear only partly because I had no ability to control the plane. More importantly, I could not prevent myself from feeling the way I felt. That loss of ability to have control over the situation gave rise to another fear: claustrophobia. Claustrophobia is the fear of being in a confined area where there is no room to move about at will. A flight in 1998 was the worst. Not only did air pockets make for a bumpy ride, but the descent was horrible—steep, rather than gradual, and interrupted by many sudden drops. The lights even went out briefly, and the flight was altogether worse than I had expected.

However, that bad experience was most interesting and revealing in what it taught me about dealing with my individual fear. My family and I were flying to Jamaica for my first trip back in twenty-nine years. The main reason it took me so long to visit was because I abhorred plane rides. This abhorrence can be justified in my eyes, at least, by the experiences I have related. When we boarded the plane and I sat down, I wanted the plane to begin the process of taking off immediately. That did not happen. You see, if the plane had begun taxiing down the runway immediately, I would have had no time to gaze at the interior of the plane and think about how little space I had to maneuver. Inactivity and confinement in such a restricted area combined to bring on a claustrophobic feeling.

I was so overcome by that fear that I had to find a way to continue looking outside, where I could see a lot of space. I concentrated on what was out there rather than my situation inside. I was on the verge of panicking. If the door of the plane had not been closed already, I might have gotten off the plane and possibly—I say possibly—not have returned. My only help at that time was to pray and comfort myself with some words from Scripture.

Among the passages that came to mind was Psalm 91, verse II "He shall give his angels charge over thee to keep thee in all thy ways." Psalm 23 was another. Repeating those and several other passages neutralized my fear enough to endure waiting in that confined area. While I ant not professing to be fear free, I know what to do when the situation gets tense.

Show me a person who has never experienced any form of fear, and I will show you a robot. Some of the bravest people have experienced fears at different times and in different ways. Obtaining relief from fear depends on recognizing the feelings and fearful behaviors that have taken up residence in the mind.

Therefore, it is important to understand that whether you are of the introverted, extroverted, or biversional type, your reaction may be far different from what you now think if fear is given the opportunity to have its way in your life. After that event has transpired or you are out of that situation, you may say in retrospect, "How foolish I was," or "Why did I not do such and such?" However, many times we do not learn from our experiences, and we only need another fearful situation to react the same way or worse.

Fortunately for me, as I grew up, I learned not to throw any more stones at passing cars. And as to the other incidents, I learned to prepare myself mentally before traveling by air. Planning to avoid, if possible, situations that make you fearful is wisdom; recognizing when you are about to experience fear gives you the opportunity to take action that may minimize the fear impact or completely eliminate the experience that precipitates that fear.

CHAPTER 4

HOW TO RECOGNIZE THE ONSET OF FEARS

t is indubitable that humankind suffers from fear. The sooner one comprehends that fact, the greater chance one has to address those fears in a manner that will make one's life more pleasant.

Fears exist because of sin. Fears are anchored in the result of actions. These results include unpleasant experiences such as physical pain, anger, anxieties, embarrassment, and emotional trauma. The ultimate feared consequence is death.

Yet, if there were no sin, none of these consequences would exist. In a world without sin, a person might fall over a five-hundred-foot cliff into a lake of volcanic lava or onto some jagged rocks—if such things would be present in a sinless environment—yet experience only joy and not painful death. We might not have fear of heights or anything else we now consider harmful. The power that brought about sin and its consequences—fear, pain, and death—would have no control over humans. Hence, we would have no need to fear anything.

Survey of Individual Fears

In my research, I discovered two interesting phenomena. First, people never fear the past; they only fear the future. Second, there is no correlation between the age of a person and the fear experience. The survey was conducted in Texas, and the sample population is considered a microcosm of the United States because it included various cultures and people from many states. I designed the survey to obtain information from people of diverse economic, cultural, educational, religious, and geographic backgrounds. It was administered to:

1. University students, both day and evening students with either a part-time or full-time load
2. High school students with diverse economic, ethnic, and cultural differences
3. Professionals with diverse economic, ethnic, and cultural differences
4. Faculty; staff, and students at a religious-oriented higher educational institution with diverse economic, educational, ethnic, cultural, and geographic mix (including people from all over the United States and at least nine other countries)
5. Members of the general public.

The survey asked respondents how they felt about fear, whether they had experienced fear, and whether they believed most people have felt fearful at some point in their lives. They were also asked if they were concerned or fearful about violence and the future of this country. Using the Likert model (questions that require the respondents to indicate the level of agreement or disagreement), they were asked to rate their level of fear about family problems, finances, health problems, death, and hell, along with a catchall question titled "Other problems." The survey showed that more than 99 percent of us feel a degree of fear. Also, of the 350 respondents, 349 stated that they have experienced fear in the past or are fearful of some future events. This is a 99.7 percent (349/350) affirmation that virtually everyone has a degree of fear in his or her life. The distribution of the survey respondents by entity is listed in table 1.

The distribution of the respondents for the entities survey is as follows.

Entity	Respondents	No. Indicating	Percentage
University	118	117	99.15%
High School	121	121	100%
Professional (Religious)	81	81	100%
General Public	30	30	100%

Table 1

Thus, almost 100 percent of the population has experienced fear and is fearful of some future event. Further breakdown of the data, however, revealed some other interesting observations. Approximately 62 percent of the respondents were females and 38 percent males. Table 2 shows the gender distribution among the entities surveyed.

	Female	Males
University	67	49
High School	72	48
Professional (Religious)	47	32
General Public	26	4
	212	133

Table 2

In figure 2, it was observed that the number of females in the 18 to 35 age group was twice as many as the number of females in the under 18 age group. The responses about being fearful from the 18 to 35 age group for females was also twice the number of responses received from the under 18 age group. This means that those in the 18 to 35 age group were not more or less fearful than those under 18 in the female category.

The same was true for the male category. There were about three times the number of male respondents who were 18 to 35 as those under 18, and they responded likewise (see figure 2). Five of the individuals did not indicate gender and were not included in certain calculations.

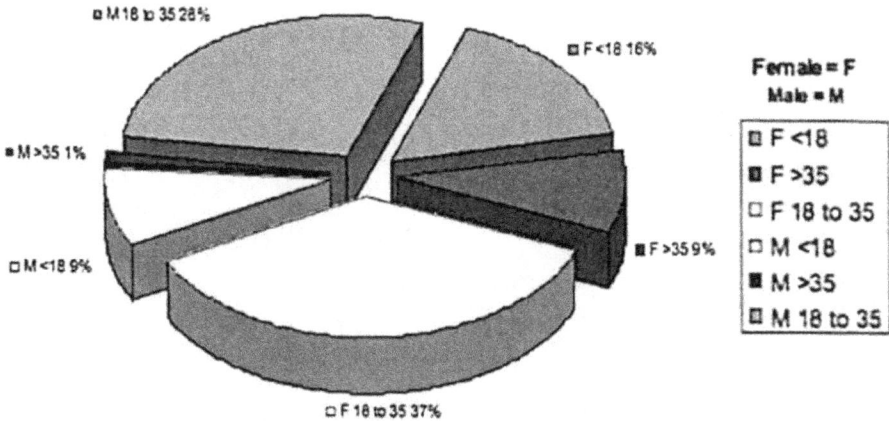

Figure 2. Gender Demographics

In the United States and in some other countries, the 18 to 35 age bracket is a time when adults become increasingly aware that they must assume more of life's responsibilities and be more independent. Most people in that age bracket have already made plans for the future. This awesome realization of their responsibility can create anxiety and fear of the future in many people. Some of the questions that arise are: How will I manage? Will I get married? Will I have children? Am I capable of raising children? Will I get a good-paying job? These and many other questions create anxiety and some degree of fear. Also, some people become very anxious if they have a close bond with their parents and the parents are ill.

In any event, all age groups exhibited some fear, but none in any way more substantially than others. Let's look at the overall fear levels of the respondents shown in figure 3.

Overall Fear Level

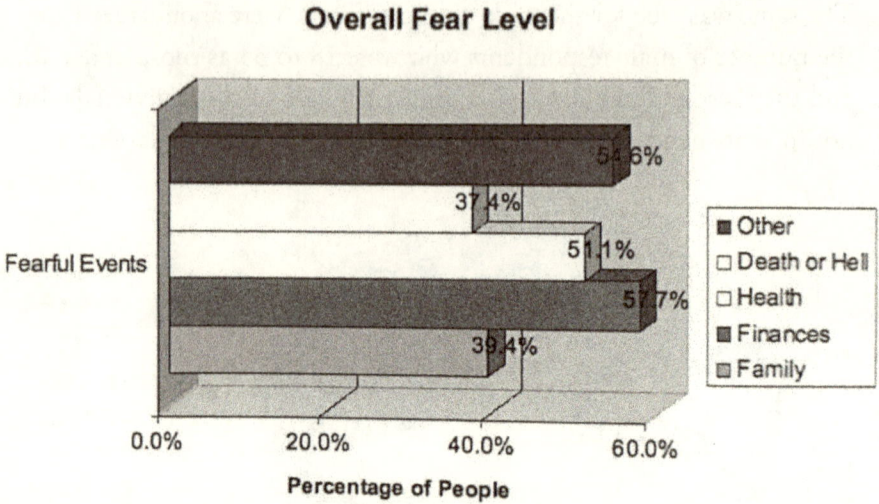

Figure 3. Overall Fear Levels

The overall fear levels of the respondents show that more people had greater fear about their financial situation (57.7 percent) than about their health (51.1 percent) or death (37.4 percent). The point could be made that those who do not have health-related fears may also not be concerned about death yet. If one is healthy, there is no immediate and foreseeable reason to expect death. Most people do not concern themselves about death unless an illness or some major catastrophe is involved. Virtually everyone is aware that death could come at any moment, but until there is some reason to suspect its imminence, people generally fail to be alarmed about it. Yet, in the end, God will say of the person whose greatest concern is about financial matters and not about his soul, "Thou Fool, this night thy soul shall be required of thee: then whose shall those things be, which thou hast provided?" (Luke 12:20).

On the other hand, it seems reasonable to believe that as long as one is alive and sane, one is conscious of financial obligations. There is concern and, in a great many people, a fear regarding fiscal matters. This appeared to be evident in both the male and female 18 to 35 age groups. The second highest fear level was in the "other problems" catchall category designed to capture items that respondents were fearful of but that were not listed on the questionnaire. Nearly 55 percent said that they were fearful about other problems. Fear about family, situations was 39.4 percent.

People's fears relate both to things that are significant to most people as well as things that are insignificant to many. A person with no reservations about fighting an army might be extremely fearful of a mouse, cockroach, or lizard, or of not meeting a spouse's expectations.

It was also interesting to note that females were slightly more fearful about violence in the United States than males (see figure 4).

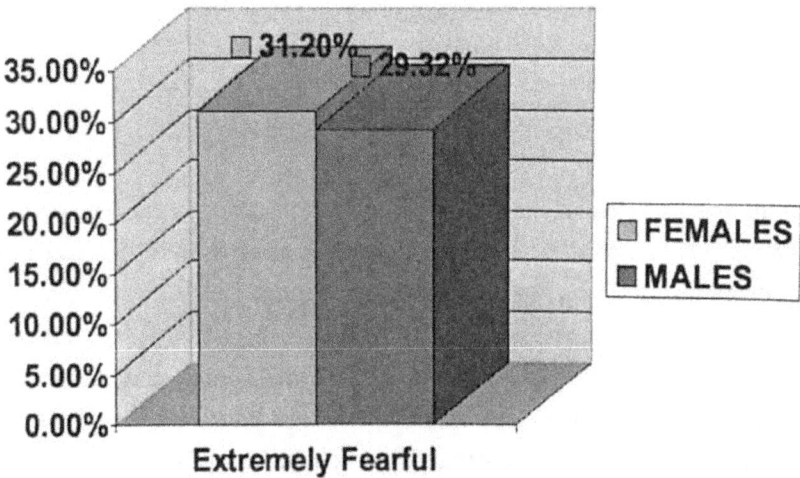

Figure 4. Fear Level of Violence and Country's Future by Gender

Finally, the survey showed that individuals in the 18 to 35 age group, on a scale of one to ten, with ten being most fearful, chose fear levels of between seven and ten twice as many times as individuals under 18 years of age (see figure 5). This seems to indicate that as individuals leave the age of adolescence and become young adults, the awareness of responsibility for their own lives and the implications, create a fear of the future.

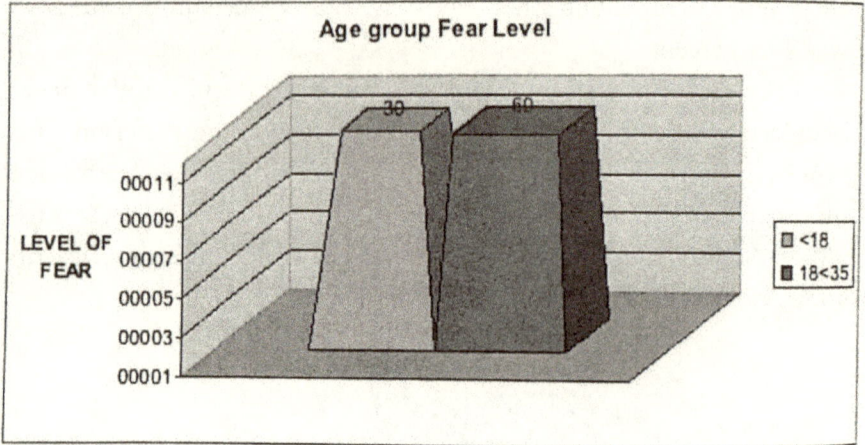

Figure 5. Age Group Fear Level Between 7 and 10

Perhaps further study should be done to compare the degree of fear between parents and students in schools across the country so that educators might develop curricula to address such fears. Fear in domestic situations can impact a child's learning ability as well as the parent-child relationship. Violence in schools across the nation is a related issue. Nevertheless, the prescription can provide a basis for relief from those fears if it is assimilated in each person's lifestyle. If school administration, faculty, and staff infuse the principles articulated in this book into the culture of the school, they could do much to quell some of the violence and lessen the fear that exists in this country.

Even up to May 2007, television news, radio talk shows, Internet blogs, and newspaper articles expressed on a daily basis the fears of the people in the United States. These include fear about various shootings that have occurred in schools and could be repeated, a porous border between the United States and Mexico, U.S. foreign policy and its potential ramifications, the negative signals that disunity in Congress sends to other countries and domestic issues that impact individuals in various ways. I will not address issues related to the post-September II mind-set that the United States and other countries now have. My central thesis remains: fear is universal and multidimensional.

Discovering Your Fears

Not everyone is fully aware of the fears or phobias in his or her subconscious mind. One may categorically deny the existence of one's fear until placed in a situation in which one has no control. If events generate unpleasant experiences, including the threat of death, one quickly realizes a degree of fear. It may be difficult to convey to someone, especially a person who is convinced that he has no fear, that he is really fearful.

A person's adamancy about not having any fears may be an indication that he is posturing in order to avoid a discovery. Such denial—and that is what it is—may come from lack of knowledge about basic human cognitive processes and responses. Or it may stem from either suppression, a conscious activity, repression, or a subconscious activity: There is only one step between him and fear: the knowledge of the reality of death or imminent severe physical or emotional trauma (pain), be it temporary or permanent. In some cases, it may not be either death or injury that causes fear but the process by which they might occur. That event of suffering may concern someone other than oneself; such as a relative or other individual held in high esteem.

Many people are afraid to discuss their fears because of the impact of the reality associated with the recognition of the discovery. It may amaze the reader to know how fearful some people are about things that others consider insignificant or benign. If a person believes that he has no fears, the first place to begin discovering the reservoir of subconscious imprints of fearful experiences is childhood. Unacknowledged childhood fears may simply lie in wait for the right time and place to display their potent forces.

It is true that some childhood fears don't necessarily return to haunt people. They do not always resurface with the same intensity that existed when they first occurred. However, if they do return at the adult stage with a magnitude equivalent to what was experienced during childhood; the emotional pressure becomes as real as when it was first experienced. Unpredictable reactions could ensue.

The discovery of fears in the life of an individual can be very unpleasant. Many times help is needed to go through the process of discovery. On their own, many people do not want to know their negative thoughts or feelings. They would like to believe that everything is all right and that present conditions are merely temporary and will soon recede.

As a Christian counselor, I am convinced that most people have undiscovered fears in their lives. A symptom of the presence of these fears is a refusal to do certain things or go to certain places or to meet certain people. Some people may respond by saying, "I don't feel like going (or doing that)." Such people may also fear counseling because they don't want to risk others discovering their past. They may fear the shame they will feel. They have an unwillingness to give themselves the opportunity to discover their fears, accept that they exist, and explore various solutions. I call this alleophobia—the fear of giving themselves or the counselors permission to wade into an exploration of their lives in order to help discover their fears and alliophobia—the fear of allowing themselves or others to explore the fears they discover.

It is unwise and unsafe to calculatedly deny oneself needed information that would lead to more knowledge and preparation to deal with life. Some people have espoused a philosophy of "what I don't know can't hurt me." But the reality of life is that what people don't know may hurt them severely.

Take, for instance, a fifty-year-old male who is fearful of being diagnosed with cancer. In order to avoid dealing with the fear, he goes around as a happy-go-lucky fellow, not worrying about anything. He knows that his father and his uncle died from colon cancer in their early fifties. His brother has recently been diagnosed with the same disease. Yet because he does not want to face the fear associated with a possible diagnosis, he does not think about it on the conscious level and does not visit his physician for preventive checkups.

When he begins experiencing excruciating abdominal pain, he decides to see the doctor. His subconscious fear now becomes a reality; he is diagnosed with cancer that is in the late stages. Help could have been obtained, but he has lived in the zone of unacknowledged fear for too long. After discovery, acknowledging the fears in one's life is the first step to the neutralization process.

Power Over Panic

Clinical psychologist Dr. Archibald D. Hart wrote a profound article in 2000 in Christian Counseling Today titled "Power Over Panic." In the article, he articulates some of the symptoms and problems associated with panic anxiety disorders. He states that panic disorder is characterized by unexpected and repeated episodes of intense fear accompanied by physical symptoms that may include "chest pain, heart palpitations, shortness of breath, dizziness, or abdominal distress, often mimicking the symptoms of a heart attack or other life-threatening medical condition" (Hart 2000, 14-15). He further states that panic disorder can appear at any age, though it is more likely to begin in early adulthood.

In this article, Dr. Hart does not mention sweaty palms, dry mouth, and incoherency, or having your mind go blank. These symptoms are within the ambit of my philosophy because I contend that almost every person, at some point in his life, has experienced one or several of them. Dr. Dziegielewski mentions additional symptoms in the book DSM-IV-TR in Action. She says that "Frightening symptoms occur that often accompany... intense fear or discomfort; palpitations; heart pounding; sweating; trembling; shaking; feelings of choking, nausea, or abdominal distress; feeling faint; and derealization (feeling that what is occurring is not real)" (Dziegielewski 2002, 281). These symptoms are manifested because of some underlying fear. Most likely, further investigation into the life of one having such experiences would reveal a past event that induced fear and had a similar psychological or physical effect.

Most attacks last only ten to fifteen minutes (Hart 2000, 14-15). The continuation of panic attacks can lead to a number of phobias. It is believed that most minor panic attacks go undiagnosed. In a study that Dr. Hart cited, 36 percent of those having panic attacks said that they diagnosed themselves (Hart 2000,54-55). It is, therefore, possible to discover one's fears by listening to a panic attack's symptoms. Those symptoms are telltale signs that will point toward an underlying problem that triggers the existing reactions.

Such symptoms generally coexist with other conditions. These may include "depression, mitral valve prolapse (MVP), hypoglycemia, illicit drug or alcohol abuse (could be self-medicating), thyroid disease, and a relatively rare condition called pbeochromocytoma (a tumor of the adrenal gland)." These conditions require referral by counselors for appropriate treatment if they are able to detect them when they suspect conditions out of their scope of operation (Hart 2000, 14-15).

Discovery of or awareness of panic attacks and their associated or underlying fears is a significant part of the process of neutralization. There may be times when one has to step back, as it were, and ask, "Why do I feel this way? Why are my hands trembling? Why am I sweating or feeling these pains?" Asking questions like these is where the discovery process begins.

Biblical Examples of People Discovering Fears

When we look to the Bible, we find examples of people discovering their fears. For example, I believe that Mary Magdalene (Mark 5:1-15) and the man out of whom Jesus cast the demons (John 4:7—18) had problems with what today we might call OCD, manic depression, and bipolar disorder. These figures, it appears, had multiple personalities that were revealed at different times through conflicting verbal expressions and conduct. For example, when the demoniac man approached Jesus, he exhibited a calm composure even though he sometimes dashed himself against the rocks and cut himself. He began worshipping and at the same time panicked when he (in actuality, his demons) expressed fear that Jesus had come to torment them before their time. This kind of conduct is manifested by a person with multiple personalities.

Another example of OCD is the woman at the well of Sychar (John 4:7-18), who claimed that she had no husband. Jesus answered that she had five husbands, and the one she was living with was not her own. Today, she would probably be diagnosed as having sexual addiction. Her disorder revolved around sex. Her life was empty, and she was seeking to fill that void. OCD was not a disease; it was a choice exercised. She made a decision to seek her own solution instead of a divine one.

Until these biblical figures met Jesus, they were hopelessly locked in an impossible situation. No medication or therapeutic sessions could cure those conditions; only Jesus could and did. He can do the same today if you believe in him, accept him as the solution to life's mental and emotional problems, and call upon him for help.

Depression and bipolar disorder could be the result of a chemical imbalance, and they may even be connected with nutritional deficiencies. However, they could be the result of guilt, which is also a cause of low self-esteem. Individuals affected in this way are generally fearful of disclosing the situations or circumstances that led to those feelings of anger, guilt, and shame. Sometimes they are not aware of the reasons for their mood swings and depressive feelings. That's why it is important to both discover and trace the reasons for the fear of being open or transparent.

Tracing Fear's Genealogy

Once a fear has been discovered, its genealogy should be traced to see how it came about in the first place. By tracing its genealogy, I mean going back to where it first started. In some cases, the occurrence of one event can be so potent that it forms an indelible mark on the mind. This imprint is revived every time the incident is remembered or a similar situation is seen or discussed.

Other events or objects sometimes become associated with the occurrence and become an anchor that links the fear and the experience. Therefore, whenever the person sees anything connected with the fear, he or she re-experiences the event and the related trauma. In many cases, it is important to travel with the individual back to the place of occurrence. This journey might not be literal, of course, but the verbal recounting of the experience is in itself a journey. A counselor is usually careful in this mode with the counselee to provide biblical consolation to address the issues encountered. There are times when the counselee may need to be referred to a professional with the training, experience, and capacity to administer medication and sustain long-term treatment. The journey must be taken in order to determine the source of the fear.

This concept of journeying into the past is really a scary one. Some people's past's are like a dark tunnel that is full of surprises as the traveler winds his way back to an emotional land of unpleasant memories. On the other hand, some people's pasts are like a walk in the meadows on a sunny day with only a few insignificant, unpleasant encounters that are overshadowed by the fragrance and ambiance of the idyllic landscape of life. The roads are different, depending on the times in and the circumstances under which a person was raised. Everyone should discover and address the fears in his life to avoid the trauma of being handicapped by those unwelcome thoughts and feelings that could produce physical immobility. Tracing the genealogy allows one to discover root causes of certain anxieties and unearth hidden concerns that serve as inhibitors to wellness and a holistic life.

In any event, the past cannot be overcome or dealt with until the issues are clear and the strategy for resolution understood. For example, in order to be able to forgive, one must know what it is that must be forgiven. In order for the mind to be purged, forgiveness must occur. The forgiver and the forgiven can then be in harmony with each other. In other words, both individuals will be on the same level—neither is indebted to the other.

Determining When Fears Affect You

It is not very difficult to determine when you are affected by a fear because it is a unique experience. Only the mention of a given place or situation can immediately triggers the memory of what was experienced. For this reason, many people try to avoid placing themselves in certain situations. Knowing one's fears and when one is affected by them makes attempting to prepare for their occurrence easier.

For example, people have been killed by crowds in soccer stadiums. The people who died were the victims of a stampede and were trampled to death by others trying to escape injury and death. That potential reality is faced by the sixty thousand to one hundred thousand people who attend such gatherings. It is easy to see how someone who has been in such a crowd could develop agoraphobia, the fear of crowds.

That individual may elect to watch the games at home on television rather than going to the stadium to join the cheering thousands. Mind you, this is not a question of anxiety it is real fear, and the incidents of stampede and death at soccer matches are even common in some countries.

It is not a figment of the imagination. Yet this individual may not be afraid to attend a church service with thousands of other people. Why? Because there is more discipline. The agoraphobia in this case seems to relate more to the conduct of the crowd than the crowd itself. The point is that some people may be diagnosed or perceived as having agoraphobia when their fear is related to something different. However, when one knows the circumstance under which this phobia attacks, one can exercise more caution.

When I fly in an airplane, I am usually very tense because I anticipate the effect of air pockets. Such incidents almost always occur. The probability of those incidents occurring seems far greater than their not occurring, in my experience. Consequently, most of my traveling is done by automobile. The fear is not of the plane itself but the effect of the activity of the plane when it runs into an air pocket. This situation is similar to someone who has ridden on a rollercoaster and was so terrified by the ride that he is afraid of riding it again. It's the effect that is feared, not the object itself. So it is with people who fear going to the soccer game because of the possibility of a stampede; it is not really agoraphobia, as suggested by the definition, but the fear of being trampled. It may not even be death that is feared but perhaps that specific manner of death.

Usually, a person becomes fearful when an incident that is dreaded is about to happen and the person has no control over the situation. If one could control every situation, decide when such situations occur, and control the process and the outcome, one would hardly have reason to fear. Thus, by determining the circumstances under which certain fears surface, one can make an effort to assess the progression of the feelings that lead to the outright experience of fear.

Assessing Your Feelings during the Experiences

Some of those feelings of fear may disappear, depending on what is currently taking place in the person's life and how the person responds to those issues. However, some of those phobias become latent hurdles that could prevent a person from soaring to success in the arena of life. All of us are subject to the whims of our memory, which at times imposes on us the unpleasant task of facing reality. Because doing so may be unwelcome but inevitable, the choices of denial or suppression can be very tempting. Yet at some point, we must address the issues that lodge so firmly in our unconscious mind and that serve as a motivation for some of our subconscious behaviors. Extroversion, introversion, a state of melancholy, being a class clown, inadequacy in marital intimacy, and being afraid of making commitments are some of the behaviors and mood changes manifested.

Let's look at another example: a woman who finds it difficult to engage in intimacy with her husband. She has tried hard to be fulfilled and to be fulfilling but to no avail. She loves her husband and wants to meet his needs, but she becomes frigid every time they come together to express themselves in conjugal rites. She does not understand why. In fact, when they were courting, she was filled with optimism and desire for him. She could not imagine being without him. When she began feeling a little impatient about the engagement period, her desire for him became so overwhelming that the couple decided to shorten the engagement and get married.

After the wedding, they went straight to their honeymoon, but when the marriage was to be consummated, she appeared to lose interest. She found some excuse not to be conjugally involved with her husband. Things got serious enough that she had to attend counseling sessions. During one session, she became very conscious of an incident that took place when she was twelve years old.

One afternoon, when she was alone in her classroom studying and waiting for her ride home, a trusted and supposedly respected male teacher offered to help her with her homework. Unaware of his intent, she accepted the offer. However, instead of solving the problem she was working on, he sexually assaulted her and threatened her if she dared to expose him. The molestation continued for several months until he left the school for another job.

Her trust in men was eroded, and she became fearful of them. Any time a man came close to her, she had a "creepy, crawly, shivery" feeling, and all her emotional and sexual expressions became dormant. It was those feelings that led her and her husband to believe that something needed to be uncovered and dealt with for the marriage to be a true success. Hence, they sought counseling.

Most women may not have had such an experience, but many have had other traumatic experiences to the extent that they are plagued by guilt and shame. They don't know why they feel so angry when they are brought into certain circumstances or why they feel so fearful when they are asked out on a date.

I know of a young lady who was constantly ignored by the boys in her school. She wanted to be accepted, but everyone appeared not to want her in their company. She felt so inadequate and downcast that she began to modify her attire in an effort to find acceptance. That appeared to draw more criticism and may have created more alienation. Her transitional year from high school to vocational training did not prove to be much better as far as her social life was concerned.

In counseling with some of her peers, I discovered that they felt that she tried to cling to them too much. Obviously, she craved attention and security. She wanted to feel loved and accepted. Her peers were fearful of having her around because they thought she would never want to leave or let them out of her sight. She, on the other hand, was so fearful of being friendless that she tried very hard to hang around and keep up with their movements from place to place, all the while wondering why they were trying to escape from her. Their fear of being with her and her fear of not being with them created a sad contrast.

In order for individuals to neutralize their fears, they must first recognize their existence and the onset or circumstances under which those fearful feelings are experienced. Only then can they begin to understand the nature of the problem and become motivated to find a solution.

CHAPTER 5

THE POWER OF FEAR ILLUSTRATED

No-Fear Attitude: Courage versus Stupidity

Some people confuse courage with stupidity. I like to think of courage as acting with vision and without fear under fearful circumstances. Conversely, I think of stupidity as jeopardizing one's life or reputation by ill-advised action under fearful or dangerous situations. Almost everyone will flinch and flee in terror when that special unnerving challenge appears. Doing otherwise would be like standing unmoved at the foot of a mountain whose volcano has just erupted while molten lava is racing downhill.

One kind of stupidity is sexual promiscuity. Despite knowledge of the AIDS virus and the potential for its contraction, there are those who flirt with this disease by acting promiscuously. Many of today's youth are engaging in unprotected sex without regard for the possibility of becoming HIV positive. Even "protected" sexual activity is not as protected as it appears. Nevertheless, some appear to see sex outside of marriage—or multiple sex partners—as a demonstration of popularity and great accomplishment. From the Christian perspective, however, such behavior is nothing short of immorality. Promiscuity involves taking a dangerous risk that could bring bitter fruits in the years to come.

A sobering fact is that a person may contract a sexually transmitted disease and continue with life for some time without any knowledge of imminent danger. The friendship formed between a man and a woman during this period could blossom into a love relationship that culminates in marriage. After this event, the result of the wayward lifestyle comes home to roost. The pain of having to watch a spouse waste away from a deadly disease is unimaginable unless, God forbid, one is a partaker of that experience. Such could be the result of a no-fear attitude that propels one into a life of perdition.

An intriguing story of such a no-fear attitude is the one about the pharaoh in the days of Moses. According to the biblical account, Pharaoh was afraid of the Israelites. He feared that they would become so large in number that they might engage in an uprising and possibly overthrow him; therefore, he enslaved them. When Moses and Aaron went before him to request that he let the Israelites go so that they might serve the LORD their God, Pharaoh responded, "Who is this LORD that I should obey Him?" (Exodus 5:2). At that point, his fear was only of the potential problems the Israelites could cause instead of what their God could do to him. Even after many plagues devastated the land, he was angrier at what their God was doing than fearful of Israel's God. That did not change until all the firstborn of Egypt, including his own son, died. One could, indeed, mistake stupidity for courage

What Fear Can Do to a Person

In October 1978 or 1979—I don't quite remember the year, but it was Halloween—I got out of bed as usual, performed my daily rituals, and headed off to work. I was working at a manufacturing corporation in the Bronx in New York City Audrey, the controller, worked next to my office. She was a short, good-natured, mild-mannered woman who appeared to be in her late forties to early fifties. I was Audrey's Assistant. Judy, a six-foot-two Jewish blonde in advertising, worked across the hall from my office.

That October morning, I went to my office as usual and began my routine functions. Sometime between ten and eleven o'clock, while

I was deep in concentration, my head bent over my desk, working ardently to accomplish the day's tasks, I sensed a presence in my office doorway.

To understand the magnitude of the incident, it's important to visualize the configuration of my office. My' office had only one entrance, which also served as the exit. The door opened into my assistant's office, and one could proceed through that office to mine. However, my office was separated from my assistant's by a partition that had metal at the lower half and glass at the upper. That way, I was able to sit at my desk and look into my assistant's office and also view any activity that transpired in the passageway. My office had one window behind me. The safe was to my right.

When I sensed the presence, I raised my head and looked toward the door. The sight was very, unseemly and terrifying. It was a huge bear standing before me at the door. I had no time to transition from my thoughts of the day's activities to my actual predicament. Consequently, this uninvited and unwelcomed visitor seemed ready to snatch my life away. It stood there looking at me, lips spread back, teeth grinning like a dog or a wolf ready to pounce and make a good meal out of its prey.

I became so fearful that I believed my life was about to end. The giant bear stood in my only path of escape. I froze. Instantly, I accepted my fate. In that split second, I resigned myself to destruction in the fiendish jaws of the bear.

However, the bear that I was looking at was Judy from across the hall, dressed in a bear costume. It was so startlingly real to me that I was immobilized. Judy did not notice my reaction to her presence because I sat and stared at her with a smile still on my face. But deep inside of me, fear had taken over. I had already calculated that there was not enough time and distance for me to mount a defense.

Fear can paralyze an individual. Fear can render one helpless at a time when one should be mobile and ready to act. Fear can produce various responses in an individual, resulting in disdain for cowardice or recognition for bravery. Sometimes, as we are about to see, bravery results from fear.

Traumatic Events: Process and Results

No one should impugn the valor of a soldier who valiantly fights for his or her country and whose loyalty has helped secure freedom. Regardless of the soldier's motivation, however, the enemy regards neither bravery nor cowardice. All are the same on the battlefield. The emotions that sometimes occur at that moment no one but the soldier understands. He or she may not wish to recount such feelings afterward, and the trauma can be so great that it results in amnesia.

Imagine a soldier creeping with his troops through the jungles of Vietnam. They are approaching an enemy hideout. They are filled with optimism and expect success, planning in just a few minutes to storm an enemy camp and take them out. Before the soldier was drafted or enlisted, he had seen on television the heroics of brave men who fought and won military victories. He had seen, that is, how platoons and companies had gone into hostile territories and decimated the enemy. He had envisioned himself among those who would dare to be brave. Of course, back then he was among friends and families. He was not living with the other troops out in the jungles of Vietnam. War was a world of fantasy to him.

Now, however, it is reality. He is in the jungle. He can see and touch the leaves of the trees around him. He is holding a real automatic gun. He has on a real camouflage outfit. He is away from his friends and relatives. He will not be able to go to the cinema that evening to watch a movie with soldiers fighting on the screen. He is approaching the real enemy, and any mistake could cost him or his comrades their lives. Life as a soldier is not vicarious now; it is real.

As he and his comrades approach the enemy in a stealthy manner, all his training returns to his mind. His platoon is cautious but confident that everything will go as planned. Suddenly, one of his men trips on an enemy mine and is blown to smithereens. The explosion signals the enemy to begin firing. The soldier's friend and comrade, beside whom he has trained, fought, eaten, laughed, and dreamed of going back home to enjoy life and reminisce about the war days—a friend whose wife and two young children are at home waiting for him—is ripped apart by machine gun fire. That friend, who was by his side, only a moment ago, is gone.

Fear fills his mind. It occurs to him that he too may never make it back home. Men are dying all around him. He sees that he may be next. His fear turns to anger. He is angry that the enemy has killed his friend and deprived him of the opportunity to go home to his family. He is angry because their mission appears to be failing and the enemy is enjoying success. He analyzes the situation. He could turn around and try to escape. He could call off the mission. But he remembers his friend's death. He remembers the others whose lives are in danger, not to mention his own. All these thoughts come into his mind in the space of only a few seconds.

His thought process was not one of cowardice. It was not one of a defeatist attitude. The fear was actual fear, not anxiety or worry over whether an unreal situation may occur. It was a legitimate fear of what was actually in progress. When he concludes that this must not continue, he resolves never to retreat or surrender but to see the job through. The soldier's anger turns into courage. He rallies his comrades, storms the enemy, and defeats them.

Fear of what is about to happen can serve as a motivator to take action and meet with success. Fear turned into anger can become the resolve that leads to actions we would all recognize as courage or bravery'. The scenario I gave about anger leading to courageous 'acts should be carefully understood because that anger, misdirected can lead to devastating results. People who are unable to control their anger have, on the battle field committed genocidal acts, or other atrocities worthy of prosecution. Similarly, in civilian life, many people who do not control their anger find themselves committing crimes or destroying friendships or engaging in acts which they later regret. I have known people who are so fearful that their anger may get out of control that they have sacrificed some pleasure to avoid confrontation with certain individuals.

I became acquainted with a Christian man whom I have counseled on occasions. He confessed to me that he has had an anger problem for many years. In fact, one morning, as I was preparing to participate

50

in the worship service, he came into my office with a somber face and was very emotional. His heart was burdened because he had allowed his anger to get the better of him and had become physical with someone dear to him. He was embarrassed to share the incident with me and was remorseful over his actions. He had been trying for years to control the anger and expressed how fearful he had been about losing his cool.

After counseling with him and praying with him, we parted. Subsequent conversations with him indicated that he had not had another bout with the anger problem. If you allow yourself to be controlled by the principles of heaven, you do not have to be afraid of challenges that ordinarily would arouse anger. You will channel your energies in the direction that benefits you and others. The Psalmist said: "I will keep my mouth with a bridle, while the wicked is before me" even though "My heart was hot within me." (Psalm 39:1, 3). And St. Paul said: "I keep under my body, and bring it into subjection" (I Corinthians 9:27). If you are struggling with anger, you do not have to be fearful that your anger will get out of hand if you follow those biblical principles. Don't hesitate, begin today.

The Impact of Fear on Some Prominent Individuals

Trauma is powerful and usually has lasting effects. Many people are walking around with a montage of emotional and physical scars from the impact of trauma. U.S. Senator John McCain is a good example. As a result of being held as prisoners of war in Vietnam in the late 1960s and early 1970s, he and fellow countrymen have suffered emotional scars. It was reported that when Senator McCain went back to view the place years later, he asked the people who were with him not to close the door behind them.

The trauma of being locked up and tortured for a long time without any assurance that they would ever be free again created a fear for that kind of environment. From a psychological perspective, it is conceivable that the experience etched in his mind the subconscious belief that if he were to be locked inside that place again, the same experience would reoccur. Hence, his request that the door be kept open makes perfect sense.

Another U.S. senator, Edward M. Kennedy, experienced tragedy in 1969 when he drove off the road on Martha's Vineyard with his companion, Mary Jo Kopechne. Miss Kopechne drowned in that mishap. In the aftermath, many people speculated that the reason it took him several hours to report the accident was because he panicked and feared the impact that tragedy would have on his ability to become president of the United States. That idea became a reality because the public never allowed him to forget that night. He abstained from entering the presidential race in 1972 and 1976 and was defeated by Jimmy Carter for the democratic nomination in 1980.

The year 1972 is famous for the break-in at the Democratic National Committee office in the Watergate Hotel. President Richard Nixon and his team feared that full disclosure of the facts could result in criminal charges, so when a full-scale investigation was considered, he and his advisers began a series of cover-ups. Lying became a norm. Documents were shredded, and the tape recorder that was installed in the Oval Office to tape the president's conversations was tampered with. About eighteen minutes of the tape was erased—a gap that became a focal point of suspicion. When the investigation began closing in and the web of phony alibis and false statements began to fall apart, President Nixon's worst fears became a reality: he would have to resign or be impeached. He resigned and spared the nation the agony of an impeachment that he might not have survived.

A more recent impeachment, the story of the moral lapse of President William Jefferson Clinton, is one that America will not soon forget because for some, it's still a reminder of national pain. And yet, although the moral tenor of that epoch was one of repulsion and shame, some find humor in recounting some of those events. Nevertheless, for the purpose of this book, the Lewinsky incident exemplifies what fear can do to prominent men in political life.

President Clinton had a sexual relationship with one of the female interns at the White House and denied it. Many people wanted to believe him, and many Americans hoped that the accusation against him was false. The president assured the American people that he had never had sexual relations with "that woman"; however, later evidence proved his statement to be false. After a lengthy investigation, the president finally admitted that he had made false and misleading statements. His fear was realized, in part, because he was impeached; although he survived the impeachment, his reputation was irredeemably tarnished. His survival was due to party loyalty and a disagreement about the constitutional interpretation of "high crimes and misdemeanors" for which a president may be removed from office. The whole process engulfed the religious arena, and religious leaders began calling for a president who could show moral leadership in our country: They were fearful that the country was becoming morally bankrupt and that the wrath of God might be the result.

Out of this scandal, an interesting question surfaced: How do religions respond to the erosion of morality or lack of cooperation with their wishes or dogmas? If many of our religious leaders had their way, Clinton would have been replaced because he had disappointed them and minimized the prestige of the Oval Office. Even though some religious leaders stood by him, fear of the future—what might happen to the country and the hope of strengthening religion and morality in public life—caused many to engage in sarcasm and show much intolerance. Therefore, the question that was posed becomes relevant not only to the Christian community but also to other religions. We explore that question in summary form in chapter 11 because time and space are not available for elaboration.

At this point, we should try to determine some of the causes of fear so we can reach back to their origins and apply the counseling principles that individuals can use to bring about a change in attitude in themselves, their organizations, and their religions to neutralize the effect of these fears.

CHAPTER 6

ROOT CAUSES OF FEAR: AN ANALYSIS

In addressing the issue of fears in individuals, we cannot look only at what people are experiencing (symptoms); we must also look at the origins of those fears. For example, how did the person begin experiencing these fears? What are some possible root causes? A root cause is a conscious or subconscious unpleasant experience or event that one does not want repeated, including a negative perception based on certain observations that may have occurred in childhood or adulthood. Hence, the person must search for a root cause to determine how these fears could have developed.

Perception of the World Based on Early Environments

One's early environment can produce a worldview that takes a tremendous effort to reverse, depending on the person's education and social circle. It does not matter that a person is born and raised in the inner city; those formative years are significant and do influence the child's future and world-view. He may be raised in a one-parent home with one income derived solely from government aid. The attitude of that parent might be that "they owe me." The child may grow up believing that the world owes him a livelihood. He does not see himself as obligated to strive to obtain through hard work what he desires. Although much of a person's worldview may be traced to the early childhood and young adult years, some people do change, and education, social interaction, and religion can modify one's worldview. Nevertheless, those early years are the foundation for the journey into the future and may lead a child to be fearful or confident as he strives to attain his life's dreams.

Negative Childhood Experiences and Repression

Although some fears are the result of traumatic incidents experienced in later adulthood, most of our fears have their foundations in childhood and early adulthood. The instabilities and hurtful situations of the early years create emotional scars that sometimes never heal. In fact, sometimes the memories are so painful that they are repressed. It is as though the mind, unable to deal with an experience that is so overwhelming, establishes a defense mechanism to force that experience into the subconscious.

In her book Examination of the Personality, Dr. Nancy Roeske says that repression is one of the most common mental mechanisms. She states that by this mechanism, impulses, desires, and ideas that would ordinarily be incompatible with the individual's conscious awareness, such as unacceptable sexual impulses, remain inaccessible in the unconsciousness; therefore, they are unable to be recognized by the personality. Roeske further states that repression is not a deliberate or conscious effort of rejection by the individual. It is an involuntary response or repudiation that occurs automatically (Roeske 1972, 41-42).

One can readily see, then, that a person in an accident or who has witnessed a heinous or despicable act could be so overwhelmed that the unconscious mind would hide it away, as it were, so that it could not form an obvious part of the individual's daily life. Some of the experiences likely to be repressed involve self-esteem issues, guilt, and shame. An individual who has such repressed memory is not aware of those anxiety-producing motivations. Indeed, some of those effects surface when the person is brought into a situation that causes a traumatic effect similar to the one that occurred when the repression took place. The phobic reaction to frequent reoccurrences of these effects is not anxiety but an experiential knowledge of the reality that is repulsive to the individual.

In today's society, one cannot take things for granted. The unthinkable occurs every day. Neighborhoods are changing, and the destructive forces in society have infiltrated all areas of our environs and every strata of our economic system so that it is not uncommon for one to fear that which heretofore appeared nonthreatening.

For example, I lived in a certain neighborhood in a suburb of a metropolitan city in Texas. The neighbors were wonderful. The ethnic diversity was considered good. There was no perceived fear of break-ins, devaluation of property, or physical assaults; that is, until one of my next-door neighbors moved out, and Mr. K moved in.

Mr. K had some huge dogs in the backyard that barked continually night and day. They were always attempting to come through the fence into our yard. Mr. K also began doing automotive work on many different cars in his driveway and then on the street. Many strangers started frequenting Mr. K's home, whether for work on their automobiles or for other reasons. Many of the neighbors now feared property devaluation and perceived a potential threat to our children and homes. One neighbor even expressed concern that there might be a drug connection.

These experiences could have set up a profile in the subconscious minds of our children that would make them fearful of dogs as adults. They might also become so uncomfortable in a neighborhood that has large nonthreatening dogs and engines that are a little louder than theirs that they move from community to community out of fear.

One of Dr. Roeske's significant observations is that repression is not always pathological. She believes that if it operates smoothly without undue effort, it may result in a well-adjusted life. The repressed material, as she describes it, may be dealt with rationally if it can be "made accessible to the scrutiny of the consciousness through other defense mechanisms" (Roeske 1972, 41-42). I believe that one such way of dealing with these repressed materials is through discovery and then application of spiritual principles. A personality that is impacted by the resurfacing of repressed material or fears resulting from unresolved issues needs introspective focus and analysis. Resolution is significant because those issues are brought into the everyday interactions and influence the activities of that individual's social and economic life. They also affect the home life, and most times, there is a carryover into the person's leadership styles in the workplace. Some of these experiences have their roots in childhood.

In some instances, children who have been locked up in closets deliberately or by mistake become claustrophobic or fearful of being in closed areas where it's difficult to get out. The same thing may be true of someone who has been locked in the trunk of a car, in a dark room, or in an elevator. These unpleasant experiences sometimes establish a foundation for fear. The fear is not of the place itself but of the emotional experience and, therefore, the inability to release oneself from that experience—inability to have control at will over entrance and egress.

Bad Dreams Interpreted as Reality

When I was a child, I heard many people relate their dreams and attach much significance to them, as if they were an infallible guide to the future. I recall seeing either a book or a magazine titled Dreams and What They Mean. I was surprised at how many people believed it to such an extent that they regulated their activities based on what they read.

When children are constantly exposed to such beliefs and practices, they accept them as normal. They incorporate them into their belief system, which forms the basis for their philosophy and outlook on life. People have reported seeing their dead relatives in dreams in which those relatives instructed them what to do or not do. Many times, people follow such instructions in detail yet never achieve what they were supposed to have achieved.

I am not suggesting that dreams should never serve exclusively as a valid warning to individuals. From a biblical perspective, nothing surpasses Jesus Christ in power or quality of being (God incarnate). And what does the Bible say about answers to life's questions found in dreams? God will "pour out my spirit on all flesh and your ... young men shall see visions and your old men shall dream dreams" (Acts 2:17). However, some dreams stem from mental exhaustion or from having various preoccupying concerns. From those subconscious thoughts come dreams that are of no valid meaning but are construed by some to be of great importance.

Additionally, since God can and does give dreams according to his word, Satan, the archenemy of God, would naturally try to deceive mankind by also giving dreams that attempt to contradict God and his Word. Trying to predict future behavior, actions, or events, barring a revelation from a divine source, would virtually be engaging in fortune telling, which is unreliable and without credibility.

I believe that some dreams have no real meaning but are a result of some physical or emotional condition. Adler believes that "dreams are considered projections of a client's current concerns and mood [and] represent rehearsals for possible courses of action" (G. Jung 1997, 33). There are those who would decide to drive their blue car to work rather than the red car if they dreamt that they were arrested for driving a red car. Fear of the dream coming true causes them to modify their plans for that day. It is amazing how much credibility is placed on superstitious dreams (much like the horoscope). These individuals need not fear the future but should redirect their focus and reliance on the one who holds the destiny of all mankind. Only God is able to provide protection and direction to those who are drifting, as it were, on the sea of life without a compass.

Exposure to Media Reports of Crimes

On a daily basis, the news media have saturated the entire United States with the horrors of tragedies perpetrated by those with depressive behaviors and psychological disorders. The airwaves are filled with reports of rapes, kidnappings, robberies, and other crimes that speak fear to the hearts of those who hear or behold them. Many a woman is seen on television crying for a lost daughter or son who has been bludgeoned to death or shot by intruders.

Churches are burglarized, burned, and robbed at gunpoint. Crimes cause many people to relocate from neighborhood to neighborhood, yet many still are unable to find peace and security and the assurance that their homes or families won't be the next statistic. Many parents and guardians, in trying to protect their minor children, transfer their fears to them.

In early 2003, I was preparing to conduct a seminar in a small town south of Dallas, Texas. This seminar was designed to address certain individual and societal issues that affect urban communities. I asked a few volunteers to extend an invitation to the community. We spoke to a particular young man about the seminar. He promised to attend. When I noticed that the young man did not attend the seminar as promised, I inquired about him and received the sad news that he had died from a gunshot wound a few days after the seminar began.

The report of that crime heightened the fear level of the community and traumatized some of the young people. It also served as a motivating factor for some adults and young people to begin attending church services to avoid dying without being prepared to meet their Maker. While some people seek religion out of fear, some become almost paranoid because of reports of the crime in their communities. Still, the true psychological effect on the children may not be determined until they reach adulthood and begin their starch for residential locations. One thing that parents and guardians can do to lessen the impact of these reports on their children is to maintain a positive attitude toward life and obtain assurance from Scripture that God has sent angels to protect those who trust in him.

Movies and Horror Stories

Some years ago, when the movie titled The Exorcist began showing in the theaters, some viewers reportedly experienced some of the things that the characters in the movie were experiencing. Many people decided not to see it because they were fearful that they might experience similar effects. Horror movies can tap into the root causes of fear in some young people, whose tender minds are easily impacted by such external stimuli.

Not all those who are affected by these movies are young people; some of them are mature adults.

I have met many people who are afraid of the dead because they seem to believe that corpses may get up and scare them. Therefore, entering a room where someone is deceased becomes a very fearful proposition. The stories that many of these people heard or watched in their youth serve as root causes of some of these fears.

Parents and guardians should remember that their children's minds are very impressionable, especially in the formative years. Even teenagers are susceptible to what they see on the screen. Some of them try to emulate what they see and either wind up dead or incarcerated for hurting or killing others. Therefore, if children are allowed to watch certain movies or read horror stories, parents and guardians should discuss the plots with them.

Bring them from the land of fantasy and make-believe to the land of reality. Explain to them the difference between what they are reading or watching and what is real. If what they are reading or watching on the screen reflects reality, help them understand how to avoid the pitfalls outlined in the plots and guide them as they try to make sense out of what they are experiencing. Remember, even with your guidance, there is no guarantee that some of the fearful scenes will not be internalized and play out in the years to come. They can also impact how children view life and how they should respond to certain events. At least you will have planted seeds of realism and positivity in their minds that you hope will germinate in the future, making them optimists and not pessimists.

Negative Mental State

A life insurance company conducted a study of policyholders who lived to the age of a hundred years or more. When they were asked to name the most important lesson they had learned in their long lifetime, the most frequent answer was to love thy neighbor as thyself." Dr. Norman Vincent Peale, quoted in Douglas M. Lawson's Give to Live, explains, "They live longer... because they have freed themselves from deadly negative influences such as anger, hatred, suspicion, guilt, and anxiety? These toxic emotions, he says, can lead to cynicism, hostility, and isolation. He further states that Dean Ornish, noted heart specialist, calls these traits major components of heart disease, high blood pressure, stroke, and probably cancer (Lawson 1995, 6). As these diseases set in, the victims become fearful of the prognostications of their quality of life and, eventually, their mortality:

The discussion about the relationship between a clear mind and a healthy body is well documented. According to the Random Acts of Kindness Foundation's Web site, Allan Luks, in his book The Healing Power of Doing Good: The Health and Spiritual Benefits of Helping Others, discusses a survey he conducted of three thousand people of various ages in over twenty organizations across the country'. He states, "Helping contributes to the maintenance of good health, and it can diminish the effect of diseases and disorders both serious and minor, psychological and physical." He goes on to say, 'All we know at this point is that different states of mind do affect the immune system?

The Web site also mentions that heart specialist Dr. Herbert Benson tells of how people have used altruism as one of the techniques to "experience decreased metabolic rates, lower blood pressure, lower heart rates, and other health benefits" (The Random Acts of Kindness Foundation, under "Kindness: How Good Deeds Can Be Good for Your).

In his article, "The Faith-Health Connection," registered clinical counselor and marriage and family therapist Dr. Chris Kempling wanted to determine whether personal faith has an overall impact on a person's health. He asked the question, "Can religious faith help to keep a person 'whole' or restore them to 'wholeness' when they become ill?" He reports a study, led by William Harris, of coronary patients, 466 of whom were prayed for and 524 of whom were not. The results of the study were later published in the Archives of Internal Medicine. The researchers approached the study with the view that God does respond to prayer. The result was that of the people studied, those who received prayer "faired eleven percent better" than those who did not. In another study, Harold Koenig (1999) found that those who had no religious affiliation spent "fourteen more days" in the hospital and incurred "$56, 000 more financial costs, with concomitant use of professional services" (Kempling 1999).

These researchers have documented how religion plays a vital role in the cure or prevention of diseases through its emphasis on charity, an altruistic attitude toward others, prayer, and a healthy lifestyle. A very interesting phenomenon is occurring in our country: Sarah Glazer, writing in the January 14, 2005, issue of The CQ Researcher, asked the question: Can spirituality influence health? The result of the research is that "scientific consensus has been reached on only one finding: Church goers live longer [and] a majority of the nation's one hundred and thirty-five medical schools now teach about spirituality, and many hospitals ask patients about it" (Glazer 2007). It stands to reason that a person with a healthy mind and body is able to deal with stress and fear from a stronger position than one who is not as healthy.

Figure 6. The Fear Circle

The very essence of this book lies in the questions that demand an immediate response and a solution: Can fear be neutralized? If yes, then how? From the previous discussion, one can readily see that neutralizing fear could be difficult for people whose daily lives are filled with menacing obstacles based on these root causes. At times, many of them do not know why they are so grumpy, feeling low, and believing that their world is closing in on them. They need help. They need direction for their lives. They need a way to short-circuit or neutralize their fears, relieve their stresses, and become happy again. I say to such folks: help is on the way. Before we discuss the principles of effective neutralization of those fears, both men and women need to understand some of the issues dealing with marriage and the family. These are a world unto themselves, but it is important to study these issues, though not exhaustively, because they also serve as root causes of fear for some individuals.

CHAPTER 7

FEARS REGARDING MARRIAGE AND FAMILY ISSUES

Unwise Parental Training and Unhealthy Relationships

P arental behavior can serve to build and strengthen a child's character or to produce a warped personality. What parents do matters a great deal in their children's development and well into adulthood. Many families stand at the bottom of the honor roll, so to speak, because the parents did not invest the time and energy in nurturing the young mind and instilling the virtues learned through good parenting skills. Unfortunately, such children may grow up believing that they should try to achieve their parents' model of behavior. The child is bereft of understanding what is right and acceptable both socially and spiritually.

For example, a father who beats his wife is telling his son that it is acceptable to be a wife abuser. He is saying to his daughter that a woman should expect and accept abuse in order to feel that she is loved. Hence, the son grows up and finds a woman whom he can mistreat. The daughter may fear marriage, expecting the treatment her mother was subjected to, or she may find a mate who exhibits the same traits as her father. The culture of abuse that was taught by example to the children is perpetuated. In many cases, the cycle is never broken through many generations.

The same thing is true about parental discipline. The nature of the punishment meted out to the children and the severity with which that punishment is applied will give direction to them as to what is expected or acceptable. Unless children learn how discipline can be administered with love, balance, and good judgment, they will fall in the same trap as their parents. Here again comes the fear factor. Some adults vow not to discipline their children in the manner in which they were disciplined because they fear that their children will feel the same resentment that they feel against their own parents.

The fearfulness that results from abusive childhood punishments can also play out later in the workplace. Many managers and supervisors inflict the same emotional punishments on their underlings as were inflicted on them in their childhood. Unable to retaliate when they were being abused and punished as children and forced to comply with unreasonable requests, they now find bitterness and resentment festering in their hearts. Perhaps they were unable to express lordship over anyone in their teenage years, so now that they have the opportunity to supervise or govern, they do so with an iron hand. In fact, this can explain why good suggestions by lower-level employees are often not accepted: the supervisor wants to be the big boss all the time and to let no one else share the glory. Such a dynamic exists not only in the workplace but also in other social structures, including church life. Resolution of these problems lies with the individual. An organization may be crippled by the baggage its administrators carry from childhood. Dr. John Gray's classic book, Men Are from Mars, Women Are from Venus, gives an example of how childhood experiences impact adult life. He talks about a woman he called Cathy. She and her husband, Harris, wanted to improve their marriage and attended one of his seminars. They went home and began practicing the suggestions they learned. After two weeks of living "in love," the process got stymied by what Cathy called her husband's withdrawal and her feeling of abandonment, which led her to discontinue her "opening up" to him. Dr. Gray said that:

> By not fully trusting and opening up, Cathy had spent years protecting herself from being hurt. But during

their two weeks of living in love she started to open up more than she ever had in her adult life. Harris's support had made it safe for her to get in touch with her old feelings. Suddenly she began to feel the way she felt as a child when her faller was too busy for her. Her past unresolved feelings of anger and powerlessness were projected onto Harris's watching TV. If these feelings had not come up, Cathy would have been able gracefully to accept Harris's wish to watch TV.

(Gray 1993, 123)

These childhood impediments impact people in their adult life until it sometimes takes extraordinary circumstances to uncover them. The sufferer must confront and unload them before life can go on as it should.

Neil Anderson offers the example of a young lady who found freedom as she discovered the source of her fears and dissatisfaction with herself. He relates an incident from one of his counseling sessions in which a woman who had been led into a life of prostitution by her mother remembered that when she was very young a fortune-teller had told her that she had a beautiful face and body. "That," the fortune-teller continued, "will help you make it through life", (Anderson 1984, 153).

These remarks—some deliberate and some so-called innocent—create an indelible impression on the minds of the young. They can help form certain philosophies that serve as a foundation for their perspective on life, leading them to actually fulfill spiritually unacceptable roles and create fears and anxieties that last a lifetime.

Many parents remember certain mistakes from their childhood or youth and loathe the result. Therefore, they endeavor to instill fear in their children by being controlling and over-protective. The children become dependent on their parents, so emotionally attenuated that they fear decision making because they do not want to make any mistakes. Dr. Henry Cloud relates the story of Burt, the twenty-five-year-old son of Christian Parents who was never allowed to make spiritual decisions for himself. They made them for him; they told him when to attend church services and supervised his attendance.

"When Burt left home, he went wild." He drank and partied in an attempt to convince himself that he was now in control of his own life. By approaching life that way, he was "losing control" rather than gaining control. The fear of seeing their child make mistakes had driven his parents to the extreme in making decisions for him. Unless something changes in Burt's life, he will try to control his children's lives so that they don't make the mistake of going wild and experiencing the shame and guilt that he may feel at the end of his escapades (if he survives and becomes a productive citizen) (Cloud 1992, 137).

Dr. Frederic Neuman made an interesting observation that corresponds to a large extent with the idea that most fears originate in childhood. People are concerned, he writes, about reports of trains sliding off embankments, buildings burning down, and people being mugged or raped. These things really happen, but the phobic, who is anxious in general, takes a closer note of these incidents than other people and exaggerates their frequency and significance (Neuman 1985, 18-19). Some of the "don'ts" that parents express to their children from the underlying cause of their fears as adults, Dr. Neuman provides corroboration that the root causes of many fears lay in childhood or young adulthood.

Some examples of "don'ts" are: "Don't take the car; it's dark out. Don't take the car; there will be traffic. Don't take the car; driving is dangerous." Dr. Neuman contends that it's just a short step from these warnings to a full-blown driving phobia. He further mentions that the phobic person considers a person's physical health to be a precarious matter, as if the human body is a machine that is not up to the challenges of daily living. Any deviation from the normal physical routine is considered dangerous (Neuman 1985, 18-19). Such individuals, I might add, are not living a God-ordained, productive life. They are too focused on themselves to the exclusion of the source of freedom, happiness, and spiritual strength.

The beginning of the process of neutralization of these fears is for those individuals to engage in visual achievement. They must look away from the self and become transfixed on him who has the power to defeat the spirit of fear and uncertainty: By engaging in this focused activity, one is able to dispel negative thoughts and feelings and receive strength on a daily basis to live a normal, productive life.

If, on the contrary, people retain or nurture these negative thoughts, they may ultimately acquire defective personalities and experience unhappiness and illnesses that otherwise would have been avoided. In the 1970s, a psychiatrist named Aaron Beck became known for treating depression by examining the thought patterns associated with negative moods. This approach, applied to the treatment of panic disorders, is called cognitive therapy. Cognitive therapy notes that many feelings that appear to arise suddenly actually originate with a thought.

Dr. Beck states that in some cases the thought is fully conscious but mistaken (Ross 1994, 76). Now, that is what I associate with anxiety and not feat. Anxiety is an assumption of false facts (events not likely to occur), whereas fear is an awareness of real facts (events that have a great probability of occurring). I will add that even with the awareness of real facts, fear would not exist if there were no negative thoughts about them. Many of these negative thoughts find their roots in childhood and are confirmed along life's road.

Dysfunctional Families and High Expectations

The dynamics of dysfunctional families demand multifaceted approaches and creative solutions. Often, problem-solving techniques must be used individually as well as collectively to achieve the desired solutions. For example, every family consists of a family unit made up of individuals. In some cases, one person in the family may have certain problems that impact the family as a whole. Therefore, that individual needs personal counseling, but the family' may have to be treated as well.

The fear of family members defacing a positive image developed over many years by the patriarch or matriarch becomes a real issue. Hence, each child and grandchild is coached and expected to engage in conduct worthy of the family name. I recall former president George Herbert Walker Bush saying during the 2000 presidential election that he had raised his children well—by the highest standards of years ago as well as today. His statement was made in support of his son, George W. Bush, who was a presidential candidate. Lesser-known families also have established traditions and family names that they vigorously protect and defend. Every family should be able to mount such a defense. Unfortunately, in some cases, the rigidity employed in the process of ensuring that the image is maintained engenders defiance, rebellion, and a result that is counterproductive.

A very important point that should not be ignored is how people view dysfunctionality. The term dysfunctional families usually is cast on poor families with little to eat and not enough money to survive. Such families may also be thought of as comprising parents and children who are on drugs, are in abusive situations, have divorced families, and so on. But there are families with bountiful supplies of everything material that one could offer except for the constant, tender care of a loving mother and the presence and guidance of a compassionate father.

In many cases, some of the most prominent families in the world lack these essential features. They may allow their children to he raised by other individuals. The time they designate as quality time is budgeted and so constricted that it falls far short of what is required. That's a major reason children who are raised under those circumstances have so much difficulty blending with their spouses and producing wholesome families.

Many of these marriages end in divorce or exist in a conflict-habituated state. The couples remain together for the children's sake or to protect their image. The fear of breaking up and shattering that facade of harmony and allowing everyone to see their empty, unfulfilled lives drives some of them to engage in public, superficial displays of love.

Many children who grew up under those circumstances tend to repeat them in their adult relationships unless, somehow, the cycle is broken. They have observed and experienced the trauma. Even though they did not really understand the nuances, dynamics, and fragmentation of the relationship, they perceived the contradiction between the public and private lives of their parents or guardians. By beholding such contradiction on a continuing basis, they have subconsciously assimilated the behaviors that eventually become their paradigm of existence.

Rejection During Childhood

The impact of rejection during childhood is greater than some people realize. Many children are shouted at and spoken to as if they were little nobodies. Things they consider achievements are ignored or criticized for not being more perfect. Some have been denied genuine affection and an atmosphere in which they can share their problems, hopes, and aspirations. Such circumstances lead children to develop self-doubt and low self-esteem. Early rejection can significantly affect a person's later outlook on life, work habits, and relationships with others.

The result of love denied—the psychological trauma of always being criticized for not being able to make one's parents or guardians proud—sometimes generates an overbearing attitude and intolerance in the workplace. Very rarely do these people realize that their behavior is a carryover from childhood. They only know that somehow their subordinates are not working efficiently enough to please them. They always seem driven to find something that is not being done right.

Childhood experiences are not generally considered when marriage is being contemplated. Because people do change—not everyone is held hostage by the baggage of unpleasant childhood experiences—some expect childhood rejection to have little effect on a marriage. Yet some of the negative symptoms of repressed childhood rejection may not surface until certain stressful situations develop within the marriage. Prospective marriage partners might not be truly able to predict a spouse's future behaviors.

Consider the following two examples, outlined to me by two adults who have given me permission to relate their experiences. Let's call them Nora and Yvette. Nora says, "Growing up for me was not what you would call a model childhood. From early on, my parents [were] divorced. My father (an alcoholic) and my older brother went to live with my grandparents, and I stayed with my mother, who remarried soon after the divorce. The man she chose to marry did not want her children around ... [so] I was shifted from house to house. Eventually, my mother decided [that] she would bring me to my grandparents to stay. However, my grandparents had enough ... burden on their hands, and a distant cousin [and her husband], whom I actually referred to as my aunt and uncle, took me in.

"Although for the majority of the years, these people were good to me in terms of providing for my needs and a roof over my head, I never did feel a sense of love. I always felt like I had to walk around on tiptoes and did not have a voice. They had a son who was the same age as I was. Although I was young, I realized [that] they treated him much differently than they did me. I can understand [that] this was their [biological] son, but it was difficult to feel like [a] part of the family unit.

"I was very much an introvert but excelled in school. I guess you could say that was my way of proving to the world [that] I was a 'real' person. As I grew older, in my high school years, I became rebellious in many different ways. This route ultimately led to my aunt and uncle's giving me a choice to change my ways or leave. I chose to leave ... thinking that I had found or would find 'real love.' This newfound love was short-lived. I believe [that] at that point I had become even more resentful of the world and the people in it, not knowing who to trust and having that feeling of being used and unloved."

Its obvious Nora suffered from severe self-esteem problems. She became fearful of developing relationships with others because she could not trust anyone. The ones she trusted disappointed her. She had looked to them for love and affection as a child but did not receive it. Instead, she felt like a second-class child; she felt as one who was not important and whose feelings were not to be taken into account. She felt abandoned. Fortunately, she trusted in God and was able to marry and is raising a child of her own.

Nora is attempting to give her child that love she wanted so desperately but was denied. However, even now, at the age of forty-two, she says that she often "looks back on my childhood and (asks the] question: how could a mother and filcher 'leave' their child?" Had Nora remained single, she night have continued to experience the profound depths of abandonment, mistrust, and fear of associating with others in attempts to avoid developing any relationship that might lead to disappointment. This approach could have led to loneliness and depression.

Yvette's experience, though different from Nora's, had a certain thread of commonality. They both felt rejected. However, each tried to achieve her objectives in different ways. Where Nora shied away from relationships to avoid rejection and disappointment, Yvette sought relationships in order to feel accepted and overcome the feeling of rejection. Yvette says, "As a child I felt rejected by my biological family. I grew up living with a neighbor of my grandmother's for reasons that were never explained to me. I went to live with my grandmother at the age of nine, [at] which [time] I learned of my biological mother, father, brothers, and sisters ... I never told anyone of my fears, but [I] always wanted other kids to like me. So I was completely other oriented. Everything I did in life was based on getting everyone to approve of me. I would see my brothers and try to get their attention but not be successful.

"Two years later, I moved to another city to live with my aunt. The thought of rejection was even stronger; here again, my grandmother sent me away. Starting all over again to gain new friends was very difficult, but I managed to gain attention by sharing myself and resources with everyone [with whom] I came in contact. My own mother didn't care about me no matter what I did, but [of the people ... whose affection I tried to obtain] I thought, Maybe I can Will him or her even if I can't win my mother. So I always strove to please. If I didn't do what others wanted—or what I thought they wanted—the only alternative was rejection. In dating, I picked difficult, demanding, hostile men who used and rejected me ... because I was trying to get acceptance in the wrong way ... I did not [remain] single for long because I wanted someone to love me. I met this man whom I thought was kind and generous. We got married [and] he told me [that] he would love and cherish me the rest the rest of his life.

"After the first six months, I noticed a pattern of verbal abuse. Then came the physical [abuse]; I was convinced that no one in this world accepted me. (The feeling of] rejection grew into bitterness, and

I developed a very low self-esteem. No longer did I have a social life. I constantly created scenarios in which people rejected me. A friend asked my opinion about buying a new car; I told her what I thought she wanted to hear. She didn't like what I said and she never talked to me again. For months, I agonized over [the) desertion. I decided to give my life to the Lord in its entirety. I am now fully recovered from the fear of rejection. And I have made every effort to locate and develop a wonderful relationship with my biological family."

The two experiences fit perfectly into the fear confirmation diagram in Figure 7. The left oval represents childhood. The right oval represents adulthood. The rectangle represents the crossover from childhood into adulthood. Thus, the area where the two ovals intersect represents adolescence into young adulthood, when many childhood fears are confirmed. I do believe that at this time in a person's life (possibly up to early midlife), some of the fears that were repressed in childhood or new fears that reemphasize old fears become real problems that must be addressed.

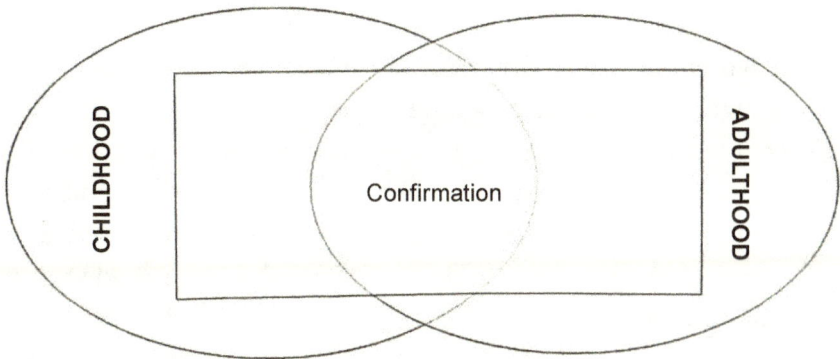

Figure 7. Fear Confirmation Diagram

I believe that people in their later years become more focused on the immediate environment and not so much on the broad spectrum of life. Therefore, it may not be important to address specific fears. General comforting and assurance of safety and hope are needed. At that stage, most of those fears no longer affect the individual. A study on how much childhood fears continue to affect people who are, let's say, in their fifties and beyond, might be an interesting project. Nevertheless, the diagram was designed to show how fears are carried over from childhood as root causes and are confirmed in adulthood.

From Nora and Yvette's stories, we see again how in many instances some of the same incidents from childhood are repeated in adult life, causing those early fears to resurface and restore the pain of the past. I call this confirmation; it confirms in a person's mind that his or her life will forever be antagonized by those incidents. People in those situations seem to see no resolution to their problems. They have insecurities and are never really free until those issues are dealt with and resolved. They keep re-experiencing aspects of their childhood, a confirmation that the trauma will never end. Childhood trauma should not be ignored; some form of counseling should be obtained.

The scars from the trauma of negative childhood experiences can and do create havoc in the lives of untold millions of people in their marriages, work environment, and social interactions. Sometimes the fear of repetition of childhood trauma is so overwhelming that the person abdicates the quest for a happy life. A can't-do attitude is assumed. The pain experienced by Nora and Yvette is shared by many whose symptoms are just emptiness and apprehension that follow them in the night and in times of solitude. They are hesitant in expressing the conflicting and disturbing thoughts for fear of rejection. Yet they desperately need someone in whom they can confide and find acceptance and peace. These experiences of rejection, coupled with poor parental examples, are a recipe for waywardness, fear, and various vices in children.

Bad Example Producing Fearful, Rebellious Children

It is ironic that some behaviors parents' exhibit are the very ones that they detest and do not want their children to exhibit. Some adults have told me that that's why they do not want to have any children. They fear that their children will become as rebellious as they were. Others have expressed that when they grow up, they will not treat their children the way they were treated. Yet some of them get married and deal more harshly with their children than their parents dealt with them. Why? Because when they were engaged in the conduct that their parents considered reprehensible, they were not satisfied. They knew they were rebellious but were only doing those things to get back at their parents or to be accepted in the "in group" that was in conflict with parental mores.

Children are very wise in their assessment of adults. Parents, at times, seem to underestimate their children's ability to see through them and to determine what they really stand for. It is one thing for a parent to tell a child to resist peer pressure in regard to smoking, illicit sex, taking drugs, and fooling around. But it is another thing when that child sees the parents smoking or taking drugs. This hypocrisy does not sit well with children. Sometimes, out of an inability to express themselves clearly to the parents about how they feel regarding this conflicting message, they engage in the same conduct, as if to say, "Do you see how I feel about what you are doing? And yet you are telling me not to do it?"

The rebellion that a child exhibits is usually a way of reaching out for help and guidance. If the child does not see the right example in the parents or guardians and if the rebellion continues for a certain period of time, it develops into a lifestyle and becomes part of the child's character. It is then that you see overt defiance of law and order and an attitude that says, "I don't care." When such conditions exist, the road back to civility is very hard because the person is dealing with a chronic condition. Only biblical principles can help bring about a change of heart and rehabilitate the individual.

These individuals are really spending their lives under the heavy burden of sin. They are laboring, they are tired, and they need rest from the activities in which they are engaged, but they see no way out. They are committed to a gang, to a cause, or to themselves as a tough character, and they want some relief but do not know where to turn or how to obtain it. The Bible indicates that Jesus knew of that condition. That's why he said, "Come unto me ye that labor and are heavy laden and I will give you rest" (Matthew 11:28). Unless the woman who is fearful of having children is aware of this help that is available, she may opt to remain childless rather than risk having children who may become rebellious.

Other People's Experience of Being Married and in Pain

Information disseminated widely by the news media has done much to educate the public about the rate of divorce in this country. We also know much about the problems of some prominent figures in American life. Additionally, those who have been raised in homes where they witnessed marital problems and abuses firsthand know the results of conflict and disorder. Out of fear, some of them have vowed not to marry. They are frightened by the possibility of emotional and perhaps even physical pain by an abusive spouse.

Unfortunately, some women are unable to trust men because of the disappointment experienced by their mothers or by their own experiences. The reality of the trauma in their lives cannot be overlooked or taken lightly. A woman who loses trust in men or who has been used and abused by them is more likely to be withdrawn from other men, bitter, attempt to find solace in relocation to other environments, or become preoccupied with material things or individuals. Make no mistake; even a practicing Christian could lose focus under such circumstances. The lack of moral direction guided by a higher code of conduct may lead the disillusioned, jilted, cheated woman to depression, other mental disorders, or various forms of deviant behaviors. I counsel such individuals to trust in the God of heaven and remember that "He will never leave you nor forsake you" (Hebrews 13:5), but, "I will strengthen thee; I will help thee; I will uphold thee with the right hand of my righteousness" (Isaiah 41:10).

When one partner in a marriage discovers that the other is unfaithful, a painful and fearful process begins. The very thought that the unfaithful partner may no longer be in love is almost overwhelming. Yet the thought of losing that unfaithful partner is not acceptable to the injured spouse. This ambivalence creates a psychological dichotomy that sometimes produces nightmares, insomnia, and a feeling of hopelessness.

Though crushed by the betrayal of the unfaithful spouse, the grieving spouse (for that is the nature of the experience) does not want to see that spouse again yet does not know how to go on living without him or her. More often than not, the injured spouse needs time to regroup, forgive, and begin the process of acceptance and healing. If the cheated spouse decides to walk away from the marriage, sometimes the unfaithful spouse panics and goes overboard in an attempt to win back the spouse.

In cases in which a person is no longer attracted to the spouse and a new relationship is begun, the rejected spouse has a similar reaction. The pain, anguish, and frustration lead that spouse to take action that drives the errant spouse even further away. Dr. James Dobson, writing of the tragedy of divorce, states that "long before a decision is made to 'fool around' or walk out on a partner, a fundamental change" has begun to take place. The change is so subtle that the little telltale signs are not noticed, but "now we begin to see why groveling, crying, and pleading by a panic-stricken partner tend to drive the claustrophobic partner even farther away. The more he or she struggles to gain a measure of freedom (or even secure a little breathing room), the more desperately the rejected spouse attempts to hang on" (Dobson June 2000, 2).

Neutralization of fear in these circumstances requires a complete trust and confidence in God. It requires a belief that recognizes that only the power of the Holy Spirit can change a vile, sinful heart and make it truly repentant and free of guilt. A pouring out of the heart to God as one would bare one's soul to a friend will help relieve the mental pain and stabilize the emotion to allow for further maintenance.

The experiences observed in childhood can become root causes of fear regarding a commitment to relationships and marriage. Yet singleness, too many of these people, is similar to being incarcerated.

The Thought of Being Single Forever

In general, men and women seem to believe that at some point they are likely to get married. Over many years of observations, interviews, and information from various sources, I have concluded that most men are not as fearful about remaining single for the rest of their lives as most women. Professor and former dean at Rutgers University, David Popenoe, and author Dr. Barbara Dafoe Whitehead, co-chair of the National Marriage Project, in their research, found that women are faced with "time pressure" to get married so they can bear children, fearing that the years of fertility might pass them by.

Men, on the other hand, can afford to wait until they are ready. The Popenoe research shows that going back to the mid-1800s, 90 percent of women were married, and by 1960, 94 percent of the women alive had been married at least once by the time they were forty-five years of age. However, there is growing pessimism or fear among the young about how permanent their marriage will be. In fact, many men and women are looking more favorably on alternative lifestyles, such as cohabitating or single parenting (Popenoe and Whitehead 2002).

In reality, the ratio of women to men makes it possible for virtually all men to marry if they so choose, or even if they were forced to select any woman at random, though she might not be the woman of their dreams. The 2005 U.S. census shows that there were approximately 288 million people in the United States. The breakdown by gender shows 147 million females and 141 million males, a ratio of 1.042 females to each male. Theoretically, accounting for aspects of compatibility; age, or attraction, men could marry virtually whomever they choose. Their primary inhibitions to marrying appear to be (not necessarily in this order) unpreparedness, available alternative lifestyles, age, financial or educational issues, not finding the right person, a desire to "experience life" before they settle down, or disinterest (Popenoe and Whitehead 2002).

On the other hand, a great many women fear being single forever. They want some form of companionship, so some go the traditional route and marry, others have children out of wedlock, and some have live-in boyfriends, some choose same-sex relationships, and, of course, some have not yet found the right person (Popenoe and Whitehead 2002).

"[In the 1980s,] Merritt and Steiner (1984) looked at motherhood without marriage and found that most women wanted to have a child but had not been able to find a man with whom they wanted to spend their lives" (Kin near 1999, 4-9). In effect, these women wanted a family situation but settled for a modified one.

I believe that the bottom line is that women, in general, envision themselves being married, and most of them desire to have children and raise a healthy, happy family. Although I am not endorsing her book, Better Single Than Sorry, the sentiment Jen Schefft expressed in promoting her book on the Web site "Better Single Than Sorry: A No-Regrets Guide to Loving Yourself and Never Settling" seems to reflect my comments about women and their singleness (Schefft 2007).

The circumstances that inhibit that expectation of companionship, however, are dealt with in different ways by different people. Psychologists, pastoral and professional counselors, therapists, and other professionals try to emphasize to single women that their singleness should not be considered a misfortune and that it does not reflect negatively on them. While some console themselves that it is because the right person has not yet come into their lives, others indicate that it is because they are not ready. Still others tend to think that something is wrong with them since they have not been chosen. This is especially true of some women who had previous relationships that were broken off and whose ex-boyfriends have married other women.

In an attempt to enhance their beauty so that they can be accepted, thinking that unattractiveness caused their competitors to get the tipper hand, some women become inordinately concerned with their attire, makeup, and general demeanor. Sometimes the statement they make with their garments or body language is so pronounced that some men detect it from afar and shy away from a potential close relationship. The fear of not attracting a suitor or not being able to maintain a long-term relationship that could blossom into marriage leads some women to compromise their self-worth.

Some women accede to the demands for premarital sex with the hope that the men will see that they are cooperative and willing to please. This, some women do not realize, is the very means of driving some men away or assisting them in their reluctance or inability to commit to a lasting relationship that could result in marriage. Unmarried women in their thirties may feel more pressure and may be more vulnerable because of the passing of time, the desire to get married and imminent physiological changes. My Spiritual Euphoric Therapy has principles that are relevant to these situations.

Retirement Issues

It is amazing to see, at times, how far into the future we project. The future, though no one knows it, is very important. Therefore, we must anticipate and plan for it. When I was a child, I did not see myself getting old and retiring. That did not cross my mind as far as my recollection is concerned. I suppose the reason was that I was interested in the present and the immediate, not some distant future. Hence, my thoughts did not expand that far.

Eventually, men and women do think about the future—the distant future—their retirement time. For many, this thought process takes place early in adult life, allowing adequate time for planning. Unfortunately, some do not face the reality until their forties or fifties— late but not too late, depending on the circumstances.

The picture of a happy retiree sitting in a well-landscaped yard with grandchildren running around may not be all that attractive if neither children nor property ownership currently exists. Without strategic planning consistent with biblical principles, fear about a successful retirement is a real issue. (The Bible encourages us to do whatsoever our hands find to do and not to be slothful in business.) The fearful thing about retirement is not so much the initial years after retirement but the later years. Many people have accumulated a decent sum of money that they can live on for a long time in retirement. Some have been fortunate to have generous pension plans. Others have, on their own, engaged in investments that have generated large retirement assets. Still others possess wealth by means of inheritance.

Yet while individuals with adequate funds available in their retirement years may not be concerned about money, some are fearful of being put away in retirement communities and nursing homes where neither friends nor relatives visit. The fear is really about loneliness in their golden years.

It is reasonable then to state that even those who have achieved financial success have fears about the retirement process. They dread feelings of uselessness, isolation, and loneliness. The fear may be all the more pronounced if health problems are present. Perhaps the spouse is deceased and life has taken on a different meaning without the usual companion. Maybe the person has been single for a lifetime. Whatever the case, entering the last stages of life alone can he a fearful situation. If these individuals are in an environment where there are activities and others with whom to associate, the feeling of loneliness can be lessened.

I have known of elderly women who have been fortunate to have had a good life. They met the men of their dreams, married, had their expectations met. Now their loneliness seems to be overshadowed by pleasant memories and reflection, as they spend their time in quiet contemplation. Their fears were not realized to any great extent. Fears that could have been pathological were jettisoned because of the fulfillment of what I call the "What Factor." Unfortunately, that is not true for everyone. Those fears that become root causes of other fears are more problematic. This leads to inquiry into other root causes of fear about marriage and women's expectations. How can those expectations be met and fears alleviated? The answer to those questions can be found in chapter 8, where we address the issues involving women's needs, their wants, and their fears about the What Factor.

CHAPTER 8

WOMEN'S FEARS ABOUT THE WHAT FACTOR

Women, Marriage, and the What Factor

Generally speaking, all women have certain needs that are intrinsic to womanhood. All women have the same reproductive and physiological capabilities. Of course, we are not dealing with aberrations due to natural causes or that are human induced. The physiological structure of women lends itself to certain attitudes in men. Generally, men are sexually attracted to women and have a basic desire to possess and enjoy them physically. These responses are derived from a nature that men inherit. They are God given. Nothing is wrong with those desires. However, such desires must be subjected to the control and guidelines of Scripture, and the sexual expression should be viewed only in context of marriage.

At the outset of a relationship, the man, in most cases, does not perceive the needs of the woman. Instead he is more concerned about his needs and the satisfaction of his desires. He tends to cater to her with the hope of satisfying her so that she can, in turn, satisfy him. Since this approach is selfish, which many women are astute enough to recognize, it leads her to wish, hope, and wonder when and if he will recognize her needs and desires so that she can be truly fulfilled. As the woman gets older, the fear (which may have originated partly in childhood) that this fulfillment may never be realized is sometimes overwhelming.

Once the man begins to understand that he must fulfill the woman's needs, he may not be ready or qualified to handle or determine what those needs are and how to address them. Therefore, a man needs to know and distinguish between what a woman needs and what she wants and endeavor to meet her needs and satisfy her wants to the best of his ability, hoping that she is understanding or godly enough to overlook and sympathize with any deficiency.

What She Needs and Wants

As a minister and counselor, I have done research on women's issues over the years. I have involved myself in cultural and cross-cultural observation and gained much insight from attending workshops and seminars, books, periodicals, journals, personal interviews, being party to women's conversations, etc., and of course, information from my wife. I have come to the conclusion that a woman has three basic needs. All other needs seem to fall under those three categories. They are the need to be loved, the need to feel secure, and the need to be reassured.

In addition to the many women who have supported my conclusion about women's needs and wants, on May II, 2010, I received feedback to my question about the validity of my conclusion from a few female nurses and doctors who have had between twelve and forty-one years experience each, dealing with hundreds, if not thousands of women, in a hospital setting as well as private practice. All but one, agreed fully with my conclusion and some provided additional information which falls under the heading of security. Even the one, who appeared to only partially agree with me, unknowingly, expressed her agreement in her explanation. She is K. W., a registered nurse (R.N.) from New Jersey. She says that "I don't need to be reassured. I am comfortable in my own right. [Then she added that] we can read each other without question. Love, trust [and] security are important, you know it [and] feel it without question." In other words, all those things she mentioned are being experienced on an ongoing basis and really serve as reaffirmation and reassurance of love which strengthen the security she enjoys.

I will not mention all the positive comments I received, only those from two medical doctors—one in private practice and the other a physician at a hospital, and another nurse. Dr. Angela Wimmer, practitioner, agreed with the three categories of needs. She stated that the woman also needs "a purpose," which really falls under either security or love. Dr. Claudine Sylvester also agreed with my assessment and added other dimensions of the woman's love. Finally, Paula Morrison, R.N., agreed wholeheartedly with my assessment and added that "a woman also needs to be comfortable with who she is and to love herself." The above comments indicate that when a woman places value on herself and feels valued by her spouse, it creates an environment where she feels secure in being herself and expressing herself in ways that are beneficial to the relationship. The fear of making a mistake or not measuring up is not an issue. Men should take note of these important statements.

Love

A woman's needs and her wants are two phenomena that must be addressed in that order unless, of course, she does not understand or she does not have her priorities together. Her needs were predetermined when God created the first woman. Later, they were reaffirmed but with different dimensions because of the sin that Adam and Eve committed. This truth is reflected in the statement God made to Eve after they sinned. He said, "Thy desire will be to thy [for your] husband and he shall rule over thee" (Genesis 3:16). Therefore, she is not expected to put aside or jettison those needs at will. Her wants, on the other hand, are her dreams, her hopes, and sometimes her passion. She sees herself possessing these dreams and imagines them as a reality: Consequently, she strives to obtain them or hopes to obtain them from the desired source: her husband.

What are the needs of a woman? A woman needs love. She needs to be loved. She needs to know and feel that she is loved. Even when a girl is raised in a dysfunctional family, that dysfunctional circumstance does not prevent her from having the need to be loved? Therefore, she seeks the one whom she believes will show expressions of love and who will, in fact, demonstrate that he loves her. Unfortunately, most women who have been abused or molested suffer from lack of self-esteem. Many of them attempt to make themselves pleasing to men who indicate that they love them by overcompensating for the void within them. This gives rise to sexual promiscuity, prostitution, and other forms of immorality. Many of these women become abusers themselves and are unable to obtain the satisfaction of being loved. They even see themselves as being taken advantage of as opposed to being genuinely loved by their spouses.

The woman who is not impacted by those unfortunate circumstances needs and seeks a relationship in which she is assured that she is loved. Sometimes this is difficult because she may feel fear and hesitation in transitioning from one lifestyle to another. Although there are exceptions, girls traditionally envision themselves growing up, getting married, and having children of their own. The idea of getting married is based on the need to have someone love them. They want that love to he expressed in a permanent way: marriage. Being married assures a woman that the love is stable and lasting. Divorce is not anticipated. If it does occur, it is an unfortunate mishap that is devastating.

The woman needs not only love but also a certain kind of love: an unconditional love. While this love includes in its portfolio love among family members, such as filial love, it runs deeper. She needs to be loved by a man as he loves himself because she is one with him and he wants to unite himself with her both physically and emotionally: The foundation of this love is agape (agape is a Greek word expressing the love from God). Therefore, love is manifested when she sees and understands that he accepts her as she is and not what he wishes her to be. When he looks into her eyes, she needs to see that look of tenderness, a look of longing for her, and a look of caring that is not stern. When she looks into his eyes, she needs to feel that she has found him for whom she has longed; she should find a sense of fulfillment and comfort there, not fear and apprehension.

Security

A woman needs to feel secure. Security comes from trust. Until a man marries the woman with whom he is in a relationship, she will continue to wonder whether he is serious about this relationship. She cannot be certain that it will be a permanent relationship until she sees actions that indicate permanency. The age of the individuals involved is not even the issue, although most of us are aware that before a certain age, one is not mature enough to make certain lasting commitments. Every woman, young or old, who is involved in a relationship with a man whose company she enjoys hopes that the relationship will continue. She is hoping—though sometimes it is a futile hope—that the experience of having found someone with whom she feels secure will never end. Many people, without realizing it at the time, actually meet their spouses in their early years—high school, elementary school, and sometimes even kindergarten.

Further, regarding the eligible bachelor, the woman wants to know that he can provide for her and the family and that he is able to defend her and the family against danger. At times, fear or uncertainty about the future is relegated to the back burner of her heart because even against her better judgment, she is unable to see how the present situation could change to an unpleasant one. Related to his ability to provide and defend is implied his willingness to do so because of the love she perceives he has fir her. Security, then, is the feeling of abiding love with financial and personal protection.

There are those who are not financially able but are perceived as having the capability to accomplish the task. (Some could argue legitimately that some of these early relationships are only youthful attractions that may not last.) Nevertheless, with the idea that "He will take care of me," some high school girls marry someone without the financial stability needed for support of a wife or family.

In some cases, people obtain certain fears from other people. By listening to and assimilating the negative experience of others and buying into the fears those people possess, they take on those attitudes of negativism and fear. Georgette Mosbacher, in It Takes Money, Honey, related her disappointment with her marriage to ex-husband Robert Mosbacher. She expresses her disillusionment with the man she thought was honest and trustworthy until he filed for a divorce. She claims that she had been unaware that he was unhappy. She was surprised not only by his divorcing her but also because he had kept other secrets from her.

Consequently, she seems to encourage women to believe that their husbands might be hiding secrets from them and that they should protect themselves by creating a secret stash of cash in case their husbands leave them so that they will not be left out in the proverbial cold. She states, "Should you too wake up one day to find that your honest-as-the-day-is-long husband has secrets from you, deep secrets that may cause your marriage to crumble, should you be forced to go from a nice house to an efficiency apartment ... you may live to regret the decision not to give yourself the financial means to rebuild your life" (Mosbacher 1999, 96).

This counsel, though well intentioned and born out of personal experience, is obviously not based upon a spiritual foundation. The parties involved clearly had issues for which biblical solutions were not considered.

Unfortunately, a weak-minded woman who is unable to properly distinguish between appropriate counsel and that which should he ignored may take hold of such counsel and begin to develop mistrust of her husband. She may assimilate that belief until her actions generate suspicion and create marital problems. Ms. Mosbacher may have had meaningful intentions, but the message in this case is really one of fear and distrust. This is not the true path to security.

Assurance

In a marriage relationship, trust needs to be maintained. Constant expressions of love strengthen the marriage bond. The trust-love-security tripod is maintained by a continuous assurance and reassurance. This does not have to be done by a continuous verbal smothering that becomes monotonous. Creative ways should be employed. It can be just a certain kind of look, a token gift, a rose petal, your presence—being by her side at an unexpected occasion or any other romantic and expressive ways. Then the wife feels secure, her trust in her husband is strengthened, and her love is maintained as a garden that is watered frequently. She loves him whether or not her trust is violated and her security threatened (that is, if she had truly loved him before marriage). However, a violation of that trust tears the security blanket that covers her. Her love, like a vulnerable fruit, is pierced.

A plethora of things can be done to provide assurance to a spouse. I say a spouse because we mostly tend to think in terms of the wife's needs, believing that the husband is strong and indifferent to reassurance. It should be remembered that many wives work outside their homes. Some are entrepreneurs or executives who hold positions in as many fields as do men. In such cases, these women may face a montage of problems, including sexual harassment. Some may become attracted to other men and develop a relationship, even though it's a violation of their marriage commitment. Therefore, the women who work outside the home are likewise expected to be faithful and provide continued assurance to their men that they are still in love with them and are faithful to their commitment.

Women need to understand the influence they have on their families. They are the ones who, in most cases, are responsible for the development of the children. The children receive a certain kind of nurturing from the mother that the father is incapable of providing. She knows their attitudes and keeps in tune with their feelings. They are apt to listen to her counsel and follow her suggestions. Pertaining to the husband, while he wants to know that she is in love with him, he presupposes that she is because she married him and has told him that she loved him. As long as she still lives with him and has said nothing to the contrary, he concludes that she is still in love with him. Barring any severe communication problem, his overriding need is sexual intimacy. He will do anything to remove or defeat that which will prevent him from achieving that fulfillment. Men are fearful of falling out of grace with their women. And although it is understood that love is the dominant theme, to avoid denial of the conjugal relationship, a man will do almost anything his woman wants to have done.

Now that we have addressed the assurance that men need, let us turn our attention to the needs of women. Many wives who have elected to stay at home and raise a family yearn for the expressions of love from their husbands. It is not a pleasant thing for a woman to be at home all day with the children and be neglected, slighted, or abused by her husband, who comes home with a myriad of demands without consideration for her feelings or her needs. This kind of behavior leads the wife to wonder whether her husband is still in love with her. The level of trust can easily be eroded.

In order to maintain a budding love relationship, a man must learn to be understanding, caring, and sensitive to his wife's feelings and needs. He needs to be observant of her moods. Even after thirty-seven years of marriage, like many men, I am still learning and doing my best to add and keep flavor in my marriage. My wife and I are friends. We trusted each other before we got married, and we continue to trust each other. We have not always agreed on everything; however, we try to be understanding and iron out our disagreements as we grow in our relationship, Our love for each other remains immovable and our faithfulness unwavering.

I constantly remind myself that I must demonstrate my love for her in tangible ways. A man must show in deed as well as in word that he loves his wife. He must do the little things that indicate that he is paying attention to her. Admittedly, many of us are not exemplary in this area.

The reason some marriages are invaded by outside parties and eventually fall apart is because the wife cannot get any meaningful attention from her husband. Fear of losing her man drives her to seek solutions from other sources. She bares her soul to anyone who is willing to listen or show interest in her and that person becomes her friend. If that friendship is developed with someone of the opposite sex (which should not be), he may take advantage of her vulnerability and cause her to violate her marriage vow.

Even with a situation as has been described, if the wife is a committed Christian, her response will he one of prayer and continued, dedicated service to her husband and family, believing that in due time, God will make things right. She should seek friendship with other committed

Christian women who can provide support. Marriage secrets should be guarded. They are not juicy materials for the public. Oh, that some women could learn this; they might save themselves from illicit affairs and divorces. When men provide continued assurance to their wives— that they love them, care about their needs, desire them—and support the verbal expressions with appropriate actions, they provide security and stability for the marriage. The fear of losing such a husband will not be entertained.

The What Factor

When two people are courting, each has certain expectations. If we should focus for just a moment on the expectations of the woman, we would observe a very interesting phenomenon. But first let me say that a man, in most cases, expects his wife to love and care for him and the children and keep the house in order (unless she is a professional and they have agreed otherwise). If those things are being done and his conjugal relationship is going well, from his perspective, that's really all he requires. He does not think of her feelings toward his friends until the question comes up.

A woman, on the other hand, has a great many concerns. She has certain fears that must be addressed as she approaches the question of marriage; she is entering a great whirlpool of love all by herself with this man in whom she is placing all her hopes. The great question that is involved in all of her expectations is what I call the "What Factor." What will he give me? What will happen when I get it? And what will happen if I don't get it? Her whole life is wrapped up in these questions as she sees herself going into the relationship and living with this man.

What Will He Give Me?

Included in this question is a multiplicity of thoughts. It is not a one-item shopping list. She is entrusting her entire future to a man that she, in many cases, has only known anywhere from a few weeks (not the general rule) to several years. Some couples have been intimately acquainted with each other for years. Even in those cases, though, life after the marriage takes on a different meaning. So the woman approaches this delicate issue very cautiously. Her excitement is mingled with questions that are concealed from her groom-to-he. This dichotomous feeling brings an inexplicable ambivalence because all her questions cannot be enumerated or adequately articulated.

Some of the questions that surface involve intimacy.. There is much trepidation about this subject because it is usually difficult for one spouse to verbalize such concerns due to fear of offending the other and risking a rift in the marriage. However, the concerns are real. Questions she poses to herself are: What satisfaction will I get sexually? Will I be fulfilled or disillusioned? Will he continue to love and care for me if we move away from to parents and my friends? What property will we possess? If he alone works outside the home, will he give me enough money to care for the family, or will he control everything? If both of us are working, will he expect me to give him my money? Will he find me fulfilling sexually? What will he do if our honeymoon is not what he expected? I know I love him, but what am I really getting into? I am excited about our marriage, but I don't know; there are so many questions. I'm scared. These and other questions about her husband-to-be may pass through her mind. Most often, no one else is privy to them. She tries to relegate those thoughts to the back burner of her heart and convince herself that she is doing the right thing. Then she moves ahead, confident and satisfied with her decision to marry him.

What Will Happen When She Gets What She Expects

As she ponders the question of what kind of life her husband will give her, she discards, or tries to discard, negative thoughts. She envisions herself obtaining all the thrills and pleasures associated with the marriage. In that state of future happiness, she sees him as a loving, caring husband. lie means everything to her. He will defend her; he will supply all her needs; he will not leave her but will be always by her side. She sees him lavishing all his love on her and the family. In a sense, she sees herself in a utopian and euphoric relationship, and no one can convince her that things will be any different. Not all women have all those thoughts, but most have some or all of them.

Intimacy

When a woman perceives that her husband is in tune with her and recognizes and understands her feelings, she is well on her way to achieving intimacy. Intimacy to a woman is not only sexual intercourse. That is just the culmination of the whole process. Intimacy is both a need and a want in a woman's life. She is, more than anything else, looking for an emotional connection that creates a bond between her and her husband. This bond is the fulfilling experience that finds its full expression in the climactic achievement of the conjugal event.

Another cardinal fact that should not be taken lightly is the satisfaction that is desired in physical intimacy. A plethora of attitudes can result from the physically unfulfilled wife, and her fears about her emotional dissatisfaction can be projected into her future. In other words, if this unfulfilled experience continues, she begins to wonder whether this is how things will be for the rest of her life. Men should also be aware that if there is physical fulfillment but emotional abandonment, marital homeostasis cannot be achieved.

In the early stages of marriage, every husband must learn about what I call the "marriage circle" (see figure 8): bedroom 101 (preplay), bedroom 201 (foreplay), bedroom 202 (engagement or consummation), bedroom 301 (postplay), and bedroom 401 (replay). Since this book is not dedicated to marriage therapy or sexuality, I will not give much space to discussion on these issues. Suffice it to say that preplay has to do with preparation for conjugal activities. This priming of the relationship involves tender loving care to the wife, reflected in attention to the little things: touching, hugging, and expressions of appreciation as well as performing the manly duties that are expected.

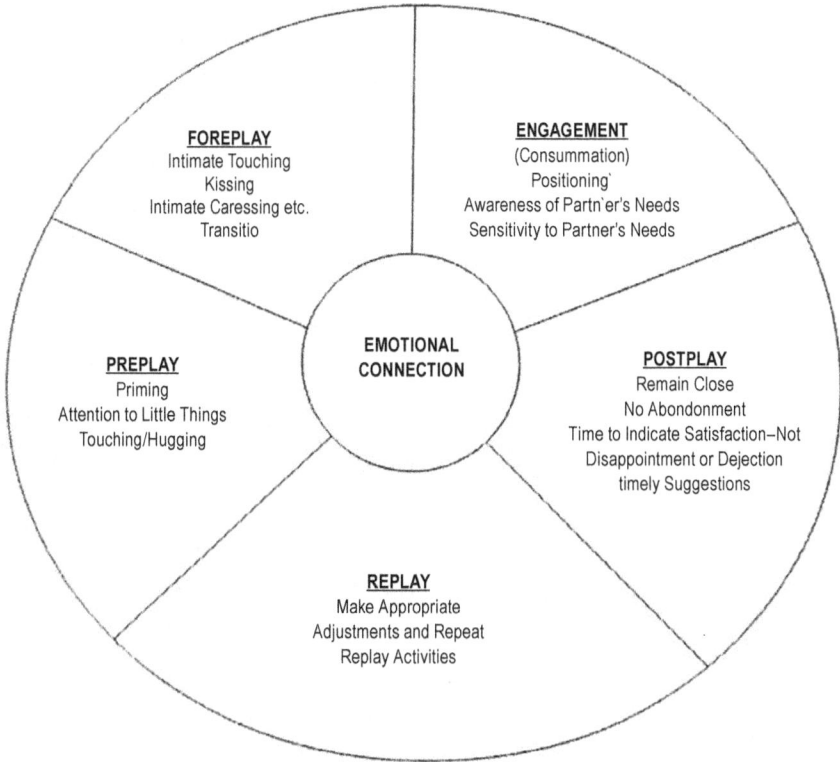

Figure 8. The Marriage Circle (Wheel of Intimacy)

Foreplay relates to a deeper, physically intimate communion that serves to stimulate the sensitivity of appropriate anatomical areas, culminating in the highest expression of lovemaking and ecstasy. Post play is the subsequent action and attitude that is exhibited following the one-flesh activity (intercourse). A husband who enters the bedroom and proceeds with his lovemaking endeavors without any meaningful demonstration of love and affection for his wife is disregarding her feelings. As soon as he is fulfilled, he abandons her, falls asleep, and gets up the following morning and is off to his daily task. Many women feel used and develop a low level of self-esteem if they are abandoned after the event that is supposed to be the most profound expression of love.

The wife, after the event, needs to still feel him close to not feel she has been used. Another point is that if the wife is made to feel secure in her relationship with her husband, she can help him understand her sensitivities and positional preferences to ameliorate the experience. Often, the husband will be fulfilled, whereas that may not be true of the wife, so a little listening and practice can enhance the situation. However, the wife must be very wise in her approach to her husband. If she is not tactful in sharing her intimate feelings regarding how he could help her feel more fulfilled, he could feel that she thinks he is inadequate. That can actually affect the relationship in a negative way.

Some women are so fearful of losing their husbands that they would not attempt to make such suggestions; they' would rather endure the continued less-than-adequate experience than offer a solution that might improve their marital experience. However, bear this caveat in mind: a man should never ask or require his wife to perform sexual acts that are inconsistent with biblical teaching and good moral judgment. This includes the departure from the "natural use" (Romans 1:27) and the performance of deviant acts. I will attempt to discreetly say that God gave mankind the gift of speaking, singing, and eating with his mouth and the ability to excrete with the organ designated for that purpose. We should glorify God with our whole being according to how he has made us.

Replay is the repeat of the preplay. This begins after the conjugal expression. The husband should continually strive to increase his wife's happiness. Then even the same old things done in different ways gain new significance.

What Happens If Her Expectations Are Not Met

Life is not usually exactly as one envisions. In many cases, not all of the woman's expectations will be met. Many areas may be on target or reasonably good enough for her to be able to live with, but her husband may be unable to meet some of her expectations. If the husband is unable to fulfill her expectations because of slothfulness or other self-induced deficiency, her disillusionment may lead her to vent her frustrations in ways that may be misinterpreted. In turn, her husband may feel that she is a nag or question her loyalty to him. This could initiate serious discord in the marriage. If the husband becomes abusive, her world is shattered, and fear and hopelessness could result.

Many expectations, however, are unrealistic. When they are not met, the wife berates her husband and sees him as less than what she bargained for. She may continue to criticize whatever he does until he feels that he cannot do anything to please her. Sometimes this leads the husband to adopt a don't-care attitude. He says to himself, "If I do it right, it's never right, and if I don't do it right, it's not right." He then will either not do what is expected or do it the way he wants and not care what she says.

This situation in a marriage does not lend itself to harmony, peace, and goodwill. Both spouses need to review their attitudes in light of the teachings of Jesus and confess their faults to each other so that their marriage can be healed. Yes, when a woman's expectations of married life are unrealized, without Christ in the heart, the marriage could become a difficult one.

Couples need more education and personal counseling before entering into the marriage relationship. While counseling may not prevent the problems that a marriage will encounter, it can help the individuals deal more rationally with the issues as they appear. Otherwise, their examples could serve as a basis for fear of entering into marriage by their children and those who look to them as mentors. Surely other people's failure and divorces serve as a root cause of fear to those who opt to abstain from marriage for the above-mentioned reasons.

An example of how unmet needs and insecurity play out in a woman's life can be seen in a study published in the British. Journal of Obstetrics and Gynaecology by Dr. Terhi Saisto, an obstetrician at the Helsinki University Central Hospital. Researchers questioned 278 couples consisting of pregnant Finnish women and their mates. The study found that women who were most fearful of vaginal delivery were those who were also dissatisfied with their relationship and were evaluated as being anxious and having low self-esteem (Saisto 2001, 492-498),

Hilde Nerum and others conducted a study that was financed by Norway Regional Health Authority Clinical Research Fund. "A psychosocial team was established to meet the needs of an increasing number of pregnant women referred for fear of birth who wished a planned cesarean. [The] conclusions [were]: impending birth activates previous traumatic experiences, abuse, and psychiatric disorders that may give rise to fear of vaginal birth" (Nerum, Hilde 2006, 221).

Thus, concerns that some women have about their pregnancies do not seem to come only from dissatisfaction with their relationships or self-esteem; they involve lifestyle issues. They have fears about how certain behaviors affect their baby. In his book 1001 Health-Care Questions Women Ask, Dr. Joe S. Mcllhaney Jr. responds to a question about how smoking affects a baby during pregnancy: "Cigarette smoking produces a number of abnormalities in a mother's body ... When you smoke, your bloodstream absorbs the smoke-caused carbon monoxide from your lungs. The lack of oxygen that results ... literally strangles your baby [during vaginal birth]" (Mcllhaney 1998, 257).

In a related question on whether smoking was harmful during pregnancy, Mcllhaney responds that "These problems [miscarriages and ectopic pregnancies] include an increased chance of the baby being very sick or dying before it is born, during [vaginal] childbirth, or right after delivery ... This necessitates getting these babies out by C-section more often [as opposed to attempting the normal vaginal birthing process]" (256).

The causes of the dissatisfaction with their relationships and the anxieties that caused these women to be fearful of vaginal childbirth were not stated. However, it seems obvious that these women were afraid of complications that could result in some form of incapacitation to them and/or the children. This, they fear, would render them incapable of taking care of themselves or the children, further damaging their relationship or causing them to he left alone in such a condition.

A woman's need of assurance and feelings of security are greatly impacted by the unfulfilled expectation from childhood that married life will be one of bliss and contentment. Indeed, fears abound in all aspects of people's lives, though some of them only surface at specific times. There is truly a need for educating people about their fears and how to neutralize them.

CHAPTER 9

NEUTRALIZING FEAR USING SPIRITUAL EUPHORIC THERAPY

Many therapeutic approaches have been used to address issues dealing with specific fears. Psychologists, psychiatrists, and other mental health professionals have dealt with various fears using various applications. Some of these approaches have provided some degree of relief to many individuals. Many counselees have found themselves on certain long-term programs that seem to have no end in sight. Spiritual Euphoric Therapy (SET) is a lifestyle reorientation approach that provides lasting benefits to those who consistently utilize its application. However, we need to look briefly at some of the other therapeutic approaches to understand their focus and what they are about.

Therapy

Let me shock the reader by saying that every person who lives on planet Earth was born brain damaged and is consequently mentally ill. What? Yes! Everyone is mentally ill and suffers from all kinds of fears. Well, how is that so? The answer may surprise you. Hang on a moment, and I will explain as succinctly as possible. The Bible states that after God made Adam, God brought all the creatures that he had made to Adam to see what he would call them (Genesis 2:19). And Adam named the creatures exactly as God would have named them. Mankind was thinking like God—perfect thought, meaning not erring in his thought process. He and his wife had no anxieties or fear of the future. They were not afraid about what God would do to them because they were without sin, in a righteous environment, and in a happy relationship with God.

However, once they disobeyed God (sinned), they became fearful (Genesis 3:10). Since that time, man's brain and his mental state have been negatively impacted. The full capability of the brain is believed to be untapped. Rather than thinking righteously, we now think sinfully. Sinful thinking is normal to us. In fact, the Bible tells us that our hearts are deceitful and wicked (Jer. 17:9). The sin principle is in us in such a way that we cannot help ourselves. The solution to our situation has to come from outside of us, not from within.

In other words, the mental defect or "illness" caused by the changes that took place in the brain due to disobedience to God is normal to us. That's the only lifestyle and way of thinking that we know. So when we say that someone is mentally ill, we are really saying that that person is acting or thinking in a way that is different from our regular abnormal way of thinking. Our attempt to apply secular therapy is designed to bring that person to our abnormal state of thinking.

That's where SET, utilized by the Christian counseling psychologist, comes in. SET is significantly different from the therapy used by secular psychologists. SET seeks to restore the "regular abnormal" thought process of the ordinary person to the original human thought pattern that predates the fall from grace, the attitude described in Philippians 2:5. If properly and consistently applied, SET also corrects the thought pattern of the person who is considered to be beyond the normal abnormality (in conventional terms, "mentally ill"). Now, if the "normally abnormal" person possesses fear, how much more does the abnormally abnormal possess?

It is natural for those who have diseases or psychological problems to seek a cure or therapy for restoration to normal health. Most people would agree that one would go to the doctor to be diagnosed and treated if one becomes physically ill. The same should be true for people with mental and emotional problems that seem to be beyond the scope of their control.

Regrettably, however, some people are not aware of their need for therapy. They either have repressed memory or are engaged in denial or suppression. The fact of the matter is that anything that is hidden in the subconscious will eventually surface. Sometimes the surfacing takes different forms. It may be in the form of depression, anger, bitterness, introversion or extroversion, always seeking to please others to gain acceptance, or many other outward signs of inner turmoil.

The fear of confronting the underlying issues may result in a facade that can only be penetrated and addressed on a biblical basis. This is not to discount the legitimate use of secular treatment, including medication, for certain cases that warrant it. In many instances, though, psychologists have uncovered problems they are unable to cure. However, there is an abundance of therapy in the Word of God that, when believed and practiced, can accomplish more than secular treatment that human wisdom provides. It must be restated that I am not negating appropriate medical treatment. Still, there are cases where the doctors have "given over" patients who, through application of biblical principles, have recovered fully and are able to live productive lives for many more years.

Let us explore the use of SET: employing certain biblical principles to neutralize the power of fear. Then we will compare and contrast some of the current methods of treatment for anxiety, depression, phobias, and other conditions by way of the various therapies that are available.

Spiritual Euphoric Therapy

This therapy developed by the author is based on what has been called the "Merry Heart theory." Its title stems from Proverbs 17:22: "A merry heart doeth good like a medicine." The Merry Heart theory suggests that if a person decides never to let circumstances dictate how joyful he should be and to maintain an attitude of thankfulness and appreciation for life, consciousness, sanity, and the ability to partake of things of this life, then that attitude of contentment and thankfulness will influence the mind to maintain positive thoughts and help to prevent certain illnesses. It will even help to accelerate the healing process of some physical ailments. This biblical principle has psychological implications.

Euphoria in this book means a joy and attitude of praise that is biblically based, no matter the physical condition of the individual. I believe that most people understand that when God asks for or says something about a person's heart (as in Proverbs 23:26: "My son, give me thine heart," or Proverbs 23:7: "As he thinketh in his heart"), He is not referring to the person's physical heart in his or her chest. That heart only pumps, through the circulatory system of the body; it cannot think. It is the mind that thinks and makes decisions for or against God.

The Bible uses the words mind and heart interchangeably, as mentioned above (or Jeremiah 13:22 "If thou say in thine heart"—the Hebrew word is Laybawb and labe which means heart or mind, even feelings, will and intellect. Also, Hebrews 8:10 says: "I will put my laws in their heart." The Greek word is dianoia which means faculty or mind). So, the mind, also called the heart, is the subject of study. It is explored in ways that allow for the discovery of its real condition and the behaviors caused by its imperfect or wayward functioning.

All human inhibitions result from fear caused by negative thoughts. Negative thoughts generated in the mind, if cherished over a long period of time, become a neurosis. In some cases, they actually cause physical ailments or prevent illnesses from being cured. Therefore, if the mind can be kept in a condition conducive to health, the individual will experience a life of wholeness—mentally, physically, and spiritually—hence the utilization of the Merry Heart theory for SET.

The scripture behind the therapy is not only Proverbs 17:22. Scripture also tells us, "A good report maketh the bones fat" (Proverbs 15:30). We are told to rejoice in the LORD always (Philippians 4:4) because all things work together for good to them that love God (Romans 8:28). One should, however, exercise care as to when and how to use this text, especially when there is bereavement. Not everyone can appreciate this concept during times of sorrow.

Furthermore, Scripture assures us there is no need to be fearful if we, like Paul, learn to be content in whatever state we find ourselves (Philippians 4:11). We must do our best to improve our situation and place our trust in God, for "the cattle upon a thousand hills [are his]" (Psalm 50:10). It is the Father's good pleasure to give us the kingdom (Luke 12:32). The most essential scriptural key to neutralizing the power of fear is what the psalmist David expressed in Psalm 34:4: "I sought the LORD, and he heard me and delivered me from all my fears."

SET could be summarized in the following formula: Believe what God has stated + Trust and obey his instructions = A happy and healthy person who obtains the blessings God wants to bestow. A compact version might look like:

Belief + Trust = Happiness = God's will accomplished.

SET can work for Christians and non-Christians alike; it works for the religious and the not so religious. On the secular level:

Positive mental attitude + Moral and healthful lifestyle = Average mental and physical health. On the spiritual level:

A merry heart + Faith in God + Healthy lifestyle = Mental, physical, and spiritual health + Divine intervention as needed.

Spiritual euphoria is not dependent on health, wealth, or the approbation of others. Unlike the euphoria brought on by a manic condition, which generates irritability or anger when deflated, it is a mental and spiritual connection with the divine. Even a person who is ill can experience spiritual euphoria through the application of the SET principles annunciated in this book.

It may be helpful for us to observe the counseling process before we proceed. The Time-Frame Release Capsule (figure 9) and the Life Maintenance Wheel (figure 10) offer graphic presentation of the phases of the counseling program.

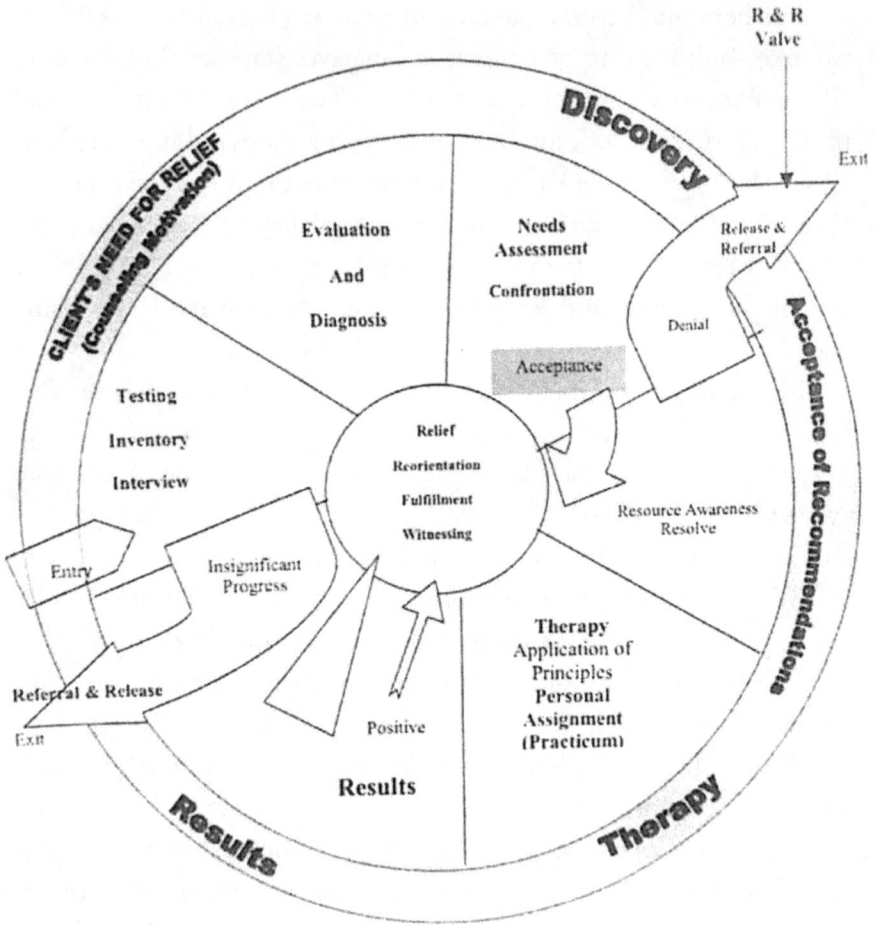

Figure 9. Time-Frame Release Capsule

Note: If the counselee cannot get past stage three, referral and release (R&R) is mandatory. The mental attitude of the individual will determine the level of positivity and result. The mind sets the tone for achieving health, happiness, or spiritual euphoria. A reentry in the program is possible and may be necessary.

The information in the Life Maintenance Wheel is part of the practicum in the SET counseling process shown in figure 9. This diagram, conceived by the author, is based on the concept of the eight laws of health mentioned in the book The Ministry of Mailing by Ellen Gould White. She states that "pure air, sunlight, abstemiousness, rest, exercise, proper diet, the use of water, trust in divine power—these are the true remedies. Every person should have knowledge of nature's remedial agencies and how to apply them" (White 5942, 127).

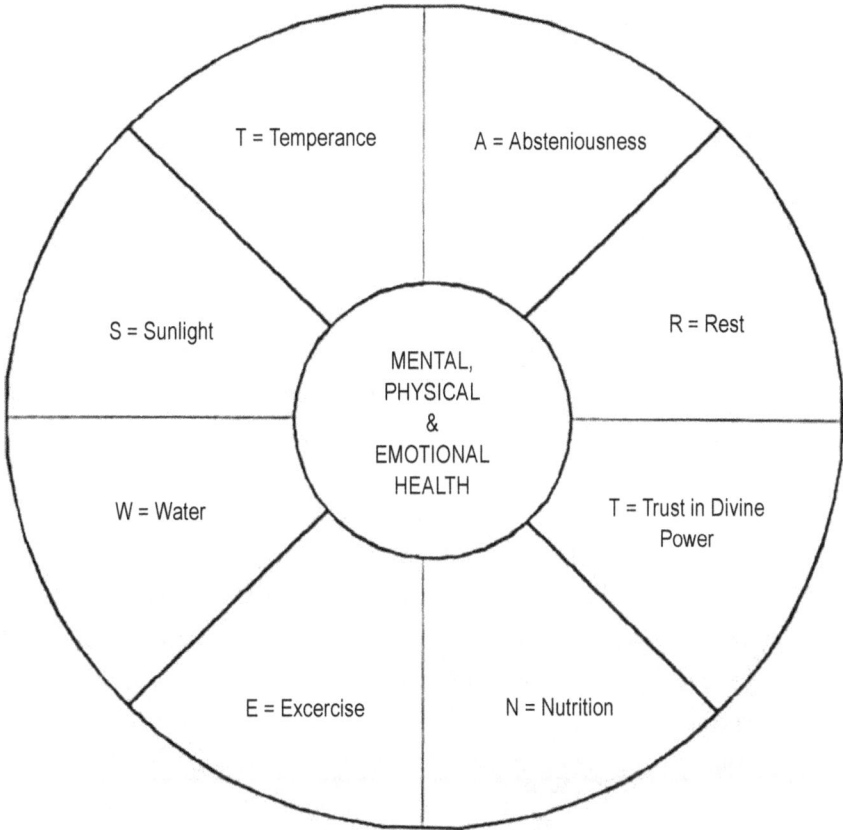

Figure 10. The Life Maintenance Wheel

An example of the positive results of having a positive mental attitude, which is part of the "trust in divine power" aspect of Spiritual Euphoric Therapy, is provided by Dr. David Felten. Bill Moyers, one of America's respected journalists, interviewed Dr. Felten and discussed, among other things, the mind and its effect on the body. The following is an excerpt from the exchange:

Felten: I'm not suggesting we abandon the high-tech diagnosis or pharmacology but that we should add more of a humane and personal touch to medicine. The art is still important.

Moyers: Because what the patient thinks and feels affects recovery?

Felten: It appears so. What we are trying to do now is find the factors that impact on the brain, which then sends signals that change the immune system. Of course, a change in the immune system makes a difference in the patient's disease.

Moyers: Are you suggesting that every time we have a thought or a feeling, hormones are released that somehow send a message to the immune system?

Felten: Yes, a constant traffic of information goes back and forth between the brain and the immune system ... and neurotransmitters are continuously talking to target cells throughout the body. There can be subtle shifts in activity in response to an individual's inner-generated thought process. Now the big question is, does that make a difference in how the immune system responds to an invader? Where these subtle changes become important is in individuals who are at the very edge of their capacity to respond—someone who's very elderly or has viral diseases or has to take drugs to suppress the immune systems. In those circumstances, the added impact of a stressor psychosocial factor ... feeling or mood could push them over the edge.

Moyers: So if they began feeling more depressed, they might go over the edge into actually feeling worse physically?

Felten: Studies suggest that ... depression does play a role in that the more severe the depression, the more likely you'll find a decreased measure of immune response.

Moyers: Are those studies showing that if I think I'm going to get worse I'll get worse, and if I think I'm going to get better, I'll get better?

Felten: That's what we're trying to find out. I'm not sure that we can generalize ... but certainly those of us who have dealt with patients know that a patient's will to live makes a difference. Yet we don't understand how that works. But the immune system is one that we're particularly interested in with regard to viral infections, bacterial infections, pneumonia, and autoimmune diseases like rheumatoid arthritis—the immune system has an impact on a lot of diseases.

(Moyers 1993, 218-219)

This discussion supports the very essence of SET, the Merry Heart theory. If the mind is kept in a state of praise, thanksgiving, and contentment, and the focus of the individual is on the goodness of God and how he can best help his neighbor, then absent any unnatural or abnormal circumstances, that person will be healthier. Chances are he or she will live longer. Such attitude of mind, however, does not obviate the need for nutrition, exercise, and maintenance of physical health; on the contrary, it's inclusive.

I must hasten to say that even a person who is not a believer in Jesus or a worshiper of Jehovah, the God of Abraham, can posses a healthy body if he seeks to maintain a positive mental attitude along with obedience to the other laws of health. God showers his blessings on all—the just and the unjust—so that all may see his benevolence and be led to glorify him. The principle of reaping what one sows is applicable to both Christians and non-Christians. Be reminded, though, that the objective in life is to obtain maximum benefits from the blessings that we have been so copiously given.

Consequently, to achieve optimum benefit and to experience miracles that go beyond material success, one must be a participant in the new birth experience. This means that the process of acceptance of the Word of God, repentance of sin, reception of the Holy Spirit, and the willingness to obey Cod in all things must be a reality in the individual's life. When that is done, when the individual allows the Holy Spirit to work, he will be able to have the spiritual euphoric experience that can actually bring about real miracles as he walks daily with the LORD. This is one of the many additional benefits that non-Christians very rarely, if ever, experience.

The Foundation of the SET counseling method is the concept of the condition of man as opposed to the nature of man. It is difficult to discuss man's condition without mentioning the biblical position as contrasting with current thinking. At times, this may become uncomfortable to counselees who are locked into traditional ideas and not open to the challenge of enlightenment by the Holy Spirit. Bucking current cultural trends is like being a part of Noah's family in the days before the flood—one man and seven followers against the millions. That's how the reader could find himself or herself if this challenge, based upon my research, is accepted. The following section takes lessons from Scripture that must he applied to one's understanding of what people are before fear can be neutralized according to SET.

Transcendent Personality

While there have been numerous discussions about many theories of personality, the trait theory is the most prominent. This theory, which comes from the ancient Greeks, lists people under the following four categorizations: phlegmatic, or emotionless; choleric, or active and irritable; sanguine, or happy; and melancholic, or depressive (Meier et al. 1997, 225).

There is, however, a transcendent personality—the personality of Christ. That personality is what Christianity is all about. Christians are exhorted to "let this mind be in you which was also in Christ Jesus" (Philippians 2:5) so that we may be one even as he and his father are one. The mind controls and generates the thoughts that become actions, which become character or a personality: The personality that Jesus wants us to have transcends any and all other personalities that may have been acquired by heredity or adaptation.

I speak of character and personality in the context that character is who a person really is and is generally reflected in the personality that the person exhibits. No matter how a person tries to mask his true character by multiple personality displays, sooner or later, the person's character will be reflected in his personality. People have the ability to mask, for a time, hideous characters with a facade of personable appearances and apparent sympathetic postures. Eventually, however, the truth is revealed.

The transcendent personality (TP) is the ideal personality. It is a personality of love. It acknowledges but deemphasizes negatives, and it emphasizes positives. TP is what causes an abusive person to become a caring, sympathetic person. It is the agent by which murderers, drunkards, liars, thieves, and immoral people become sober, conscientious, law-abiding, productive citizens who share with others the message of salvation. TP is the ultimate personality because it overrides and supersedes the negative factors in the other personalities. Until TP is fully dominant in a person, the process of refinement will continue if he is desirous of obtaining that goal. The process of the new birth mentioned in Scripture is the beginning step toward achieving TP.

It was the superimposition of this personality that caused Jan Hus, Jerome of Prague (Jeronym Prazsky), William Tyndale, Ulrich Zwingli, and the million, of Christians who died during the persecution of the Middle Ages to sing and pray while being executed or punished. It was the Merry Heart theory in operation when Stephen, in biblical times, prayed for his persecutors and assassins. Fear is effectively neutralized by SET because the body can then maintain its strength as well as its physical health. The replacement of negative thoughts with godly and rational ones, utilizing the biblical model resident in the principles taught by Christ, provides a therapy that is unparalleled.

Those who want to use the do-it-yourself approach to neutralizing the power fear has over them should apply the principles outlined above and elsewhere in this hook. Those who need guidance or counseling by a Christian counselor will he led through the Time-Frame Release Capsule (TRC) process, illustrated in figure 9, using the SET principles.

Whichever approach is used, the SET principles are so powerful that after using them for a while, the power that fear had over a person becomes weakened and virtually nonexistent. At the individual level, the principles become a lifestyle within the family; at the corporate level, they become the foundation for the character of that organization; and at the government and societal levels, they become the ways and mores of that society. At the societal level, leadership in corporate organizations and government, by promoting the principles mentioned above, inspire confidence and positive attitudes in their employees. That positivity filters out to society, thereby producing general optimism in the citizenry and reducing pessimism and fear.

Other Therapeutic Approaches Examined

While many competing psychological theories may have interesting insights into overcoming fear, none of the following present the complete spiritual package that SET, based on biblical principles, has to offer. In the book Competent Christian Counseling, Drs. Timothy Clinton and George Ohlschlager write:

> We believe that sound psychology is at best limited, and at worst useless, unless it is based on sound theology. The key to effectively speaking God's truth into people's hearts and lives is an intimate knowledge of who he is, what he has revealed to us, and who he has designed us to become... Colossians 2:8 tells us not to

allow philosophy and deception to take our thoughts captive. It's easy for Christian counselors to become so fascinated by or enamored with the theory and technique of different psychological schools of thought that we forget what is most important. While some aspects of psychology can provide helpful insights and tools for the counselor, what it means to be a whole person can only be understood within the context of a personal, life-changing relationship with Jesus Christ.

(Clinton and Ohlschlager 2002, 350)

With such foundational support for the principles outlined in SET, we will explore some of the alternatives.

The Avoidance Approach

Avoiding discussions or confrontation about existing problems is never a solution to the problems. The avoidance approach does not eliminate the fear of confrontation, misunderstanding, and sometimes, animated dialogue. The longer the postponement, the greater the tension and fear.

The individual who takes the avoidance approach is really saying, "Let's wait and see what happens." However, when dealing with fear, the wait and-see attitude in many cases is just a comfort to a fool. Fear does not go away without some direct effort or action. Why do some prefer the avoidance approach? It is a way of providing temporary hope. The idea is for you not to worry about the situation because it will go away. If one avoids those situations out of a desire to anesthetize the body against fear until one has accumulated enough courage to confront and endure the apprehension, that fear may temporarily abate but will not go away permanently.

I suggest that regrouping to obtain an understanding of what is actually taking place may help. This way, the individual can chart a course of action that may produce the desired result. In the avoidance approach, one may never gain enough courage to attack the problem and obtain a solution. This, of course, may depend on the level of motivation involved.

Take, for instance, a daughter-in-law who believes that her mother-in-law is too intrusive. Perhaps the daughter-in-law is afraid to confront her; wary that she may react in an unpleasant manner. What does she do? She pretends everything is okay and smiles when the intrusiveness occurs. In doing so, she is supporting the intrusiveness by her outward endorsement.

She also has another problem: she is fearful of discussing the matter with her husband because she thinks it will embarrass him. She is unsure how he will react. Hence, she suffers in silence and plays the part of the victimized wife under the guise of being cooperative and submissive. Her avoidance is costing her happiness, and the fear is a constant torment. Yet she feels compelled to endure this emotional trauma because of fear.

I say to such individuals, "Life can be beautiful!" Arise and discover the true meaning of life. God has a plan for you. Seek him in prayer, and in the words of the psalmist, say, "The LORD is my light and my salvation; whom shall I fear?" (Psalm 27:1). I would say to the daughter-in-law, "With such assurance, talk with your husband about the situation. Let him know that you love him and your mother-in-law dearly. Then tell him how you feel when his mother does so-and-so or says so-and-so. Use such unthreatening language as, 'I feel this way when this or that happens.'"

In that way, such situations can be resolved, not avoided. If the husband can communicate the problem to his mother, the wife's discomfort can be neutralized. Of course, there may be other factors to consider. The nature of the problem could also warrant her talking to the mother-in-law personally. Unlike ongoing avoidance, initiating potentially frightening conversations might eliminate a whole range of misunderstandings and make the mother-in-law feel grateful for the candor. It could generate a closer relationship. The mother is likely to feel that if something goes wrong, the daughter-in-law will not go around complaining about her but will discuss the matter with her.

The Head-on Approach

Those who advocate the head-on approach should observe that fear is not an object sitting in the middle of the road that can be charged by someone with a bulldozer and pushed out of the way. Some fears have been around for so long and are so rooted that it takes time to expunge them. The waving of a wand or the snap of the fingers will not cause them to disappear.

I saw a television show that appeared to have been designed to give people an opportunity to overcome certain fears. They were given certain challenges that included some of the things they feared most. In return for overcoming those fearful ventures and emerging as victors over other contestants, winners received a large sum of money. This is not a viable approach to fear for everyone. If the root cause of the fear is not determined and addressed, the person has not dealt with the real issue and moved on.

Equally true is the fact that certain fears result from events that cannot or are not feasible to be recreated; for example, a rape or other violent crime. Such incidents cannot be reenacted to help the victim overcome his or her fear of men, sex, or relationships in general. Therefore, a head-on approach might only be effective in very limited circumstances. It seems more logical to engage in some form of therapy to find satisfactory relief.

Reality Therapy

Reality therapy, developed by William Glasser (1925–), is based, essentially, on a concept called choice theory (originally called control theory). In this model, although external forces influence behavior, they do not cause behavior, because human behavior is purposeful and originates from within an individual rather than from external forces. Furthermore, it purports that our behavior is our best attempt to get what we want in order to gain effective control of our lives.

Reality therapy revolves around three Rs. The first is right—the belief that healthy people evaluate and modify their behavior to fit in some cultural norm. Next is responsibility—the ability of the person receiving the therapy to satisfy personal needs without preventing others from realizing theirs. Last is reality—the realization that individuals have limitations for meeting self-needs and that this is a universal reality experienced by everyone (G. Jung 1997, 75).

The focus, as the reader can see, is on self, or the individual, and what he or she can accomplish. The problem with this therapy is that it appears to be philosophically challenged. Humanity without divinity is a complete failure.

Rational Emotive Therapy

In his practice of "standard psychoanalysis," Albert Ellis (1913–) observed that many of his patients would say, "Yes, I see exactly what bothers me now and why I am bothered by it, but I nevertheless still am bothered. Now what can I do about that?" He became frustrated and began experimenting with "more active, directive and short-term treatments." This resulted in the development of Rational Emotive Therapy (RET) (Bloch 2006, 145). Ellis also refers to this therapy as Rational Emotive Behavior Therapy (REBT) (Koocher, Norcross, Hill, 2005, 212).

Rational Emotive Therapy (RET) is a cognitive behavior therapy that is based on the premise that cognitions produce self-talk that leads to either a satisfied, healthy, happy person or a dissatisfied, maladjusted, unhappy person. RET contends, that "human beings are born with a potential for both rational, or straight, thinking and irrational, or crooked, thinking. People, it purports, have predispositions for self-preservation, happiness, thinking and verbalizing, loving, communion with others, and growth and self-actualization" (G. Jung 1997, 67). One of RET's four key assumptions is that people have the capacity to change their cognitive, emotive, and behavioral processes. A summary statement that seems to serve as the capstone for RET is that "humans are self-talking, sell-evaluating, and self-sustaining" (G. Jung 1997, 67).

In RET, the self is reliant on self to bring about all the changes necessary to achieve the full potential. There seems to be perceived self-sufficiency and no need for external assistance. Hence, God is not a part of the equation.

Behavior Therapy

According to Dr. Neal H. Olshan, in his book Depression, the principles of behavior modification are used in behavior therapy "to alleviate symptoms in a wide variety of mental disorders. Unlike in classical psychotherapy, behavior therapy does not emphasize understanding the unconscious or release of emotional tensions." Behavior therapy, he believes, is based on the following two underlying assumptions: (1) that the personality is a collection of learned habits and (2) that disordered behavior is nothing more than the use of these habits in situations where they have no useful value. Treatment, he concludes, "consists of eliminating the maladaptive habits by conditioning techniques and replacing these habits with more appropriate ones" (Olshan 1982, 84).

Again, such a purely human-centered approach appears destined not to have lasting success. Humankind is always faltering and failing, and unless our efforts are aided by divine strength, we will continue to go over the same path again and again.

Re-Design Therapy

Gary A. Jung (1951—), a professor at Southwest Bible College and Seminary, in his textbook Understanding and Comparing Counseling Therapies, describes his re-designed therapy, which is based on a psychological model developed to "integrate psychology and theology." The model is called the design-gap theory. The belief is that mankind was originally designed to live in fellowship with God, but through an act of rebellion, man rejected God's design. As a result, man's nature is rebellious and sinful and has a strong propensity to reject God and his plan (G. Jung 1997, 4-14).

Design-gap theory is anchored in the belief that the breath of life that God breathed into man (Genesis 2:7) at the time of creation is not really breath of life but a sentient entity in man called a spirit, which is an eternal element of a person's being. It further proffers that the soul (in Greek, psuche, meaning "breath" or "life") consists of mind (intellect), will (volition), and emotions (feelings); the body (soma) is the physical clement (see Matthew 10:28). It also argues that the temperament is an inborn psychical structure given by God and is a person's foundation, which sets the tone for the personality

A basic clement of the theory is that a person must be born again as a core structure in the process of re-designing. The theory, upon which the re-designed therapy is built, poses some problems for some people, because if man has a spirit that is immortal, it means that there is no need for Jesus to come back to this world and confer immortality on the righteous (1 Corinthians 15:51-54). There would be no need for him to resurrect the saints who are already living an immortal life in heaven. While some aspects of the therapy's methodology are profoundly significant, there are certain problematic questions in its biblical foundation. Many people who lose their loved ones to death become frustrated and angry with God because they are uncertain as to whether their unsaved loved ones are burning in hell. And depending on the time they "entered hell," some people would spend a longer time in hell for less grievous sins (which is uncharacteristic of the justice of God).

Furthermore, if everyone who dies is "gone to be with the LORD and in a better place," as many preachers say, to comfort the deceased's family, then no one is in hell. If the belief is that the person who died was not a Christian and is not gone to heaven (because only Christians will be in heaven), why not disclose that to the grieving family? Why not tell them that their loved one is being burned and tortured in hell? That, of course, would be cruel, and the fear of offending the family might not allow it; although during the Middle Ages, people paid the church to get their loved ones out of hell or purgatory. Disclosure would be the right thing to do. This topic needs to be restudied by many preachers and counsel on who have tie deal with grieving individuals. A proper understanding of this issue can help to provide comfort and allay the fears caused by uncertainty or misinformation.

Psychoanalytic Therapy

Psychoanalysis focuses on the patient's unconscious thoughts and feelings as expressed in dreams, fantasies, and actions (Olshan 1982,84). Psychoanalytic theory states that the causes of many mental illnesses can lie buried deep in the unconscious. The patient meets with the psychiatrist or psychologist and talks about his or her childhood, dreams, or everything that comes to mind in an attempt to resolve problems by uncovering unconscious conflicts. This is referred to as "free association" (Brill 1965, 10). Resolution of these conflicts is viewed as curative. Spiritual concern or connection is not necessarily applicable, and certain existing fears that were not present in childhood or are not discussed may not be addressed or resolved.

This theory also teaches that "personality consists of three systems" [or facets] (G. Jung 1997, 16). These are the id (biological component), the ego (psychological component), and the superego (social component). Sigmund Freud (1856-1939) described classical psychoanalysis in 1900 when he published his book The Interpretation of Dreams, while Erik Erikson (1902-1994) emphasized psychosocial development, which is a modification and expansion of Freud's ideas.

This led Dr. C. George Boeree to describe Erikson as a "Freudian ego-psychologist because he not only accepted Freud's ideas but also the ideas about the ego that were added by other Freud's loyalists" (Boeree 2003). Psychoanalytic theory postulates that behavior is determined by a combination of "irrational forces, unconscious motivations, and biological and instinctive drives." The instincts mentioned are the libido (sexual desires), eros (desire to have pleasure without pain), and thanatos (a death instinct, an unconscious desire to hurt oneself or others) (G. Jung 1997, 16).

Erikson, according to Boeree, expanded Freud's psychoanalytic theory to include eight stages of development rather than Freud's five (infant, toddler, preschooler, school-age child, adolescence, plus Erikson's young adult, middle adulthood, and late adulthood). Boeree further states that Erikson also developed the "epigenetic principle," which states that these stages of development are predetermined, and one's personality is as the "unfolding of a rose bud" in a predetermined process toward a predetermined end (Boeree 2003). This means that only interference by the individual could cause any disruption in the process.

I believe that some aspects of the therapy are sound and that there is no overt suggestion for abdication of responsibility by individuals for their actions. However, this concept of predetermined personality opens the door for people to think that they are victims and that their actions are not all their fault. It could serve as confirmation of what I have heard some people say: "This is how I am; I cannot help it. My personality is this way and I cannot change." The theory places emphasis on the individual and what he can do to make himself better. It obviates the need for repentance and reliance on divine guidance for one's journey through life.

Jungian Therapy

Jungian therapy, or analytic psychology, founded by Carl Jung (1875-1961), espouses the idea that behavior results from both conscious and unconscious forces. It states that all individuals strive to achieve a sense of self-fulfillment by the motivation of a god that is within.

Jung proposed that the collective unconscious represents inherited, repetitious experiences of past generations that are permanently embedded in the human mind. The information is transmitted from one generation to the next; thus, the information is collected. He further states that all humans share the same collective unconscious, leading to "psychic predispositions regarding perception, emotion, and behavior." The ideas found in the unconscious are called archetypes (G. Jung 1997, 26).

This therapy is in direct conflict with biblical principles and would not be a course that the Christian community would recommend. The focus is on self and what humans, of themselves, can achieve. The chances of a person neutralizing the fear that is within him by trying to access something that is within—a thing that may in itself be contributing to or even the reason for the fear—seem slim.

Adlerian Therapy

Alfred Adler (1870-1937) developed Adlerian therapy, also known as individual psychology. This therapy holds that humans are the masters of their own fate, not victims of life. Adler believed that although people are greatly influenced by the first six years of their lives, they have choices and are therefore responsible for their actions. He believed that a person's happiness and success are largely related to social connectedness (G. Jung 1997, 31).

Developing the person's social interest is achieved by increasing self=awareness and by challenging and modifying fundamental premises of life's goals and basic concepts. Adlerian therapy purports that clients are not mentally sick but discouraged. This therapy does not provide the proper ingredients for the neutralization of fear because it focuses on an area that is unstable (the social community). It proposes nothing of permanence to fall back on. God is not the center of this endeavor.

Existential Therapy

Existential therapy, promoted by Victor Frankl (1905-1997) and Rollo May (1909-1994), is said by some to be more an attitude toward life than a clearly defined system of psychotherapy. It purports that "humans are in a constant state of transition, emerging, evolving and becoming" (G. Jung 1997, 38). In the arena of existential therapy, the emergence of awareness, identity, and the search for meaning and relationship with others are of highest concern. The primary concern is the enabling of individuals to accept the freedom to act and the responsibility for their actions. Reliance on God for direction or biblical principles as the foundation for a meaningful and productive life is not an emphasis. There is no specific approach to discovering various fears and neutralizing them. The emphasis is on humans striving to be all they can be on their own.

117

Person-Centered Therapy

Person-centered therapy; developed by Carl Rogers (1902-1987), espouses the concept that "people are resourceful, capable of self-direction, and able to live effective and productive lives" (G. Jung 1997, 43). It teaches that humans possess an "innate striving for self-actualization." Using this therapy; "both client and therapist embark as it were on a shared journey that reveals their humanness and participate in a growth experience" (44). The goal is for individuals to become people who have openness to experience, trust in themselves, an internal source of evaluation, and a willingness to continue growing. The emphasis is on individual development that can be accomplished by and through oneself. No reliance is placed on God and what he can do for or through that person. It is humanistic in approach.

Gestalt Therapy

A term coined by Fritz Perk (1893-1970), Gestalt therapy sees "humans as living organisms moving toward the construction of meaningful wholes or gestalts to promote balance with their immediate environment" (G. Jung 1997, 47). It contends that genuine knowledge is the product of what is immediately evident in the experience of the perceiver.

The concepts of the "now, the unfinished business, avoidance, layers of neurosis, contact and resistance to contact, and energy and blocks to energy" (47) are explored. Emphasis is on the utilization of self alone to fix the self. Nothing but the now, for example, is said to exist. The therapist asks "what and how" questions to help the client make contact with the present moment. There is no recognition or awareness of sin, its psychological and physical impact on the individual, or what biblical solutions may he obtained.

Since "the adult personality can he likened to the multilayered onion, and five layers of neurosis must be stripped off in order to achieve psychological maturity" (47), the fear of making unpleasant discoveries can be very traumatic. Without reliance on divine guidance, any solutions obtained have no valid basis of permanency.

Transactional Analysis

The designer of this therapy, Eric Berne (1910-1970), espouses the theory that people can reorder and redirect their lives by making decisions in new and effective ways (Craighead, W. Edward. Nemeroff, Charles B. 2001). According to G. Jung, the three patterns of behavior, or ego states, held by this therapy are the parent, adult, and child states. In the parent, or superego state, the individual is said to experience what he imagines were his own parents' feelings in a situation, or he feels and acts toward others as parents felt and acted toward him; the "oughts" and "shoulds" are involved in this state. The adult, or ego state, is said to be the "objective part of the person which is not emotional or judgmental but works with facts and the external reality" (G. Jung 1997, 54). Jung further suggests that the child, or id state, deals with feelings, impulses, and spontaneous acts.

The goal of transactional analysis is to substitute what is called an autonomous lifestyle—characterized by awareness, spontaneity, and intimacy—for a lifestyle characterized by manipulation, game playing, and a self-defeating life script. Like other secular therapies, this approach does not feature biblical principles or divine guidance or intervention, unlike SET, which focuses on a biblical solution.

Since we have dealt with the individual's fear and recognize that it is the individual who creates and operates social entities such as corporations and governments, it will be worth to explore how fear plays out in the corporate setting, first through individuals and then to society as a whole.

CHAPTER 10

CORPORATE FEAR

Corporate culture includes both written and unwritten rules. Sometimes the expected conduct is not verbally communicated. The employees observe attitudes and mannerisms of their superiors and those who have been in the organization for a long time; by observing, they come to realize the unwritten dos and don'ts of the establishment. In some cases, the culture goes far beyond regional and corporate offices. It extends to the industry. Thus, you might hear it said, for example, "This is how it is done in the music industry." Anyone who is in business or planning to enter the business arena must be cognizant of the environment and its requirements for success.

Corporations and other organizations are very particular about image, so they take great pains in hiring employees. The fear that the prospective employee may not fit into the culture has led many companies to develop and rely on psychological profiles and extensive interviews in an attempt to minimize the company's expenses or potential legal liability. Industrial psychologists are used to ensure the health of the organization, preservation of its culture, cohesion within the company's psychosocial infrastructure, production improvement, and marketing effectiveness.

No company wants to he left behind when it comes to technological advancements, market share, or image. This is true of for-profit entities, not-for-profit organizations, and associations. The fear of being inferior or inadequate lends itself to articulation of a mission and a modus operandi. The corporate world is bulging with graduates of renowned institutions, who espouse various philosophies on how organizations are to behave in order to be successful. Although all organizations have certain commonalities, various methodologies tend to highlight the differences in approach. To add some flavor to the discussion on corporate thinking, we would do well to hear from some of the great schools of thought.

In his book The Renewal Factor: How the Best Get and Keep the Competitive Edge, Robert Waterman Jr. introduces a profound concept called "stability in motion." Quoting from Heraclitus (C. 500 BC), he notes: "Nothing endures but change." Waterman attempts to convince the reader that good management will set the organization so that it not only experiences changes but it also expects them. Change, then, he suggests, becomes the norm as the organization moves forward, and the employees do not fear it (Waterman 1987, 214-241).

The apparent underlying factor here is that an organization is dynamic—it moves forward with its mission and its strategic plans, underpinned by its purpose. This results in the need for emotional, physical, and environmental adaptation to internal and external stimuli. Those experiences may not necessarily be palatable for the employee or the corporate structure. Hence, there may be a fear of the organization's future and a fear of the individual's well-being. This fear gives rise to the concept of stability in motion. To create this stability while the organization moves, companies such as Maytag, DANA, IBM, and NUCOR have adopted policies that include soliciting ideas for better productivity, paying people for their ideas, avoiding layoffs, and retraining when displacement occurs. Since every organization may not be able to adopt those policies, there will continue to be that fear factor that adds to the existing plight of how to stay abreast with the competition.

Sometimes organizational decision making is very traumatic, especially when it relates to disciplining or terminating employees. Peter Drucker wrote about these kinds of unwelcomed decisions that management is forced to make. Management must balance what he calls "conscience decisions" with the potential impact of not making the decision at all (Drucker 1974, 458-460). If management does not carefully make certain decisions that may be unpleasant, to say the least, some employees may experience fears of demoralization.

Drucker describes the scenario of a bookkeeper who started out with a company in its infancy and grew with it until, at the age of fifty or so, he is made controller. Yet he is not capable of handling such a heavy responsibility. If management does not find a way to relieve him of his responsibility as controller, his inability to perform in this new arena will endanger the company, [and] his inadequacy demoralizes the entire management group and discredits management altogether." Drucker's recommendation is that "the man must be removed from his job" (Drucker 1974, 458-460). This could be a very fearful and traumatic experience, but it is the reality of one of the fears that permeate the business environment.

Drucker's approach to management has served as a benchmark for corporate executives. His development of the concept of management by objectives (MBO) has been widely practiced. Stephen P. Robbins of San Diego State University and Mary Coulter of Southwest Missouri State University, in their book Management, extolled this approach because they said it consists of "goal specificity [you know what you want to achieve], participative decision making [not a loner; there is team effort or collaboration], an explicit time period [not being indefinite, tentative, unsure or unconcerned about achievement time-frame], and performance feedback [need to know how we are doing and what improvements need to be made]" (Robbins and Coulter 1999, 51-52, 224).

They like the approach because "its appeal lies in its emphasis on converting overall objectives into specific objectives for organizational units and individual members [and that] studies of actual MBO programs confirm that MBO effectively increases employee performance and organizational productivity" (Robbins and Cooker 1999, 224). When this concept is properly implemented and there are employees who are still uncooperative and unproductive, according to Drucker, management cannot allow the fear of offending or even subsequent unpleasant actions by disgruntled employees to inhibit them from making tough decisions (Drucker 1974, 458-460). Even in making these tough decisions, however, certain principles of SET with available options can be used to minimize tension and help provide a smooth transition.

In 2003, Management Consulting News interviewed James Hoopes, distinguished professor of history at Babson College, about his book False Prophets: The Gurus Who Created Modern Management and Why Their Ideas Are Bad for Business Today. In his response to questions about which guru or leader he would put in the "Hall of Fame," Hoopes mentioned Drucker, even though he does not agree with every aspect of Drucker's management philosophy. He said that Drucker believes that because managers "have power that is not consistent with a democratic society, the corporation is morally illegitimate and it needs to become morally legitimate" (Hoopes 2003).

Hoopes believes that we should accept the illegitimate corporate power because we are not perfect and we live in an imperfect world with "imperfect institutions." However, Hoopes implies in his statements that, like Drucker, he believes management should use discretion and conscience when making decisions. He said, "[management has] unjustifiable power over other people's lives ... You need to be as fair and careful as you can in handling their lives." The interview further quotes Hoopes: "Only if managerial power is understood as an undemocratic but necessary evil ... does moral cautions have a fighting chance to engage the manager's conscience" (Hoopes 2003). In other words, conscience and morality should be considered when making business decisions or else there could be negative repercussions, a corporate fear.

Weeding out lazy or unproductive people from an establishment and providing an environment conducive to growth are a prerequisite for neutralizing the fear of underachievement. This is evident when we examine the business and leadership concepts found in the famous theory X and theory Y. According to theory X, people are basically lazy, whereas according to theory Y, people have a need to succeed (McGregor 1985, 6). An enterprise needs to provide the lazy ones with motivation for production (including, but not limited to, termination) and the opportunity for progress to those who have a need to succeed.

In a grid developed to show conditions and their effects in an organization, Blake and Mouton (1985, 20) describe what they call a "nine and one orientation' that spreads through an organization. The nine signifies that the organization is high on production, and the one that it is low on concern for people. Such skewed dynamics can produce an atmosphere similar to a guard-prisoner mentality. The subordinate says yes all the time to the superior whether he agrees with the situation or not. A no may be covered up with a yes. This orientation breeds distrust, and people's true feelings are never known. The resulting systemic fear usually breeds failure.

I read with great interest an article by Alisa Priddle in the December 2000 edition of the journal Ward's AutoWorld titled "Panic in Detroit: DaimlerChrysler's Jim Holden Pays the Price for Stuttgart's Jitters." The article described, and reinforced in my mind, a great example of corporate fear. The article begins by saying that you know you are having a bad day when the best part of it is being grilled by journalists about why your stock is tanking (going down the drain, so to speak). Mr. Holden, president and CEO of DC, was placed on the proverbial hot seat to answer questions regarding the disappointing performance of the company. Mr. Holden knows "he's on shaky ground in Germany after a $512 million loss in third quarter earnings" (Priddle 2000, 42). Eleven days after that November 1, 2000, interview, Mr. Holden was fired.

In regard to their image, corporations are very fearful of not meeting the expectations of their stakeholders as well as those of the public. In fact, the article clearly states that there is panic in Detroit fed by analysts who criticize DC for ambitious plans to replace 80 percent of its lineup by 2004 yet in the next breath denounce it for its aging fleet. The fear mongering is further fueled by restructuring teams looking to excise $3 billion. White-collar employees worry that Stuttgart finally will declare many functions in Auburn Hills, Michigan, redundant. If the Chrysler Group can regain cost leadership, "that's a ... lot easier job than the one we faced in 1990, 1991, 1992, which was: 'Fix your designs, fix your

quality, fix your financials, fix your loyalty rights, fix your dealers"'
(Priddle 2000, 42-43).

Clearly, when pressure is brought to bear on corporate executives,
the entire corporation will have to produce and perform. I can almost
hear them saying, "Make us look good, achieve the maximum market
share, make us a leader, and enhance our image." Fear of failure is the
result. Many suffer the consequences of not meeting the prescribed
expectations. This, in general, is the standard operating procedure in
U.S. corporate life.

It must also be remembered that some of the problems mentioned
above are not unique to large corporations. Small and medium-sized
businesses possess some of these problems in relatively smaller or greater
degrees. According to UCLA business professor Dr. Ichak Adizes,
some organizations have "pathological problems" (Adizes 1988, 12-15).
Pathological problems are those problems that management should
not have to begin with; often they are incapable of dealing with them.
Pathological problems retard the organization's ability to develop. They
stymie and entrap the organization in a particular phase of the life cycle
(Adizes 1988, 7--11).

Unfortunately, although Adizes's suggested solution of removing
the problem so that the business can move to the next stage appears
reasonable, it may not be as easy as it sounds. In some cases, the
problems are created by people who are themselves suffering from
pathological problems and have infused some of those problems into the
corporate system. These pathological problems may include "autocracy,
impulsiveness," and other behaviors inimical to morale and the "social
health of an organization." This creates fear and distrust that could
stifle an organization and eventually initiate its demise. Employees'
fear becomes more profound if their superiors or leaders have coercive
power—the "perceived power to fire, transfer, demote, and so on"
(Hersey and Blanchard 1993, 235).

If an organization is to effectively persuade its human resources
to quell the seeds of doubt and mistrust of the body corporate or soul
of the organization, it must engage in what I call "corporate self-talk."
Corporate self-talk is a continual repetition of the organization's purpose

and mission at every level. It must be used in meetings, workshops, and seminars. By constant rehearsal of the entity's purpose and mission, the employees and others associated with the organization begin to internalize them to the extent that they surface in every aspect of the company's relationship with employees, customers, stockholders, and the general public. A rebirth of the organization takes place. The soul of the organization is not only what the organization wants to accomplish, thinks it can accomplish, and is working toward accomplishing; it is also how the employees feel about the organization and their commitment to its cause.

The soul of the organization includes its strategic plans, its reaction to various environmental challenges, and its ability to withstand the impact of severe negative experiences. All of these are predicated on the entity's purpose and mission and the resolve of leadership to achieve its objectives. Quality of leadership therefore weighs heavily in the process, and the psychological problems that leaders bring to the process play a pivotal role in their thinking. Thus, their fears must be addressed before they permeate the organization. If the transfer of those fears has already occurred, the relevant recurring question seems to be whether corporate fear can be overcome or neutralized.

The answer to that question is found in the next chapter and in the other chapters (6, 9 and 14) dealing with root causes of individuals' fears, biblical foundation for fear neutralization, and neutralizing fear using spiritual euphoric therapy. Suffice it to say that the resolution appears to begin at the individual level being the basis for corporations, communities, and societies. However, before we move on with the discussion on overcoming corporate fear, two significant issues should not be overlooked. They are what I call the "corporate miasma" and the "if syndrome."

The corporate miasma results from stagnated management. When a corporation or any established entity engages itself in a product line (whether it be contracting, partnering, or the performance of a service), and management constricts itself to the basic elements of that task, ignoring the opportunity to expand through creative thinking, the corporation experiences malaise. If this condition continues without the infusion and implementation of new ideas and approaches to the quest for success, the corporation can be said to possess corporate miasma—a basic unwillingness to try other endeavors or ideas that could achieve the desired success (out of fear of failure). It cannot see or move beyond the present problems because the focus is on what is currently happening and not on where it needs to be in the future.

Interestingly, this is true of a large corporation as well as a family unit. Many companies sense this stagnation, and the fear of just "marking time" leads them to change management. The family unit is different, of course; the actions taken may include getting a new job or an additional job, improving one's skills through continuing education, or emphasizing frugality until enough funds accumulate to engage in entrepreneurship. Most of this is done to avoid poverty and dependence on others. The fear of actual poverty is real to the family unit; to the corporation, poverty means being gobbled up by the competition or death. Organizations exist to be viable and to succeed, and anything less is deemed a failure. This fear drives many to offer excuses for their inability to implement sound strategies. I refer to these excuses as the "ifs."

The "if syndrome" is really a spinoff from the miasmatic condition. It results from knowing that the establishment is in a rut, so to speak, but not knowing how to get out. The "ifs" appear as hypothetical's. If we had a better manager, we would accomplish more. If we had more people, we would feel better. If the corporate office would pay us more, production would increase. If there were less noise around, my attitude would be better. If Mary had not called me to work on this project, I would not have made this mistake. These ifs are a form of abdication of responsibility. It is always someone else's fault, never mine. The pervasiveness of such attitudes in an establishment signals underlying fears. Work needs to be done to uncover those fears and provide solutions for the individuals or the group(s) (Henry 2002).

The reader may find it as intriguing as I do that not only for-profit establishments experience such situations. The nonprofit entities that engage in charity work and fundraising are susceptible to the same malaise and fear filled attitudes. Many of those organizations might have been extremely successful had they only had the courage to engage the appropriate potential donors in the right manner at the right time under the right circumstances.

The preceding statement may seem very challenging and perhaps a little optimistic. Such a conclusion should be reevaluated. When I listened to a lecture at Loma Linda University by Dr. Lilya Wagner, the internationally known writer and fundraiser, I became even more convinced that my position on this matter is sustainable. Dr. Wagner, from her vast experience, confirmed that one of the reasons people representing a range of institutions are afraid to ask for money, is that they fear rejection (Wagner 2002). Fear of rejection has led many to shortchange their institutions and stymie the progress that would have helped them achieve some of their significant objectives.

How, then, can a corporate entity address such issues? Ignoring them will not solve the problem. They must be dealt with so that the corporation or organization can move ahead successfully. While corporate fear is a subject unto itself, the author would not do justice to the subject of neutralizing the power of fear without a few words on how fear causes these entities to behave and what can be done to overcome it.

Overcoming Corporate Fear

Paradoxical though it may sound, there is no corporate fear if individual fears do not exist. It is individuals who transfer their fears to the corporate environment. If an organization is properly prepared for the venture on which it has embarked, it will have good information on many, if not all of the following:

- A corporation's "complex." Is it inferior, superior, or equal to the competition?
- Its niche. Market research should reveal product demand, competitors' market share, advertising strategies, target groups, logistical problems (including delivery and mobility of human resources).
- A strategic master plan, both long and short range.

Finally, companies must know how they will handle the "myth of failure," so called because I believe failure is created, not imposed. Failure is experienced only when a person or an entity determines that it is to be experienced. A company needs to know when it is suffering from corporate fear because fear is an inhibitor of success even though it may be a motivator for strategic planning. The conventional thought is that failure occurs when a person tries to accomplish something and is unable to. At that point, there should be "gear changing." Apparent failure is an opportunity to engage in product modification or diversification. Otherwise, it's lost Opportunity. True failure occurs only when unrealized goals cause despair, panic, cessation of the activity, and an abandonment of effort. I call it the "sold, fold, and die syndrome."

Just as individuals make up the corporate environment, corporate entities—corporations, partnerships, families, joint ventures, and so on—are the individual units that make up society. Exploring how individuals' fear spread through corporations brings us to how corporate fears become the structural fears endemic to society.

Corporate fear is really the aggregate fear of a set of individuals. It may be derived from a group or a dominant individual who has the power and authority to transfer such fear. The power that fear has to paralyze an individual is the same power that paralyzes business entities and societies. Every thinking entity will experience fear.

I worked at one of the largest universities in what was the fourth largest city in the United States until the late 1990s. My position and location allowed me to interact with top executives as well as middle and lower-level employees. At one point during my tenure, there were layoffs and separations for one reason or another. Fear was in the minds of almost all middle and lower-level employees. They kept asking, "Who is next?" Employees sometimes put on smiling faces in the presence of their supervisors but behind their backs made disparaging remarks.

The new vice president for administration and finance seemed to have sensed that something was wrong and that discontent in the organization could eventually threaten his position. In an attempt to improve productivity and loyalty, he divided his department into two groups—an A team and a B team. The A team consisted of the ones closest to him in the organizational structure and the B team of everyone else.

He brought in an expert in organizational behavior and management to help the employees discover the areas in which they were strong, as well the areas in which they were not so strong. Some employees continued to feel a sense of distrust and even isolation because what resulted from those sessions appeared to be a form of demotion and/or isolation of some who previously had been "in the loop." Some people worked a little later and perhaps on weekends to get financial statements out but not out of true loyalty to the organization or the supervisor. They drove themselves because of fear—fear of being blacklisted, looked upon as uncooperative, thought of as not a team member, and perhaps ultimately fear of termination. Surreptitious negative expressions about management (made overtly to friends and close colleagues) persisted.

The full impact of the position changes may have been lessened, but loyalty, efficiency, and production did not increase. The strategy would have been a superb one if demotions, terminations, and apparent favoritism were not included.

The following are indicators of whether a company is experiencing corporate fear:

1. Friction or schism in the top, middle, or lower management structure.
   Friction among any combination of these is a true sign of corporate fear.
2. Pervasive or chronic disagreements among supervisors and workers.
3. Scarcity of new ideas from lower-level employees or unwillingness to discuss problems.
4. Distrust among coworkers and/or a tendency to assign blame.
5. Fear of management reflected by behaviors such as employees running to their desks if management is coming, subordinates paying undue strict attention to their work, and so on.

To initiate the process of neutralizing those fears and avoiding the fear trap, individual managers from the top down should assimilate and model the principles of the Spiritual Euphoric Therapy (SET) described in chapter 13. SET would establish a sense that management cares about the workers—worker nurturing, if you please. The result would most likely be increased production and greater loyalty. Additionally, management should begin some form of informal interaction with lower-level supervisors and, where possible, with the employee pool at large. The corporation can obtain instruments designed for group discussions and interactions that will facilitate better employee relations. These may provide valuable insight for improvement of product, service, or image. Fear is a catalyst for strategic planning but an inhibitor of successful outcomes if not negated. Consider the following examples.

Lee Iacocca's gutsy move to convince the government to pump about 400 million dollars into the Chrysler Corporation in the seventies when it was on the verge of collapse was an example of the effective capitalization of an atmosphere of fear to achieve success. John DeLorean, on the other hand, who left an arguably enviable position in a successful corporation to establish his own company, fell by the wayside. Allegedly, fear of failure because of inadequate funding caused him to resort to unsavory transactions to fund his company in order to achieve success.

Now consider the impact that the aggregate fear within governments, industry, academia, and other institutions has on any given society. The fear in each of these segments of society could create a mushrooming effect if given the right publicity. Enter the media. Fear about ominous future economic conditions could lead industry to pull significant amounts of investments out of the stock market, creating a selling spree and causing other entities to be jittery. As the fever spreads, the economy becomes worse in a self-fulfilling prophecy. Many individuals, fearing future loss of their nest eggs, panic.

CHAPTER 11

SOCIETY AND FEAR'S ROLE IN HISTORY

Theocratic entities have quicker resolutions to their constituents' fears of infiltration or destruction than do institutions in non-theocratic states. Fears are allayed by the assurance that their success is guaranteed because of their dependence on their supreme commander—God. A clarification or explanation of the term theocracy is imperative at this point because there seems to be misunderstandings about that term.

A theocracy cannot be created by human beings; it can only be rejected or maintained by them. Nations that desire to be led by leaders who recognize and trust in God, the Creator, may do so. If their activities are within his will, when they call on him, he will hear and work in their behalf. But only God can create a theocracy. In a nation that is theoretically governed, as far as strategies relating to the military for both domestic and foreign endeavors, persistent fear by the citizens is virtually nonexistent because victory is assured.

In ancient times, when the tribe of Israel was ruled by a theocracy, the leaders (judges or prophets) had only to seek God's guidance, and he gave them instructions regarding certain decisions that were to be made. For example, Joshua 8:1 says, "And the LORD said unto Joshua, Fear not, neither be thou dismayed: Take all the people of war with thee, and arise, go up Ai: see, I have given into thy hand the king of Ai, and his people, and his city, and his land." Likewise, 1 Samuel 7:8 says, "And the children of Israel said to Samuel, Cease not to cry unto the Lord our God for us, that he will save us out of the hand of the Philistines.

After they rejected that form of government when they told Samuel that they wanted a king like the other nations, God said that they had not rejected Samuel but had rejected him (1 Samuel 8:7). Notwithstanding that rejection, their kings still had to rely upon divine direction when Kings were faced with serious challenges. An example of that is found in 2 Kings 18:13-19:37. Sennacherib, king of Assyria, threatened Judah during the reign of King Hezekiah. Hezekiah became fearful and spread the letter from Sennacherib before the Lord (2 Kings 19:14). God heard his prayer and sent word through his prophet Isaiah, saying, "He shall not come into this city or shoot an arrow there" (2 Kings 19:32). God sent an angel and killed 185, 000 soldiers that night. Sennacherib was eventually killed by his own relatives (2 Kings 19:35-37).

In a theocracy, God, the creator of heaven and earth, rules. He designates by some visible signs the person or persons who are his representatives so that the inhabitants of the land, as well as those from afar, know whom to call on for counsel; God makes clear whose word should be respected above all others. Except for conditional prophecy, which must be understood in its context, the word of a prophet of God always comes to pass.

Notwithstanding such public knowledge, the messages given by God's representatives must be tested by the guidebook—Scriptures— prescribed for all mankind. Clerics and other religious leaders cannot make a state theocratic. Only God can declare a nation as being theocratic, meaning governed by him. Hence, no theocracy exists. Therefore, any nation that claims to be ruled by a spiritual power (a god) is what I call a "demiocracy" (rulership by religious human beings in the name of religion but having less power than that which is directly from God), not a theocracy. No theocracy exists today; therefore, we must concern ourselves with the systems of ideologies that are competing for supremacy in the current construct of human existence.

Ideology Overrun

Our first example of an ideology based on fear is twentieth-century Russia. When the tsars were overthrown in Russia in 1917, the Bolshevik regime was established. A Marxist-Leninist government enforced communism—a godless form of socialism—and began to expand. In some ways, however, Soviet communism resembled a monarchy, where wealth is extracted from those at the bottom to enrich those at the top who live sumptuously (as opposed to capitalism, which rewards the entrepreneurial endeavors of motivated individuals or groups). The expansion of this socialistic ideology engulfed many nearby countries and constructed closed, restricted societies.

"Since 1902, Vladimir Lenin had worked to create an elite political organization that would be distinguished from the other Russian socialist parties. Once he got the party on course it was a struggle to keep it there" (Kort 1985, 96-97). The explosive growth of the party in 1917 transformed it from an "exclusive, insulated elite" to a mass party with many committees and cells that often operated independently. By March 1917, the Bolsheviks under Lenin were triumphant over the Tsarists. The Tsarists' worst fears were realized (Kort 1985, 96-105).

In the months following the Bolshevik coup, there were severe shortages of food and fuel triggered by the expropriation of the properties of the wealthy or large estates. Production was disrupted. There were no overall plans made to address those crises. Drastic measures had to be taken; these measures became known as "War Communism" (Kort 1985, 120). That, no doubt, was the genesis of communism in Russia and the USSR, ushering in the fear that was cast upon the Russian people.

> War Communism in its essence was an unstable combination of cold and often cruel expediency born of the civil war crisis and utopian visions of recreating Russian society in [a] Marxist equivalent of six biblical days ... [There was a] "food dictatorship" decree of May 1918, which called for using force and class warfare in villages against the wealthier peasants (called kulaks,

the Russian word for "fists"), to assure the delivery of grain to the State monopoly at fixed prices ... They seized not only grain and other food but such other necessities as horses and wagons

(Kort 1985, 95-120).

After Lenin's death, Joseph Stalin gained ascendancy over Leon Trotsky. The apparent fear of losing out to Trotsky motivated Stalin to send and to take Trotsky's life. He disposed of his critics on the left and undermined or killed those on the right. Communism accelerated after World War II, and the countries under the control of the USSR eventually became known as the Iron Curtain countries. Indescribable fear of the state and fear of the secret police was the norm among the residents of that geographic area.

After World War II, observing communism's philosophy and economic achievements, Western capitalism became very anticommunistic. It also appeared obvious that communism was bent on the destruction of capitalism. The two philosophies were diametrically opposed to each other, and the globe was split, as it were, between these two ideologies. Thus, the fear of military superiority by the opposition became a preoccupation.

Fear of Attack: From World War II to Today's Middle East

No country or state wants to be inferior or to be perceived as being inferior to another. Clouds of war hung over the world because of the military capability of many nations. Categorizations appeared to define and contain fear.

During World War II, humanity was exposed to heretofore inconceivable weapons. In World War I, the weapons were rifles, swords, bayonets, cannons, and certain kinds of warships. To our modern perception, these appear easy to defend against. During the Second World War, however, the stakes became higher. Warplanes became more sophisticated, guns were more potent and versatile, and warships were faster, larger, and more lethal. To crown it all, for the first time in the history of this planet, humankind split the atom. The world would never be the same.

Ever since Hiroshima and Nagasaki, the fear factor in all societies has increased to another level. Not only did the philosophies of communism in the East and capitalism in the West threaten each other but also each side feared that crusading leadership on the other side might perceive the other as weak or vulnerable. Consequently, both sides prepared to launch an attack in the belief that either could win an all-out war.

That was what the Cold War was all about—intimidation of the enemy, uncertainty about its true capability, and instilling fear to prevent a wrong move. The stalemate gave rise to the concept of mutually assured destruction, or MAD)—one party's decision to attack the other would initiate its own destruction if each has the capability to destroy the other.

The pervasiveness of fear in our society during World War II was reflected when about 120,000 Japanese Americans, many of them U.S. citizens, were imprisoned after the attack on Pearl Harbor. FBI director J. Edgar Hoover, who had "interned nine hundred and forty-two Japanese aliens in the days after Pearl Harbor" (Morgan 1985, 625-659), was reluctant to accept the idea of a mass evacuation of those people from the West Coast, blaming the clamor for such evacuation on "public and political pressure rather than factual data." American society, ordinary citizens as well as its leaders, were fearful about the future; this fear became an uncertainty and a mistrust of Americans who were of Japanese descent. Ted Morgan's biography of Franklin Roosevelt (FDR) notes that "in an attempt to calm public fears, [Attorney General Francis] Biddle drafted a press release ... which said that ... enemy aliens would be 'evacuated' from eighty-eight prohibited area[s] in California. [Incidentally,] FDR was in favor of [the] evacuation" (Morgan 1985, 625-659).

American society was not the only one battling fear and uncertainty about the future. European countries were in the same situation. Representative of that geographic area was Winston Churchill. "After Pearl Harbor [December 7, 1941], Churchill lost no time coming to

Washington, arriving on December 22, for he was deeply concerned that the Americans would mount an all-out effort against Japan, leaving the British and the Russians to deal with Hitler." Stalin also was experiencing fear and anxiety. He "cabled Churchill on March 18 that 'Uncertainty of your statements concerning contemplated Anglo-American offensive across channel arouses grave anxiety in me about which I feel I can not be silent'" (Morgan 1985, 625-659). The era of World War II and its aftermath was indeed a time when the globe was in a state of fear, not knowing what the future would bring.

Societal fear is the accumulation of individuals' fears, but it would be naive to insinuate that fear can be eradicated from every person on the earth. The offered prescription would not be accepted by all. Furthermore, fear is intangible and cannot be destroyed by human beings; so how can it be neutralized? It must be addressed on the individual level. Individuals make up organizations and together they form society. It is the individuals—the leaders and public figures—that transfer their fears to society. Therefore, the solution starts with individuals, and it begins with the five steps mentioned previously. Through education—seminars, workshops, books, schools, churches, etc., people can learn to depend on sustainable principles (biblical principles, for example) to bring rationality and calm to society—thereby avoiding the fear trap.

I vividly recall the tenseness and fear that seemed to have gripped the world in 1962. The Soviet Union, with Nikita Khrushchev at the helm, was trying desperately to aid Cuba militarily and position itself' in the western hemisphere for a possible future confrontation with the United States. Mr. Khrushchev sent several ships with missiles to be installed in Cuba. John Fitzgerald Kennedy, elected president in 1960, net the most formidable test of his administration. He had to put a stop to what would have become a potentially deadly threat to the United States. After President Kennedy's unsuccessful attempt to persuade Mr. Khrushchev to turn the Soviet ships around and abandon the idea of installing the missiles, he erected a blockade and gave the orders that if the ships insisted on proceeding toward Cuba, they should be sunk. Not knowing how Mr. Khrushchev would respond, the world watched with bated breath. Some thought that World War III was at hand. Others seemed to have been stricken with fear beyond description. Fortunately for the world, Mr. Khrushchev backed down. Cuba was left without the wherewithal to pose a significant threat to the United States.

Fear of the future has led the United States, on several occasions, to pursue a defense system called the Strategic Defense Initiative (SDI), dubbed "Star Wars" by some. SDI would provide a shield over the United States, they said, to protect us from incoming missiles. Whether missile defense would work is difficult to tell. Nevertheless, military missile defense projects, including Patriot-type missiles, have been funded, and the defense system will continue to be refined in the years to come. It is all about fear and what can be done to protect against the military might of an enemy.

In the last leg of President Clinton's administration, the Middle East peace negotiations between the Palestinians and Israel—with the United States, Egypt, Russia, and others all in the mix—were very tentative, fragile, and tense. It appeared that in addition to other hidden factors many of us may not be aware of, a visit to the Temple Mount by Gershon Salomon, who was accompanied by several hundred soldiers, sparked violence and unrest in that region. Stones were thrown, slingshots were hurled, guns were blazing, and chaos reigned. These events, most people thought, were harbingers of a greater calamity if the peace process failed. There was great fear that some of those who were negotiating were insincere or not willing to do whatever it took to achieve peace.

On October 10, 2000, Mr. Koppel, then news anchor of ABC's Night-line with Ted Koppel, hosted a panel of Palestinian and Israeli representatives and an audience eager to ask questions in Jerusalem. The title of the program was "The Holy Land: Moment of Crisis, Nightline Town Meeting from Jerusalem." Among the panelists were those who had actually taken part in the negotiations as well as the mayor of Jerusalem. It seemed that the purpose of the meeting was for those close to the conflict to offer possible solutions to the problems.

Mr. Koppel tried to moderate as best he could, but the dominating question that kept coming back to the Israeli panelists was regarding footage shown prior to the discussions of a Palestinian man and his twelve-year-old son caught in crossfire and trying to hide behind an object. The little boy was killed by a bullet. The father was wounded but survived. The world had seen this tragedy unfold, and the picture was indelibly etched in the memory of those whose friends and families were feeling the anguish. Not being able to effectively deal with the armored vehicles that were inflicting death and heartache to those in their path frustrated everyone.

One of the Israeli panelists, in response to a statement made by a Palestinian panelist about the Israeli army, said, "Our strength has become our weakness." The same Israeli panelist, in response to another Palestinian statement that Israel is occupying the Palestinian land, inquired whether he thought the Palestinian could come to Israel and occupy its land. The Palestinian responded that the Palestinians would love to but will never be able to do it (Koppel 2000).

At the heart of their exchange lay deep-seated anger and fear—anger over the current loss of life and fear that loss of life could persist. Israel prides itself in a well-equipped and sophisticated military that provides assurance that the nation can defend itself in the event of an attack that could come at any time.

Therefore, because Israel is strong militarily, any threat to its peace or stability is likely to be met with a response from the army.

This kind of force is generally seen as an overreaction and elicits sympathy for the Palestinians from people around the world. Its strength invariably becomes its weakness. When I began writing this book, some of the events mentioned above were only possibilities. Since that time, however, many changes have taken place in the Middle East, including the kidnapping of two Israeli soldiers and a 2006 military confrontation in Lebanon. These events highlight my point: nations invest in military might and national security out of fear of being defeated by the enemy.

Beyond the military troubles of nations around the world, other factors make governments fearful. Central among these are the breakdown of law and order, moral decay, and a poor economy, which can destabilize a government. All three make a nation vulnerable to sinister leadership and outside attack.

Breakdown of Law and Order and Morality

The United States is known as a republic. Every citizen, as is guaranteed by the Constitution, has a right to bear arms. However, we see many people trying to abridge that right by wanting law-abiding citizens to disarm or to position themselves in a manner that will make it easy to be disarmed. Now, I have never purchased a firearm. I have not argued pro or con on the issue of gun control. My position does not prevent me from observing what I perceive to be facts. One of the arguments used very often by some who are pro gun control is that the restriction of various types of guns and people who may procure them is intended to prevent the breakdown of law and order and to help stem the tide of moral decay in our society. These fears, they project, are real, and the perceived threat to our society should not be taken for granted.

I must admit that the possibility of increased erosion of law and order and the decadence of our society is real. The solution to these problems, however, does not appear to be the disarming of citizens, though some people act irresponsibly with the storage and usage of their firearms. Some contend that due to the nature of our society, if the government disarms citizens, thugs and criminals will develop a black market for guns. And the very problem you are trying to solve becomes a greater problem.

Others say that with the citizens disarmed, irresponsible government could, as in some countries, perpetrate atrocities and crimes against the people. Government with a dictatorial mentality will not hesitate to squelch the cry of human reasoning when it seems politically convenient to do so. That expediency may be exercised in order to remain in power. These are some of the fears that exist with the citizenry as well as concerned voices in the halls of power.

Unlike tragedies that have transpired in some countries such as Somalia, Croatia, and even Rwanda at the writing of this book (2007), there is virtually no chance for breakdown of law and order in the United States because of the structure of the system. There have been packets of disturbances resulting from inappropriate responses by fans to the victory of their sports teams. Some of those acts could very well be labeled as criminal behavior (such as overturning cars, burning automobiles and buildings, and looting). Those were brief, localized situations brought under control expeditiously, as opposed to the total breakdown of law and order in which the government has lost control.

The days when law enforcement officers confronted the civil rights marchers and demonstrators under Dr. Martin Luther King Jr. are in the past. Those demonstrations were not a breakdown of order. They could almost be called a breakdown of law because of how law enforcement handled some of those marches due to the fear of a potential national uprising, yet those were actions relating to specific events and not a national crisis in that regard. However, unless the immigration issue is solved, there could be a repeat of massive demonstrations with their potential consequences.

The real problem is in the area of the moral decadence in our society. One does not know where to begin when it comes to listing the areas of morality that need to be addressed. Let me mention a few, beginning with what is permitted to be transmitted over the airwaves. In times past, certain words or conduct considered obscenity were either kept off the air or not aired during prime time. Today, it appears that anything and everything goes. Sexually explicit acts are shown on what seems to be a daily basis. Vulgarity in conversation is laughed at as if it's a virtue. Little wonder that people from countries that extol the virtues that we as a society once prized loathe the values we now accept, even though most of them would do almost anything to enter the United States for economic reasons.

Coupled with those issues are the number of incidents of crimes and violence and the devaluing of manhood and womanhood. There is infanticide, homicide, child abuse, and spousal abuse. I suggest that all of these are actions of the basic sinful human nature caused by fear and cause a lot of fear in society. The solution to these problems begins with the proper application of the Spiritual Euphoric Therapy (SET) as illustrated in the Time-Frame Release Capsule in chapter 9 and explained elsewhere in this book.

The Economy

In addition to law and order concerns, a poor economy can bring a nation to a point of anarchy. Thus, political parties and presidential hopefuls spar over who has the best economic program. Debate about economic programs occurs in every free country and even surfaces from time to time in countries that have less regard for the principles of democracy. Let us look for a moment on the 2000 U.S. presidential race between then vice president Al Gore and then Texas governor George W. Bush.

The question was not really how to fix the economy. Back then, the economy was booming, unemployment was at an all-time low, there was a huge surplus, and consumer confidence was high. The major points of focus were what to do with the surplus, how to improve education, how to safeguard Social Security, what to do about health care, and how to best strengthen the military. Most of these items had to do with the economy.

The way the media and the political pundits portray each candidate has an impact on many voters. Media portraits help determine the outcome of an election. People become very fearful about a candidate and what he or she might do in the future. They could also become apathetic if they believe that all political parties are the same. Most people want to feel secure about the future, so anything that generates fear in their minds will not be looked at favorably. With campaign promises of security and prosperity, people aligned themselves with one side or the other. Despite a few individuals from independent parties running for the presidency; only the major parties shared the limelight, leaving the less popular parties disgruntled. There were predictions on every side. However, no one could know the future. Uncertainty brought fear to many on all sides—fear of ultraconservatism and fear of ultra liberalism.

Regardless of the contrasting predictions, both major candidates promised preservation of the good economy and protection against policies that would set us back to the days before the prosperous and enjoyable economic boom. Why were we so afraid of having a poor economy? Among other things, a poor economy is bad for business, and if it is bad for business, it is bad for the people. When the economy is bad, people tend to make rash decisions out of fear of losing their investments. Interestingly; both candidates agreed that there was a surplus and only debated who would better manage that surplus.

On Election Day November 7, 2000, many people were anxious and fearful about the future of the country. Some said that if the Republican candidate won, the country would go back to the old days of deficits and economic woes. Others said that the country would experience more "big government," continued moral deficiency, and the appointment of liberal Supreme Court justices if the Democratic candidate won. The point I am making is that our focus was on fear: the anxiety and apprehension that came over us as a cloud during that period of American history.

On November 29, 2000, the State of Florida declared Governor Bush the winner and awarded him its twenty-five electoral votes. On December 18, 2000, George W. Bush became president by obtaining 271 electoral votes. Vice President Al Gore was unsuccessful in his challenge to the decision after the U.S. Supreme Court declared Governor Bush the winner. The general feeling among both politicians and their constituents was one of intrigue and suspense. It was an historic moment in the United States.

Responses from politicians during interviews indicated that they were as apprehensive as the general public. People were fearful about what could transpire if the election were not settled in a timely manner. As much as the situation revolved around economic issues, there was also a psychological aspect to the dispute. If the country could no longer tolerate the uncertain situation, spending decisions could have been impacted. That, in turn, would have impacted the activity of the stock market and created a domino effect on major economic strategies of many corporations and institutions.

The fears about the possible divide in the United States due to the anger and bitterness over the election results and the potential economic problems that could have ensued were not necessarily unfounded. Those concerns are not unique to American politics. Other countries have fears regarding their future. Many other countries have even more tension and fear, especially those that do not have the political system that exists in the United States. As difficult as it may seem, the nation cannot be allowed to live in fear. Fear spells bad news for the government as well as the society.

On Thursday, May 6, 2010, as I watched the news, Rick's List, on the Cable News Network (CNN) channel, there were reports that the stock market, specifically, the Dow Jones Industrial (DIJA) Average, dropped about 997 points. CNN also showed pictures of a protest taking place in Greece because of the financial crisis that country was facing. One of the journalists reporting the stories, namely, Christine Romans, stated that she learned that "a fault in Proctor & Gamble's stock quote" triggered a drop in that stock price by about 37 percent. These events, according to the reports, created fear in the marketplace and caused profound uncertainty about the future. They believe that the crisis in Greece may cause a rippling effect throughout Europe, Asia, and the United States.

A significant point that was mentioned in all of this was that most of the trading was done by electronic means—computer program driven. In all of this, the one word that these media persons kept using is fear—that people are fearful as to what will happen tomorrow and in the future. This is caused by individuals' actions, creating an unstable environment, which spills over into society as a whole. This kind of fear must be neutralized. It must be done, using the mechanisms mentioned above—addressing individuals' fears (one person at a time or in groups, which will spill over into the corporate arena) and hence, societal fears.

Religion and Its Reaction

In order to cover the full spectrum of societal fears, we must address certain aspects of the religion factor, the role it plays in society and how it handles its fears. Fear in the religious sector of society is real and should be addressed. It should be noted that people in a given society tend to live out—in whole or in part—the principles of their religion. They become very defensive and protective of that religion.

Why would people of religious orientation feel fearful that their religion is in danger? Cannot their god protect the religion? What is really at stake here? We shall endeavor to address these issues as we proceed toward discovering how religion deals with its fear. Both offensive and defensive mechanisms are sometimes employed to obtain and retain power. Such fear needs to be neutralized.

During the 2000 election, influential religious people and some religious organizations were so fearful of the potential outcome that they mounted campaigns to register new voters, provided voting records of incumbents, and made speeches about the kind of leadership that the country needed. In other words, they did everything that was legally permissible to make sure that antireligious legislator or leaders whose moral stand appeared to be different from theirs were not elected. Their concern was not whether their religion, Christianity, would be overrun, diluted, or become extinct because they knew the power of Christianity and how it survived over the centuries. They were concerned about the political and spiritual future of the country: how future legislations or court rulings might affect certain actions or practices that they believed were contrary to biblical principles and offensive to God.

That, however, is different from a religion that covers a large segment of a population, a country, or a region acting to prevent or restrict other religions or "faith traditions" from practicing their belief for fear their adherents might accept this new tradition or that their religion would become diluted. Religion, the solace of the people and the guiding light to its adherents, should react in a manner consistent with its teachings and expectations of goodwill and assurance of peace and hope by its followers.

Religion Defined

Religion is the acknowledgment and worship of a deity. That necessarily involves belief in and practice of what are considered to be the teachings of that deity. .Adherents of those teachings are expected to faithfully obey and submit to any pronouncements by the deity; they may otherwise expect wrath in the form of physical pain or death. A deity is one who is infinite, superior to human beings, omnipotent, omniscient, and omnipresent. A deity can he invisible or visible at will. A deity can destroy but cannot be destroyed; a deity is immortal. A deity can create but cannot be created. A deity does not need to be defended. A deity is not confined to this earth, solar system, or galaxy. Finally, a deity is self-sustaining, with no need for oxygen, matter, or human thought (conscious or unconscious) to exist. On the surface, this is a very fearful concept. Religion, then, is not a person or a thing; it involves a belief system espoused by human beings.

A deity is all that humans are not. Humanity consists of flesh and bones. Humanity has the capacity to think, reason, and have emotional responses to internal or external stimuli. Humanity depends on oxygen to survive and food and water to be sustained. Humanity can be created and can be destroyed; humanity is mortal. Humanity is finite. Humanity cannot, on its own, be visible or invisible at will. Humanity, for the most part, is confined to this earth and certainly to this solar system. Humanity has knowledge but not foreknowledge. Humanity has some knowledge of some of the past, some knowledge of some of the present, and no knowledge of the future—except that which is revealed supernaturally. In fact, humanity lives in time—not just time but the present time. Humanity cannot live in the past, present, and future simultaneously. Thus, since humanity does not meet any of the criteria of a deity, it would be ludicrous, even silly, to ascribe deity status to or to worship a human being.

Everyone belongs to a religion. In fact, even antagonists to religion belong to a kind of "No Religionist" religion. They worship things or people in that "No Religionist" sphere, be it hedonism, materialism, opinionism, or paganism. In my research, the only religion that I have discovered that one can depend on to provide principles that can be relied on to neutralize the fears that exist on all levels of our existence is the Christian religion. Why? Because its founder and teacher has been proven to be divine, while humans are mere mortals. Consider this: The Bible (also called the Scriptures) claims that Jesus, the Son of God, came from heaven (the cosmos) to earth in order to live a sinless (perfect) life and die in man's place to satisfy the requirements of God's law that was broken when humankind sinned. The Bible records that they crucified Him but on the third day, He rose again (not reincarnated) and ascended to heaven. There were eyewitnesses to these incidents, and they testified accordingly: One such witness, as stated in the Bible, doubted the account of Jesus's resurrection and was given the opportunity to thrust his finger in Jesus's side to verify for himself that Jesus was as real after his resurrection as he was before his crucifixion (John 20:27). After that, more than 500 people saw Him at once (1 Corinthians 15:4-8). So, unlike the leaders of all the other religions who are dead and in their graves, Christianity's leader, Christ, died and is alive again.

In contrast, those who claim to be mystics, founders or leaders of more recent religions or religious movements, do not by any credible records, claim to be able to die and resurrect themselves from the grave. In fact, media reports of those who are alive and have been threatened with imprisonment or death have tried to flee from their persecutors. Those who say they do not mind dying as martyrs have not so much as pretend to be able to bring back themselves from the jaws of death. Therefore, sound thinking and a rational choice would be to follow the teachings of this unique personality—Jesus, the Christ of the Bible, the Son of God. It is for this reason that I use Biblical principles to provide sustainable solutions to the problem of fear.

CHAPTER 12

A BIBLICAL OUTLINE FOR FEAR NEUTRALIZATION

Recognition of the Need for Help

The story is told of a child who was lost in the woods. The child had wandered away from her parents and was caught up with the beauty of the flowers, the lush and scrumptious berries, and the breathtaking waterfalls. Oblivious of the dangers of the forest, such as wild predators, the child settled down at a comfortable spot. Meanwhile, her parents, neighbors, and the local authorities scoured the place for her with a desperate urgency.

After a sustained period of time, they found her resting on a rock admiring the waterfalls and enjoying the berries. When told that she was lost and that they had been searching for her for a long time, she said, "I was not lost. I was always right here at the place where you found me." Had she not been found in time, she might have been the victim of a predator. She was lost; she simply did not know it. Therefore, she made no effort to seek help.

Generally speaking, unless physical injury renders a person unconscious or immobile or illness or disease inhibits mobility or rational thinking so that someone else has to get the individual help, recognizing one's own need for help must take place. The need for help must be a reality in the person's mind before help and healing can be realized. When someone else takes the initiative to help, unless the victim or sufferer recognizes the need for assistance, he or she will remain captive to the unfortunate situation.

The affliction of fear, anxiety, and even some physical illnesses can be neutralized, overcome, or adequately treated as long as the individuals recognize that they have a problem and must seek help. One reason many people are unwilling to admit to a problem is fear of embarrassment. People like to project an image that says, "I am in control. I have it all together. I don't need sympathy, pity, or anyone to tell me how to handle myself or my business." Consequently, they suffer in silence. In some cases, their problems are discovered only by accident. In other cases, the discovery is too late.

Many people in the United States are health care challenged. They are shut out of the system because of economic inhibitors or deliberate programming by relatives, friends, or society. They do not frequent doctors or medical facilities for fear of not receiving medical assistance or for fear of discovering illnesses that they may not be able to treat due to lack of funds. Some, due to their unfortunate economic circumstances, take a don't-care attitude toward their own health, perhaps to ensure the well-being of their children or other family members.

Whatever the circumstance, admitting a need for help and expressing the desire to obtain it provides the basis for action and the actual realization of a viable solution. After a person comes to the conclusion that he or she needs help, the next questions that surface are: What precisely do I need help with? Is help available for this situation? Where can I obtain that help? Thus, discovering the right source becomes a significant factor in the endeavor to realize one's desire.

Discovering the Source of Help

This book offers a source that can be relied upon to provide genuine, credible, and permanent solutions to mankind's problems. Ultimately, man's philosophy of life determines where he places his confidence and the sources that he relies on for assistance when fears present themselves and in critical times. Religion becomes a significant factor in that equation.

Atheists and agnostics do not rely on the supernatural for assistance. They have to rely on themselves and what other people can accomplish without recognition of the endowment of talents or gifts by God. As far as they can see, man has achieved his level of intelligence by himself and for himself. Hence their reliance upon people—people who live for a certain number of years and die like the animals do (without God and without hope). It is difficult, then, for any rational being to place substantial confidence in an entity that has no permanence, cannot perform superhuman feats, and can live for only a relatively short period of time. Religion is the only viable source to which we can turn when we are in need of help.

All the religions but one (Christianity) are either still looking for the messiah to come to earth, believe in multiple sons of God who came to earth at different times and are dead and in their graves, or do not acknowledge any son of God or messiah but worship the Great Spirit, Ultimate Reality, Allah, Mother Earth, or some other entity. Some practically do not mention or acknowledge sin and its consequences nor the need to receive forgiveness and be in harmony with God. Their holy one has not performed any acts on this earth that give assurance that he or she has permanence, superiority, or credibility and can guarantee everlasting life to the adherents.

Christianity, on the other hand, has demonstrated that Jesus Christ, the Son of God, came to this earth and performed miracles that no other person or being has ever performed, such as raising the dead so that the person resumes his normal life on earth among his relatives and friends as he used to before his death. Jesus Christ was killed (crucified) and was buried, and many witnesses were present. He rose from the grave despite the attempts of soldiers to prevent him from coming out. He was seen by his friends, relatives, and hundreds of witnesses. Then he ascended to heaven in the sight of multitudes of people. Jesus promised to return and take his people back to heaven. He gave us the Bible as an instruction book for humankind to believe and obey. It is his book, the Bible, which tells us that God created the heavens and the earth in six days and rested the seventh day. He, the Bible tells us, is above every power and authority. He is superior to all. For all of these reasons, Christ of the Bible is the only credible source for help when dealing with any matter that is beyond human capability.

No religion, person, or being can compare with Jesus Christ. He laid down his life, and he took it up again. No one could have killed him if he did not choose to allow it. Jesus was the only person to have ordered a storm to be quiet, made the winds immediately cease to blow, and the waves become calm—something witnesses saw and verified (Mark 4:39).

Saint Mark tells the story of how a ruler of the synagogue, Jairus by name, came to Jesus and asked him to come and lay his hands on his daughter because she was at the point of death (Mark 5). On the way, Jesus was delayed. A woman who was sick for many years had touched him and was healed immediately. While he was talking to her, a person from the ruler's house came and told Jairus that his daughter was dead (verse 35). Jesus saw that the man became fearful immediately, so he said, "Be not afraid, only believe" (verse 36).

When Jesus reached the house, he saw the people weeping and wailing. He asked the multitude why they were making this big ado about the girl. In fact, Jesus told them that the girl was not dead but asleep, and they laughed him to scorn (verses 39-40). Jesus had already taught that when a person dies, he is unconscious and knows nothing; he is as if he is sleeping and awaiting the time of the resurrection. Jesus went where the girl was lying and said, "Damsel, I say unto thee, arise." The twelve-year-old girl arose and walked (Mark 5:41-42).

No other religion outside the Christian religion (which includes many Jewish principles), and no other so-called messiahs, has performed such supernatural feats. It is this kind of person that one wants to rely on for solutions to one's problems. It is that kind of source that any rational being would turn to for answers and guidance along life's way. Hence, we turn to Christianity and its manual, the Bible. Can anyone, in the face of such clear-cut facts, not see that we have found the only source of help—a source that can provide food if we are hungry, clothes if we are naked, healing if we are sick, and life if we are dead and Jesus chooses to resurrect us? Is this not such a source that one wants to rely on? Surely this is an effective source for neutralization of all our fears.

Accepting the Overtures from the Source

Now that we have identified the source that is credible and permanent, not here today and gone tomorrow, not subject to death and annihilation, how do we go about demonstrating our acceptance of that source?

The first step in the acceptance of this source, Jesus Christ, is that "he that cometh to God, must believe that he is [he exists] and that he is a rewarder of them that diligently seek him" (Hebrews 11:6). The principle is clear: you must acknowledge that God exists and believe that he will reward you for acknowledging and trusting him. If you only acknowledge that he exists but do not trust him, it does not benefit you. You must believe that he can do what he says he will do, and you ought to expect him to do it. Further, you ought to hold him to his promise.

After one exercises one's faith by believing in God, one must accept his Son, Jesus Christ, whom he sent to this earth to pay the penalty for man's sin. The real scoop is that God had created man with the hope that man would choose to serve him and not the devil. Satan deceived man, causing him to ignore God's instructions and thereby sin against his maker. Lucifer was in heaven with Jesus and his Father until he rebelled against God, and Jesus had to cast him out. Since his ejection from heaven, he has had a name change. His name is now the devil, or Satan, and he has many aliases—dragon, serpent, deceiver, for example (Revelation 12:9).

Since his successful deception of Adam and Eve, Satan has influenced the minds of the atheists and agnostics to believe that there is no God or that they can't be sure that there is a God in whom they must believe. So it is imperative to observe the first principle: believe that God exists and that he will perform what he has promised. Before anyone can be a partaker of the kingdom of God and receive all its benefits, this first step must be taken. There is no exception to this rule. The wealthy and the poor must do it. The learned and the unlearned must do it. The corporate executive and the assembly-line worker must do it. The social elite and the peasant must do it. The king and his subjects must do it. There are no exceptions. Everyone who desires access to the rights of the kingdom must believe that God exists.

The second step is that a person must acknowledge that he is a sinner. In other words, because Adam, our forefather, sinned, all his descendants are conceived in sin and "shapen in iniquity" (Psalm 51:5); consequently, all have sinned (Romans 3:23). Without that acknowledgment, God can do nothing to save a person from the pitiful condition that he is in. Yes, you are in a pitiful condition. In fact, as far as God is concerned, you are abhorrent, full of sores from the crown of your head to the soles of your feet. You need to be washed and made clean. The comforting thing about this is that he extends the invitation for you to come to him. He will clean you up and make you whole (Isaiah 1:6, 16). That's why it is important for you, reader, to acknowledge that you are a sinner. Otherwise, you are walking around thinking that you are all right when, in the sight of God, you are emitting a foul odor.

The third step is for you to accept the means that God has provided to clean you up and make you appear as if you have never Sinned a day in your life. What is the means by which this can be accomplished? This can only be accomplished by your acceptance of Jesus Christ as LORD and Savior. It is extremely important for a person to recognize that he is destined to die because he has sinned, and the wages of sin is death (Romans 6:23). But God provided someone to die in our place. That person is Jesus Christ. If we accept Jesus as our substitute, it means that we have already paid the price for our sin by way of his substitutionary death on the cross; therefore, we are eligible for the gift of eternal life (Romans 6:23). Anyone who desires to live forever without experiencing the effects of sin—pain, heartache, death—must accept Jesus as Savior and LORD. Only an unwise person would understand this and yet refuse such an offer, for there is no other name given among men whereby a person can be saved (Acts 4:12).

How does one really accept Jesus as Savior and LORD? One needs only to say, with a sincere heart, "Dear Father (God), I acknowledge that I am a sinner and need forgiveness and salvation. Please forgive me of my sins and let your Son, Jesus, come into my heart and make me your child. I renounce the world and all it has to offer, and I accept Jesus as, my LORD and Savior; in his name I pray: Amen."

At that very moment, the Holy Spirit enters your heart and begins to effect a change in your life. Because your heart is sincere and you have renounced the world and its ways, you are now willing to do whatever Jesus, your new master, wants you to do. That's where he becomes LORD of your life. When you acknowledged your sin and asked him to forgive you and to come into your life, he became your Savior. After he became your Savior, your desire is now to please him; therefore, he becomes your LORD.

Everything you do from that moment is geared toward pleasing him. His acceptance of you and your guarantee of eternal life were not dependent on your pleasing him. But now that he has done what no other person or being could have done for you, namely, dying on the cross for the sins of the entire world and cleansing you and giving you eternal life, you become so grateful that you will do anything he wants you to do. He wants us to be perfect (Matthew 5:48) or matured. This means conforming to the instructions given by our newfound source of happiness and hope. At that point, fear is effectively neutralized.

Conforming to the Instructions from the Source

It is not always easy to change one's way of thinking. This is especially true of older individuals who have developed certain habits and formed a certain character. These individuals have seen life and have much to say about it. A change of lifestyle may be next to impossible to accomplish. That is, of course, if it is being attempted only by the person's own strength. Most people have experienced some difficult times at some point in their lifetime. Many can tell you that they don't know how they made it through. Most of them are unmindful that God rules in the affairs of men. God continues to give us opportunities to repent, turn to him, and conform to a more productive and rewarding lifestyle as outlined in his instruction manual, the Bible. Our challenge is to get rid of the harriers that are preventing us from what he wants us to be.

Removing the Barriers and Surrendering

To be free from the power of fear, we must remove the barriers that are inhibitors of our blessings. Some of the most common barriers to surrendering one's life to the control of the LORD Jesus Christ and the power of the Holy Spirit include doubt, pride, fear, apprehension, and anger.

Doubt

This is a very powerful tool of Satan's; it is the foundation for defeat. Unbelief (a statement of position) and doubt (a statement of condition—unsure of what position to take) are inseparable to some degree. Therefore, they are treated as one. Doubt is distrust, and it generates discouragement. If Satan can get a person to be discouraged, that person has already lost the battle with whatever or whomever he or she is fighting. Doubt weakens a person's mental capacity so that he feels incapable of performing at the level that it takes to overcome the difficulties encountered on the road to success. Doubt fosters negativity, and negativity brings contention—the catalyst for schisms and defeat.

It does not matter what endeavor is at issue; those who allow themselves to be captivated by this insidious enemy of success are bound to failure. This is true in the corporate arena as well as in the ordinary activities of life. It is also no different when it comes to acceptance of Christ and his way of life. That's why Jesus said that all things are possible if you only believe; belief is the first step to success. You must believe that it can be done. You must believe that you can achieve. You must believe that despite what others think or say, you can make it. They may not have made it because of their unbelief, so they are trying to instill in you that unbelief that caused them to fail. Don't accept it; reject it immediately and do as Jesus said: "If thou canst believe, all things are possible to him that believeth" (Mark 9:23). Within the parameters of a person's mental capacity to think rationally, that truth is the difference between success and failure.

This principle of believing rather than doubting applies to all individuals whether they are Christians or not. However, non-Christians are limited to only material achievement; they are destitute in the spiritual realm, wherein lies true success. One can achieve not only material success by accepting Christ as LORD and Savior but also eternal life. The reader is strongly encouraged at this point to pause for a moment; now, bow your head and ask Jesus to come into your life and give you the true success for which your heart longs.

If you are in doubt as to what Jesus can do for you, talk to some of those whose lives were empty and meaningless and who have found hope and comfort in Jesus. Talk to former alcoholics and prostitutes who have accepted Jesus and given up their old lifestyles for the life that Christ offers. Talk to the robber, the abuser, and the gambler who have now found a new life in Jesus. Talk to the drug addict who has now found that there is a high that is higher than the high that coke can give. Conversations with these individuals will help to inspire you to give up your doubting and believe. Your fear of taking that step to ultimate success will be allayed, and the barrier of doubt will be removed.

Pride

Many people are afraid to openly acknowledge Jesus as the Messiah and accept his way of life. They hesitate to accept the solutions that he offers for the resolution of the ills of society. They feel that identifying themselves as followers of Jesus will make them pariahs. They fear ostracism, not wanting to be shunned by their peers. They think they will be looked down on if they are unable to partake of some of the activities of their previous lifestyle. Pride is definitely a barrier to acceptance of Jesus and the experience of a transformation of character.

Fear of the Future

The inability to see or predict the future creates fear and a tentative attitude in the decision-making process. Many individuals and even organizations would otherwise be successful if they only had the courage to believe that they can achieve greatness. Rather than approaching life or a given venture with positivity and optimism, they become handicapped by the negative thought of possible failure. That is not to say that one must not examine all possible scenarios and options and choose a path that seems wisest. But to wallow in the possibility of never making it or the negative aspects of "what ifs" is to fertilize the psychological ground of mental weakness and defeat. It could very well be said that fear of the future and of the unknown is the underpinning of all other fears.

We can live only in the present. No one can live in the future, a time that has not yet come. All fears relate to what will occur or what will happen. Jesus highlighted human concern about the future when he said, "Take no thought for the morrow" (Matthew 6:34). He knew that humankind would be anxious and fearful of the undiscoverable, invisible future. The past never changes and cannot be manipulated, whereas the future always yields to the present and is always out of our grasp. But the present is flexible and manipulative. The present must be seized and used wisely if fear is to be rendered ineffective or neutralized and success achieved.

One should never be afraid of the future, which will come regardless of one's acceptance or rejection of it. Paradoxically, the future begins today—every day. Careful planning is therefore essential for daily success. I say daily success because if you do not live to see the fruition or achievement that has been planned for your organization or yourself at a certain date, each day that you lived or were a part of that entity should have been one of success. Each day's achievements should be the fulfillment of a successful microcosm of the aggregate that will be achieved. Hence, successful planning for the future involves successful planning for daily accomplishments.

When one follows that concept, the result will be the same regardless of what one does. It may involve seeking a potential mate, falling in love, and marrying. It may be planning to raise a family or making certain financial decisions for the family; the result is the same. A daily unfolding of your plans for the future represents a step-by-step accumulation of the total success that is planned for the future. Proper preparation for the future is a significant part of neutralizing the fears about the unknown.

The 2001 survey discussed in chapter 4 showed that everyone, from high school students to working adults, has fears about the future. Financial uncertainty, family problems, and personal issues weigh heavily on the minds of many. So many high school and college students are afraid because they don't know what will happen when they get out of school.

The counsel to them is as stated above: utilize the opportunity that you have to ensure proper preparation, trusting the one who holds and controls the future. Move with poise and dignity, and the way will be opened and success will be yours.

Anger and Bitterness

One of the most insidious antagonists of human health is anger. Anger has caused a multitude of illnesses, broken relationships, and other unpleasant situations. Some people tend to pride themselves on the fact that they have a temper. Others, unaware of the anger within them, find themselves acting in a manner that embarrasses themselves or others.

Anger manifests itself in many ways. It may be reflected in envy toward a neighbor or jealousy over the success of others. Perhaps the angry person was deprived of some important beneficial thing as a child. It may be that her childhood was violated by an adult, and this molestation or abuse created a deep, angry scar, a permanent personality disfigurement in her psychological profile.

People who were outcasts or who were "kept down" generally harbor bitterness. Some were never affirmed, and nothing they did was acceptable or approved of by their parents or other significant persons in their lives while others were accepted and applauded. Some have even been angry with themselves for "messing up." These and other circumstances have caused some people to walk around with a proverbial chip on their shoulders. They sometimes become intolerant of others because they are intolerant of themselves. They may never have considered themselves worthy.

These deep-seated feelings are brought into everyday life. They are reflected in the way some supervisors treat their subordinates or the way directors or managers behave in their approach to strategic planning and operational functions. Yet deeply rooted anger can be resolved. The Christian manager, director, supervisor, or worker with a whatsoever-you- dodo-all-to-the-glory-of-God perspective brings honesty, integrity, morality, positivity, efficiency, and wisdom to the activities in which he or she is involved. Their deeds are recorded in the books of heaven, so nothing short of their best is acceptable to them. A true Christian is one who does not just control his or her anger but strives to get rid of it.

However, there is a type of anger different from the kind we have just discussed. That anger is what is called "righteous indignation." A Christian experiences such anger when he hears someone taking the name of the LORD in vain or when he sees injustices being done to innocent individuals, the poor, or the unfortunate—those who are unable to represent or fend for themselves in society. That kind of anger is not related to selfishness but to a yearning for righteousness, justice, peace, and goodwill.

Some time ago, my wife went to a hospital to have surgery. After the surgery, she was placed in a private room where she could recuperate. In one instance, she needed the use of the bathroom facility, and she called the nurse. My recollection is that the nurse either told her to go and use it or did not respond. Needless to say, my wife was not pleased at all; neither was I. We did not proceed with any complaint, but the "tender, loving care" that we expected in that circumstance was not available.

Uncaring though the nurse appeared to be, she was actually doing my wife a service (though her approach could have been a little better). Fortunately, I did not embarrass myself or my wife by making a big issue out of the matter. Subsequently, I read in Fundamentals of Nursing the following: "When greater emphasis was placed on patients assuming self-care activities as soon as their physical state permitted, the nurse's role as a health teacher increased steadily. At one time, patients had almost everything done for them by the nurse. Now nurses are helping patients to learn to do as much as possible for themselves. As the values of increased activity and decreased bed rest have been noted, some authorities in physical medicine and rehabilitation concluded that the old approach of too much 'tender loving care' was actually harmful" (Fuerst 1974, 147).

Thus, if I had become incensed and demonstrated anger over the situation, I would not have been a good representative of Christ. Moreover, I would have been seeking to foster a procedure that might have been counterproductive to my wife's healing.

One Friday morning in 2006, my wife had another surgery. That very afternoon, the physical therapist came for her to get up and begin walking. It was very painful for her, but I remembered the education I received after the first surgery. I resigned myself to the thought that the doctors and therapists knew best. The fear of her collapsing or suffering more than was necessary was lessened by my confidence in the physician who had performed the surgery and the apparent competence of the rehabilitation staff. I had no need to feel or express anger at those caregivers.

I am not an anger-management proponent, per se, unless the objective of the process is to help the individual get rid of the problem. Work to get rid of your selfish anger about how people have mistreated or taken advantage of you, about mistakes you have made in life, about the hand life has dealt you. If you walk around with a chip on your shoulder, don't keep managing that anger. You need help. Those who harbor anger and hostility should obtain the appropriate therapy to address those issues.

Spiritual Euphoric Therapy (SET) is a classic example of a therapy that serves as a real change agent in a person's life. Through this therapy, one can eventually experience the ultimate personality—the personality obtained from having the new birth experience. In this mode, anger is dispensed with. The fruit of the spirit—love, joy, peace, long-suffering, gentleness, goodness, faith, meekness, temperance (Galatians 5:22)— possesses his whole being. Fear associated with anger and bitterness is then neutralized, and life becomes a day of sunshine.

Shame and Guilt

The world is full of people walking around with the baggage of shame on their shoulders. Guilt and shame are true monkeys they are unable to shake off their backs. Things they did in childhood or early adulthood keep coming back to haunt them. Unresolved issues follow them through life as unfinished business that negatively impacts their self-esteem.

Not only childhood experiences cause these shameful feelings. Mistakes made in adult life are also painful to recall. An individual may look back at a given situation and say, "How could I have been so stupid?" If that's all the individual does before moving on, that's not a problem. However, many people seem to see themselves as making and remaking those same mistakes every day. They act as though everyone knows about their mistakes, snickers, and points the finger at them as they pass by their houses, saying gleefully, "There goes the idiot!" That is how they seem to approach life. With this attitude, shame and guilt are always present.

Guilt is a very good thing up to a point; beyond that point, it is a very dangerous and damaging monster. When a person does something wrong, the mechanism that God placed in all humankind called a conscience exercises its duty. It makes the person feel ashamed, uneasy, condemned, and vulnerable, as if everyone is noticing. Guilty people feel less than acceptable to the people who are involved. They may have powerful urges to make it right by confessing. That is a good thing. However, after the person confesses, asks for forgiveness, and has given up his evil ways, he or she must accept the forgiveness that is given. Going around day after day, year in, year out, or pining over things for which one has received absolution becomes a problem that needs to be addressed through counseling.

Sometimes conflicts in a marriage or family do not happen because family members are unwilling to live in peace and harmony. They may result from unfortunate unresolved events that occurred in the lives of the husbands or wives that left them feeling guilty or ashamed. Some people have been raised in homes lacking peace, harmony, love, and understanding, where they were always spoken to in rough tones and without affection. They are, therefore, replaying the script that they were dealt.

Only when a plan for a better life is presented and accepted by them will they experience a change in their family life. An inferiority complex and low self-esteem make them feel that it was something they did to place them in this unfortunate circumstance. An alarming number of women cannot truly love their husbands because of the abuse or molestation inflicted by their fathers or other relatives.

Another guilt-related problem can be found in women who have suffered from the trauma of abortion and have been unable to dispense with a resulting feeling of guilt. They may not know how to forgive themselves because they have not asked the Lord to forgive them. Unfortunately; a lot of Christian women struggle with such guilt as well. In most cases, they harbor an unwillingness to forgive themselves even though God has forgiven them. It is not an easy situation, especially when one considers that in most cases the act was deliberate. God has promised that he will cast our sins in the deepest part of the sea (Micah 7:59) and remember them no more.

Believe it. Accept it. Act upon it. You are forgiven. Leave those sins behind. You now have a new life in Christ. You are made whole in him. Go and live it out in your daily life. That is an effective neutralization for the fear relating to the guilt and shame of the past.

The devil will try to remind you of those sins. Rebuke him in the name of Jesus, and those fears of the past will be forced to remain in the past and will have no power over you. If perchance your position in society or an organization is serving as an inhibitor to the humility of confession, you are not alone. Many have wrestled with that problem and have not yet found a solution. Seek the courage to make things right with God, who is near you. If you are willing to ask, God will give you the courage and the wisdom to approach the situation in a way that will yield the best outcome.

Don't be afraid to commit your ways to him, for that is the foundation for faithfulness to others. Although he has promised that he will not fail you or forsake you, many are hesitant in taking a stand for him because they are unsure of how long their commitment will last. This hesitancy carries over into their everyday life; therefore, the issue needs to be dealt with and resolved.

Fear of Unfaithfulness

Some people fear commitment. Perhaps they do not want to disappoint the one to whom they have made the commitment or be disappointed by him. For this reason, many relationships have been avoided. In this regard, the marriage commitment is no exception.

Many people are petrified of committing themselves to the marriage relationship. They have become so accustomed to flirting with other individuals or having illicit relationships that they are afraid to relinquish this freedom. The thought of being "tied down" or restricted by the commitment to one individual is too much to assimilate. Therefore, they lead people on, knowing full well that they do not intend to marry them. The uncertainty of knowing whether the other individual will be faithful is also cause for hesitancy for many individuals.

The fear of being unfaithful in a marriage leads some to engage in common-law relationships. They want to try out the relationship before they commit to it. Many of these arrangements end up in heartbreak and damaged emotions. Sometimes the scars are so deep that they never heal. This fear of unfaithfulness is symptomatic of a larger problem. People who have been involved in relationships that have gone sour are reluctant to embark upon other relationships. It may also be that the reason for the hesitancy is insincerity. That's one of the reasons people enter into marriage with prenuptial agreements. They are not sure things will work out, so they leave room to escape without too much hurt or loss.

That kind of fear or doubt is unnecessary when one contemplates a relationship with Jesus Christ because whatever he promises, he will do. And we have already established his credibility. Further, he has provided written assurances, which is ironic because we just mentioned that no prenuptial agreements are needed, and here he is, writing a prenuptial agreement. Why is this true? Because in Jeremiah 3:14, God said that he is married to Israel, his church.

The agreement that he is entering into, however, is unilateral. He is the one who prepared it. He alone signed it. The scripture says, "He that begun a good work in you will perform it until the day of Jesus Christ" (Philippians 1:6). So we have an unfair advantage, as it were, because it is in our favor. We can hold him to it. He must fulfill what he has promised. We, on the other hand, are free to do as we please—at the peril of our souls, of course. That's why he continues to plead with us to be faithful to our commitment to him. And all those who are truehearted will try to be faithful to him under all circumstances, for therein lies our true reward.

Not only in the family and religious arenas do people have a timidity to commit; some people just have a fear of commitment. They cannot bring themselves to make certain decisions that obligate them to anything. These individuals are, generally speaking, psychologically handicapped in that regard. Much can be lost at times through procrastinating about the decision-making process.

On the other hand, sometimes delays in decision making stem from lack of adequate information, lack of understanding of the information at hand, or the idea that the timing is not right. There is a fine line between success and failure, between greatness and stupidity, between folly and wisdom. The line between these poles is indistinguishable in many circumstances until after the event. After the event, it can only be characterized as "if." Further, with the fragility of human accolades and the basic need to be esteemed, one does not relish the thought of treading the path of uncharted areas and run the risk of being ridiculed.

Acceptance of Jesus Christ and his lifestyle, however, does not present the challenge of uncharted waters nor does it lend itself to ultimate disappointment. On the contrary, it promises freedom from the captivity of sin that breeds fear, distrust, and disappointment. It promises life everlasting and a place of royalty, righteousness, and happiness. It does, however, forewarn that if one is a coward—afraid of persecution, deprivation, ridicule, embarrassment, and death—one would be hard pressed to choose a path as challenging as the one offered by Jesus Christ. Christianity is not for wimps. It calls for commitment and conformity to biblical instructions supplied by the source of light and life. The challenge is yours; don't be afraid to accept Jesus. He can neutralize your fears so that they have no power over you, no matter how insignificant or prominent your position is in this world.

Eminence, Betrayal of Trust, and Fear of Confession

We are a society with great regard for people in high positions. In our political system, elected officials are expected to be of moral character, honest, full of dignity, and perhaps even religious (though it has not always been this way). It becomes evident from recent events that when such persons are involved with promiscuity, immorality of any kind, or any dishonest conduct, their fear of public revelation lends itself to cover up, untruthfulness, and finger-pointing.

Confession, if there is any, comes only after the truth has been discovered or when it appears that all other options are exhausted. Fear of losing the position, power, and authority that go along with the office seems more important than honesty, integrity, and a clear conscience. This does not have to be. A Christian leader should always remember that he or she is accountable to God as well as to the constituents.

In recent decades, the Christian community has suffered ignominiously due to the activities of unscrupulous leaders. Those who would critique Christianity and its activities have found ample ammunition to attack and malign the cause. One must admit that the equivocation of those involved in biblical exegesis by those with differing agendas has not been entirely in the wrong. The fear of another exposé by the media seems in those moments of vulnerability- to elicit an apparent conspiratorial consent to withhold information that might be deemed destructive to the Christian community.

The Christian's position should always be one of openness and candor, knowing that there is an all-seeing eye that chronicles all the activities of mankind. A Christian does not have to fear as long as his conduct is proper, and he is honest and truthful, that is, of course, within a society that recognizes the principles of Christianity as a paradigm. American society is generally forgiving and sympathetic to honest people who make honest mistakes. But fear of embarrassment seems to prevail in some situations.

Fear of Reprisal

Outside of Christianity, virtually all religions seem irate about their adherents leaving the religion to join another (mostly Christianity). It does not appear that the greater portion of their ire is against proselytizing, per se; it is that they are opposed to Christianity. Christians will not inflict punishment on any individual for leaving the Christian religion to join any other religion. However, the same cannot be said of all the other religions. In some parts of the world, it is a crime (even punishable by death) if one leaves the established state religion and becomes a Christian.

The fear of reprisal, then, becomes a real inhibitor to proselytization. Remarkably, there are people in China, Indonesia, Pakistan, India, Sudan, and other countries who count it a privilege to become Christians and suffer hardship. The Bible is the only book that addresses the sin problem and the only book that provides the answer to that problem. They fear not the persecutors but the awful thought of the result of not accepting life everlasting that is offered to them. They realize that they may be killed because they have turned their backs on gods that are not as great as the God of heaven. But they also know that those persecutors can have no power over them or even kill them unless the God of heaven allows it. In some cases, God has worked in many miraculous ways to save his people from the enemy. In other cases, the threat to those contemplating proselytizing is so real that many fear for their lives and the lives of their family members if they dare to accept Christianity:

Interestingly, it is a mistake to believe that the threat of reprisal is present only abroad. In these United States, where there is freedom of religion, people have been ostracized and made pariahs for leaving one denomination to join another. Of course, this is somewhat different from the type of government-sanctioned persecution described above. In the United States, reprisal comes from family members or the faith community that suffered the loss. Secondly, instead of punishment by death, people suffer humiliation. They may feel that they have lost a major portion of their lives, including the friendship of those they love and for whom they care. Nevertheless, many willingly make the transition because of their conviction.

The fear of reprisal can be neutralized by remembering that if the Holy Spirit has spoken to your heart to move in a certain direction, and you clearly see Scripture to support it, you can rest assured that God will work it out for you. Not only that, even if death comes in the process, you are guaranteed eternal life; what, then, is there to worry about?

Fear is the essence of paralysis and should not be nurtured. The Bible addresses the issue of fear and clearly states that fear hath torment but perfect love casteth out fear (1 John 4:18). When one has the love of God in one's heart, one has holy boldness that serves as a formidable force to defeat the enemy called fear. This holy boldness, however, is not without wisdom, common sense, and discretion. In this way, success can be achieved.

Fear of Failure in Business

Many people will not go into business because others who have attempted those business ventures have been unsuccessful. Others already in business are so fearful of the competition that they see themselves as grasshoppers in contrast with their competitors. That attitude is fertile ground for defeat. If you have interest in a given area, provided it's legal and morally and biblically acceptable, consider Jesus's instructions and biblical principles about how to approach the matter. He said, "For which of you, intending to build a tower, sitteth not down first, and counteth the cost, whether he have sufficient to finish it?" (Luke 14:28).

That is the core reason that many businesses fail: not adequately providing for eventualities. Perhaps the strategic planning process was fraught with inadequate or faulty data, which led to faulty assumptions and conclusions. Those conclusions became the bases upon which the projects or ventures were predicated, hence a failed business. A similar situation was mentioned in Luke 6:49 in which a foolish man built his house without the proper foundation and wound up losing his investment.

Regarding investments, I have had my share of failures. I have lost many thousands of dollars in business ventures and on investments. I know what it is like to be like the foolish man. The only bright side of some of those experiences is that it is easier for me to identify with those who are in similar situations. Knowing more, I can now provide counseling to those with less experience. Additionally, I learned that God is able to raise me up if I fall.

In his book Time Trap, Alec Mackenzie made an interesting observation that amplifies the point. He said that management by crisis means just that—management after the crisis has occurred. The best way to handle crises, he suggests, is to keep them from occurring in the first place. To prevent the crises means to anticipate them and plan for them, if possible, but if not, to strategize to reduce their impact (Mackenzie 1991, 58). My advice is: seek God's guidance, get professional advice, do proper planning, count the cost, prepare for eventualities, pray before execution, and move ahead without fear.

Fear of Obtaining or Holding a Job

Some professions by nature are service oriented. Those who feel called to serve humanity in those capacities are well deserving of accolades and respect. However, a great many people select a career as just an individual venture or for family considerations. The importance of these careers is evaluated by financial achievement, position, prestige, power, or some other value they assign.

Although financial gain may be a major consideration in the selection of employment, some of the more renowned advocates of progress have emphasized the need for recognizing the significance of choosing careers that offer opportunities to serve humanity. The late president John F. Kennedy expressed this when he said, "Ask not what your country can do for you; ask what you can do for your country." Similarly, in speaking about African Americans and what direction they needed to take, W.E.B. DuBois said, "The new generation must learn that the object of the world is not profit but service and happiness" (Gates and West 1996, 176).

It is tremendously difficult to think of entering a field of endeavor to serve first and obtain financial prosperity later. Nonetheless, it is a sobering thought. It brings to light our basic self-centeredness, that is, our emphasis on what we can get versus what we can give. The financial demands of today are so pressing that many hardly consider service a primary object of employment. My younger daughter, who majored in biology and has received her master's in public health, always considered service first. At first she wanted to be an obstetrician-gynecologist. Her objective was to serve the community and help those who cannot afford to pay their medical bills. She also wanted to educate the community on how to prevent diseases. Her desire has been to give of herself to humanity.

One need not fear obtaining or holding a position if one is prepared for that employment opportunity. Incidentally, the idea of holding a job is not very satisfactory. A better concept is that one is engaging in a certain occupation, area of employment, or profession. This provides more value significance that enhances the way one feels about that area of endeavor. The Bible says, "Seest thou a man diligent in his business? He shall stand before kings" (Proverbs 22: 29). Be prepared in every way you can and be diligent. Do your work well, adhere to company guidelines, and trust in God. Then you need not fear, for nothing happens without God allowing it.

Fear of Loneliness

Countless thousands of people in cities across the United States suffer from loneliness. The news media, ever so often, reveal the tragedy that befell some lonely person living in a dilapidated residence. Some are seen in nursing homes, wondering when their imaginary, long-lost relative will come and visit or take them home. The problem of loneliness is real, and many people dread the day when they will become a victim of the aging process. Some fear the day when they are set aside and relegated to the fate of society's "useless and unproductive" class. Yes, sometimes it seems that the treatment that some of these formerly most productive individuals endure does make them feel useless. Some have little desire to keep on living.

Society moves at a fast pace today, and many people have no time for those who cannot keep up. The fast lane of this decade is littered with the moral remains of those who would achieve at any cost. A philosophy of relativism and materialism augments the onslaught of humanism. It appears that even some adherents of Christianity have laid their robes of purity on the steps of expediency and capitulated to the forces that desire to establish a politically correct society.

It is so easy to become lonely even in a crowd. The path that one chooses in this epoch of American history determines the level of sociability that one may enjoy. Consequently, as one counts the cost of bucking the prevailing trends, one could become fearful of the price that must be paid. Whether the loneliness comes from being old and dwelling in a nursing home with few visits from family or friends or just from being single, the effect is virtually the same.

Others may feel loneliness when they fear a potential divorce. They may feel unattractive and attribute their loneliness and failure to be noticed by the opposite sex to that. It may seem that everyone but them is sought out to participate in certain activities. Any number of things can precipitate feelings of loneliness.

I have good news for those who are lonely or who fear the day they may become lonely. We revert to the Scriptures for the solution to this universal problem. The Bible assures us that God has promised to never leave us nor forsake us (Hebrews 13:5). With that promise in mind, you can go through life with boldness and confidence, knowing that you are not alone as long as you let Jesus become your friend. Loneliness is real, and many fear it. Nevertheless, those who utilize the principles of the Merry Heart theory will never walk through life alone.

Fear of Traveling

If the fear of traveling by air, sea, or land stems from fear that one might die, then that individual actually fears death, not traveling. Sometimes we must discover the real causes for concern; we cannot assume that what a person complains of or what he says he is afraid of is really the problem. Some fears are effects or symptoms of underlying problems that must be resolved before the symptoms can disappear.

It must also be remembered that a physical reaction to a certain situation may not necessarily be a psychological problem. For example, if a person has motion sickness when he rides in a car or flies, it may be merely physical intolerance of the effect of the bumpy feeling, not the ride in a car or airplane itself.

However, if one is afraid of traveling, for whatever reason, one should remember this promise: God will instruct you and teach you in the way which you will go; God will guide you with his eye (Psalm 32:8). Moreover, "The LORD shall preserve thy going out and thy coming in from this time forth, and even for evermore" (Psalm 121:8). Trust in the LORD Jesus Christ, and you will be safe from the schemes of the devil. For, "Yea, though I walk through the valley of the shadow of death, I will fear no evil: for thou art with me; thy rod and thy staff they comfort me" (Psalm 23:4).

Nothing can harm or befall you unless God allows it. If God allows anything to happen that humankind would consider unfortunate, God has a reason that will be for your good and his glory. Therefore, you don't have to worry about traveling because everything will be all right. Remember that he is the God who creates, sustains, and restores life.

Fear of the Empty Nest

As couples progress in years and their children are grown and gone, the empty nest syndrome sets in. In some marriages, not enough time was spent with each other previously. This time—when no one is around but the two parents—can become very awkward. This is especially true when constant disagreement and emotional estrangement left behind unresolved issues. Strong relationships may even have developed on the job or elsewhere. The process of re-acquaintance with this long-despised spouse becomes a challenge.

To rekindle the spark of love and readjust to this new life, a process of recommitment must take place. It is a good time to be retrospective as well as introspective. Couples must accept the reality that something more than just human effort must have sustained the union and the family during those difficult times. Unfortunately, if unfaithfulness to the marriage vow was involved or if abuse or neglect of the family was a part of that experience, many do not find it in their hearts to forgive.

The fear of the empty nest pertains not only to the couple that will miss having the children around. It also pertains to the couple that is planning to split after the children are gone. Divorce or separation is very traumatic, and no one relishes going through such painful experiences. The effects could be similar to when a loved one has died. The empty nest could really be more than that; it could be a deeper emptiness that is not easily filled. Unless a person has a relationship with the LORD and a strong support system, the fear of not making it could be overwhelming.

Fear of Widowhood (Or Being a Widower)

It is believed that married couples who live together for many years and lose their spouses in their late senior years die within seven years of such loss. Of course, there are exceptions. However, many fear losing a spouse because they cannot see how life can continue without him or her. Thus, one spouse's illness can take a tremendous toll on the other—not just because of the illness but because of the possibility of losing that spouse.

Much care and attention should be given to the elderly by their relatives and those charged with administering care in their declining years. The way sec treat our seniors is an indication of the condition of our character and our moral fortitude to defend the defenseless. Some look upon the condition of those in nursing homes and dread the day when they may become helpless and dependent on others to care for them. Even if a mental illness has overtaken that person, it is well to read scriptures of hope and assurance to him or her. Alzheimer's disease and senility may be present, but the Holy Spirit can penetrate the heart through the reading of the Scriptures. Hope and buoyancy can still be theirs.

The Bible says that God looks upon his church as a bride. Therefore, God says, "Thy maker is thy husband" (Isaiah 54:5). The day is coming when those who wait on the LORD "shall renew their strength; they shall mount up with wings as eagles; they shall run and not be weary; and they shall walk, and not faint" (Isaiah 40:31). "And God shall wipe away all tears from their eyes; and there shall be no more death; neither sorrow, nor crying, neither shall there be any more pain: for the former things are passed away" (Revelation 21:4). Be not afraid; you are in God's hands.

Fears Related to Disability

One who was able to see and becomes blind must really feel a tremendous sense of loss. How does that compare with someone who was born blind? Many will never know, nor is it something that anyone wants to experience. I have had occasion to interact with blind individuals. It is remarkable how much courage, optimism, and insight many of these people have. I have read about a well-known hymn writer by the name of Fanny Crosby. She was born with sight but became blind due to an unfortunate incident. She, however, managed to transcend bitterness and disappointment and lived to write the lyrics to many hymns from which the Christian community has obtained hope and courage, such as "Blessed Assurance" and "Tell Me the Story of Jesus."

Likewise, Joni Eareckson Tada, a Christian quadriplegic, has been sharing her story of hope and positivity on a daily radio show across America for over twenty years. After a diving accident in 1967 that left her without the use of her legs and arms, she spent two years in rehabilitation. Rather than being bitter and withdrawn, "she reentered the community with new skills and a fresh determination to help others in similar situations." As of December 2006, she has "over a million listeners a week [to her] daily five-minute radio program." She brings hope to thousands who are incapacitated by life's unfortunate circumstances. She has also provided inspiration to many who are living normal lives but need to hear a word of encouragement. Tada did not let her circumstance get her down. With the support of her church, she maintained her faith in God and used biblical principles to weaken the power that fear would have over her (Tada 2006).

People with optical problems who fear going blind wonder what will happen to them if that occurs. Technological advances can prevent or postpone some illnesses, but until a person hears that he is cured of a disease or that a doctor's examination turns out negative, elements of doubt and apprehension linger.

God told Isaiah, his servant, "Say to them that are of a fearful heart, be strong, fear not: behold, your God will come ... and save you. Then the eyes of the blind shall be opened, and the ears of the deaf shall be unstopped. Then shall the lame man leap as an hart, and the tongue of the dumb sing (Isaiah 35:4-6). Those are comforting promises to those who trust God.

Other Fears

Here, I will discuss a few more selected fears and how to avoid them, as well as some of God's promises that should be used to offset them when they arise.

I know of many parents who have been emotionally drained by the frustration of the uncertainty of their children's spiritual health. They burn with the desire to see them accept Jesus as their personal Savior and become a part of the fellowship of his people. Many blame themselves for not doing a better job of training them. Some are fearful of having children at all, feeling incapable of raising them as godly children. They desire to prevent them from being a part of the world rather than a part of the church. To them, it is a very fearful thought.

The punishment that some people mete out to themselves before they even do anything to deserve it is very sad. It is counter to their Christian heritage, which teaches faith in God, obedience to his Word, and claiming the promises that he made in the Scriptures. Once a person follows the instructions that God has given in his Word, God is obligated by his own Word to perform what he has promised to perform (in the context of our surrender and the glorification of his name). I say that not because God would renege on his promises but that we might be assured that God, who cannot lie (Hebrews 6:18), has sworn by himself because there was none greater (Hebrews 6:13) that he would perform his promises. And this he has said, "I will contend with him that contend with thee, and I will save thy children" (Isaiah 49:25).

If you have done what the LORD has asked you to do, you can, with confidence, lay hold on these promises. They will be fulfilled. If you have been unfaithful to him in the past, confess now your sins and ask his forgiveness. Ask him for a miracle in your life and in the lives of your children. He is able to do for you "exceeding abundantly above all that we ask or think according to the power that worked in us" (Ephesians 3:20). The power must be allowed to work in us and then the promises will be fulfilled. He will surprise you every time.

Some fear deprivation because even here in a society where there is so much, not all are able to provide enough food or clothing for themselves or their families. Although our blessings are so plenteous that we have been known to pay our farmers subsidies not to produce certain crops in abundance, this is still a society where charitable organizations set up soup kitchens and goodwill centers. There are Americans who go to bed hungry at night and who live as if in a third-world country. Many people are just a paycheck away from homelessness.

Some of these unfortunate circumstances stare us in the face on a regular basis. Yet many of us ignore homelessness and hunger. Like the scribes and Pharisees in the Bible, many pass by on the other side. We need not fear homelessness or privation. God is saying to those who "walketh righteously, and speaketh uprightly... (that] his place of defense shall be the munition of rocks; bread shall be given him; his waters shall be sure" (Isaiah 33:15, 16). Jesus re-enforced the Christian's faith by stating in Luke 12:28 that if God clothes the grass which is here today and tomorrow is cast into the tire, how much more will he clothe you?

My exhortation to the reader is that the devil wants us to be fearful and distrustful. We must reject that suggestion and trust the divine one. To maintain our communication with God, we must keep in touch on a daily basis. Through this mechanism, our strength will be renewed daily.

SET Principles at Work

Dwight L. Moody, Dr. Billy Graham, and other evangelists have told many true stories of how dependence on God for help, healing, and provision has resulted in miracles. Evangelist Mark Finley, in his devotional book, Solid Ground, told a story about a young woman who, prior to becoming a Christian, suffered many traumatic events that could have caused her to lose hope and give up. Her parents were divorced when she was ten. She left home at fourteen because of abuse and was in and out of mental and penal institutions" (Finley 2004, 66) by the time she was eighteen. She got married and then divorced. She went deeply into the abuse of drugs and alcohol and suffered some abusive relationships. She hated herself and did not trust God. She married a drug addict in 1993 while she was homeless, but they got divorced in 1994. That brought her to the realization that she needed help, and so she checked herself into a drug rehabilitation facility. Finley recalled her saying:

> There I met John. When we left the facility, we moved into an apartment and both got jobs. We seemed to be doing fine. The only problem was that there was nothing to take the place of the drugs and alcohol. Four months later we were consuming them again. One night after an argument we discussed what we had learned about a higher power. We got down on our knees and said the most sincere prayer of our lives! The next day, when John was tempted to take a drink of alcohol, he heard a voice say as plainly as if someone was right next to him, "You asked Me to take it away, and I took it away".

> (Finley 2004, 66)

That direct manifestation (a divine intervention) started them on their journey to Christianity. They began reading their Bibles and experiencing greater knowledge about God and his plans for their lives (Finley 2004, 66). That couple experienced the essence of one of the eight principles of health—the result of trusting in divine power—a cardinal part of the Spiritual Euphoric Therapy principle. While every case is not the same, many people can be delivered from drug addiction, prostitution, sexual addiction, alcoholism, and other vices and mental and emotional disorders if they desire to be free and receive proper Christian counseling and guidance. SET principles can be applied constantly without long-term visits for contemporary secular psychological counseling

CHAPTER 13

HOW TO APPLY SET

I f you are a counselor and want to introduce your client to Spiritual Euphoric Therapy after you have gone through the counseling process (TRC described in chapter 9), you will have already determined the biblical principles to apply to the individual based on the specific need. You are now ready to recommend SET. If you are someone who is seeking self-edification, the possibility of improved health or just wanting to be a better person, practicing the eight principles (laws) of health is the best approach to get what an old acquaintance of mine called a "NEW START." These eight laws of health are shown in the Life Maintenance Wheel in chapter 9.

The first phase of SET is inventorying the issues that the person has and, after assessing the needs, applying counsel based on biblical principles. For example, the person is suffering from guilt because of an abortion due to an unplanned pregnancy. Show the person where God has promised, "If we confess our sins, he is faithful and just to forgive us our sins and to cleanse us from all unrighteousness" (1 John 1:9). He further states, As far as the east is from the west, so far hath he removed our transgressions from us" (Psalm 103:12). Teach them how to cast their cares or unburden themselves before the LORD and let him handle their stresses.

Through Christian counseling psychology, teach them how to forget or nullify the guilt of past mistakes. Teach them how to dispense with negative thoughts through what I call linkage and minimalization—linking each negative thought with a positive one and intentionally making the negative thought insignificant. Let them know that God said that he will forgive their iniquity and promised to "remember their sin no more (Jeremiah 31:34). Tell them that since God will forget their sins when they confess them and ask for forgiveness, it does not make sense for them to keep reminding themselves of those sins. That only adds more stress and anxiety to their lives. Provide this and other counseling information to them and encourage them to get a new start. Then add phase two, which is the NEW START program. The acronym NEW START is easy to remember. This is what it means:

N is for nutrition, the first law of health. Today; many people suffer from serious nutritional deficiencies that immobilize them both physically and mentally. A balanced diet is what the body needs. However, at times, many of us are so busy that we tend to want things right away and either cannot or will not spend the time to prepare a healthy meal. Depriving the body of the required nutrients will eventually make the body susceptible to diseases.

It may surprise you to know that according to the Bible, humankind's first diet consisted of only fruits, grains, and nuts (Genesis 1:29), and the animals were given a vegetarian diet (Genesis 1:30) were herbivorous. However, after humankind sinned, God added herbs (vegetables) to humankind's diet (Genesis 3:18). Things got worse and the inhabitants became corrupt (Genesis 6:5), "and the LORD said, I will destroy man [humankind] whom I have created from the face of the earth (Genesis 6:7). So God sent a flood upon the earth that lasted forty days (Genesis 7:17), and every living thing that was upon the earth died (Genesis 7:21-22), except Noah, the seven people, and the creatures that were with him in the ark (Genesis 8:1). When the flood ceased, God sent Noah and all that were with him from the ark (Genesis 8:15-17). He added flesh as food to humankind's diet (Genesis 9:2-3), but he stated that some animals were "not clean" and were not good for human consumption (Genesis 7:2 and Leviticus 11:2-31). Think about it for a moment!

Before man became subject to death (sinned), he was given a certain diet and was not subject to death (Genesis 2:17). After man sinned, but before the flood, even though humankind became subject to death, it seems as though the diet they were on, perhaps along with the environmental condition, allowed them to live as long as 969 years (Genesis 5:27). However, after the flood, when there was a change in diet to include flesh meat, humankind's lifespan shortened tremendously. It dropped from six hundred years (Genesis 11:10-11) to 205 years (Genesis 11:32) and continued to decline until David, king of Israel, stated, "The days of our years are threescore years and ten [seventy years]; and if by reason of strength they be fourscore years" (Psalm 90:10).

Proper nutrition produces a healthy body and a clear mind and protects against diseases. In our era, there is much pollution. Although we have all sorts of formulas, concentrated minerals and vitamins, and genetically engineered foods, the threat of contamination or disease is real; therefore, one has to be very careful in the selection of foods.

Medical doctor Aileen Ludington and public health doctor Hans Diehl, in their book Health Power: Healthy Choice Not Chance, say, "It turns out that fruits and vegetables are loaded with compounds called phytochemicals and antioxidants that demonstrably lower the risk of cancer. Phyto is Latin for plant. These food chemicals cannot be obtained from animal products" (Ludington and Diehl 2002, 134). They further indicate, "Seven out of ten Americans suffer and die prematurely of three killer diseases: heart disease, cancer, and stroke." They quote Dr. C. Everett Koop, former U.S. surgeon general: "the Western diet was a major contributor to these diseases." Koop asserts that the "largest source" of cholesterol and saturated fat come from animals and that people cat these foods "'at the expense of complex-carbohydrate-rich foods such as grains, legumes and vegetables'" (Ludington and Diehl 2002, 182). Proper nutrition in Spiritual Euphoric Therapy is a vital part of obtaining and maintaining health to fully experience the benefits of SET.

E is for exercise, the second law of health. The body requires exercise in order to maintain its physical fitness. Everyone's physical condition is not the same. However, regardless of your situation, some form of exercise will acid more years to your life. As a medical doctor, Larry

Altshuler, in his book titled Bottom Line's Balanced Healing, makes the following statement:

> If someone told you there is a method that would take just two or three hours a week to prevent disease or improve your health, wouldn't it make sense to do it, and avoid all the trials, tribulations, and expenses of being ill? There is such a method: exercise. A number of studies have conclusively proven that improving or maintaining adequate physical fitness significantly decreases your risk of dying from all causes ... Even if you are in pain, have a disability, or are older, there are types of exercise that you can do and from which you can benefit ... [However,' before beginning an exercise program, get a thorough checkup from a doctor. This is especially necessary if you have heart problems, injuries, or other health conditions [or] if you haven't exercised in a long time. [To begin] stretch slowly and stretch all your muscle groups for at least five minutes. [Do it daily] because of its many benefits, even if you're not doing any other exercise that day.
>
> (Altshuler 2004, 83-85)

Start the process today if possible and be consistent, and you will begin to feel better in a very short time.

W is for water, the third law of health. Water is an extremely important part of the SET program. One cannot live without water. People are being told constantly by health professionals, media reports, and laypersons who are interested in promoting health that our bodies cannot survive any significant length of time without water. The larger portion of the body is water, and we need to keep that level of water in the body for health and survival. Suzanne Winckler of the University of California, Davis, Groundwater Cooperative Extension Program, states, "Water composes half to four-fifths of you, depending on how much body fat you have" and that your brain consists of up to about 85 percent water (Winckler 2000, 122-125).

Additionally, because 80 percent of the human blood is water and 70 percent of the brain, we need a flow of water to replenish and to cleanse the system. All the toxins and waste that accumulate in the body need to be expunged, and water is the agent that does this job. "Cool, clear water keeps the human engine running. Conventional wisdom tells us to drink eight eight-ounce glasses of water a day, but a recent medical research suggests that ten or eleven servings a day increases water's health benefits" (Winckler 2000, 122-125). Water also has other uses, such as hydrotherapy. It can be used externally for cleansing, to reduce tension, to stimulate the pores, and to invigorate the body.

S is for sunlight, the fourth law of health. I, like so many people, learned very early in life that sunlight provides vitamin D for the body. Vitamin D is essential because it helps protect the body against cancer. This is clearly stated by Drs. Susan Male Smith, Arline McDonald, Annette Natow, and Jo-Ann Heslin in their book Complete Book of Vitamins & Minerals. They write:

> In one study, people with the lowest intakes of Vitamin D and calcium were those who developed colon and rectal cancers during a year long period. Vitamin D deficiency causes rickets in children. Because vitamin D is crucial to proper calcium absorption, the hallmark of rickets is the undermineralivation of bones. One of its common signs is bowlegs. Another sign is beadlike swellings on the ribs—a condition called rachitic rosary. Teething is usually late in children with rickets, and what teeth do develop are susceptible to decay. Vitamin D deficiency in adults is called osteomalacia. It involves the loss of calcium and protein from bones [in this case, only mineral is lost, not bones].

> (Smith, McDonald, Natow, and Heslin 1996, 69, 137)

Additionally, people have shared many experiences with me as to how sunlight tends to lift the spirits and dispels, even momentarily, feelings of gloom and despair. Sunlight is an important part of SET, and barring adverse medical or psychological reasons that inhibit people from exposing themselves to sunlight; it should become a part of their regimen.

T is for temperance, the fifth law of health. Everything that a person does (that's good) should be done in moderation. Intemperance has done much harm to many individuals, yet so many people engage in excesses. The Apostle Paul encourages us to be "temperate in all things" (1 Corinthians 9:25). And we are not only to be temperate privately, but we are to "Let [our] moderation be known to all men [humankind]" (Philippians 4:5) by the life we live.

I believe that a temperate person will be more perceptive and disposed to exercise better judgment than an intemperate person. Temperance calls for a person to avoid starving one's self, overeating, overworking, pushing the body during exercise beyond the limits that the body is capable of handling, staying too long in the sun, depriving the body of adequate rest, and so on. These are only a few examples of intemperance.

Temperance also includes abstemiousness. Practicing abstemiousness means abstaining from things that are harmful to your physical body, such as alcohol, tobacco in its various forms, and foods that are injurious to health. By restraining one's self from ingesting things that are harmful (in the long or short run), one endeavors to protect against premature death, inconvenience or grief to others, burden on the taxpayer, and other situations deemed avoidable.

Temperance can be defined as abstaining from that which is harmful and using in moderation that which is good. Abstemiousness is that part of temperance that avoids the use of those things which we should not put in our bodies. We have focused on the physical, but we should not ignore the spiritual and psychological aspects of temperance. People ingest psychologically impure materials that pollute their minds, create addiction in some cases, and make them a threat to both themselves and society. Temperance is an integral part of SET.

A is for air, the sixth law of health. Fresh air is like a tonic to the body. Even governments recognize the need for clean air to promote health for their citizens, and many have enacted and implemented clean-air legislations. Humans need oxygen to survive, and we get our oxygen from the air. Impure air, however, causes respiratory problems and various diseases that could be fatal. The Web site "U.S.-Canada Air Quality Agreement 1996 Progress Report" states that:

> In 1991, the U.S. and Canada entered into an agreement to address transboundary air pollution, whereby pollutants released at one location can travel long distances, affecting air quality at their sources, as well as many miles away. The 1991 agreement led to reductions in acid rain in the 1990s, and was expanded in 2000 to reduce trans boundary smog emissions under the Ozone Annex.

(U.S.-Canada Air Quality Agreement 2007)

Many companies are also aware of these issues and have designed indoor purification systems for better indoor air quality. Going outside in the open air, if there are no health risks, and doing exercise and deep breathing can be very helpful, especially to those who are always indoors. Some may need to consult their physicians before they engage in some of the activities referred to in these eight laws of health. But know this: health is very important and anything that will promote health should be given some consideration. Healthy people are happier and are in a better position to fully experience the Spiritual Euphoric Therapy.

R is for rest, the seventh law of health. Rest is absolutely crucial if one is to carry on a daily routine inside or outside the home. Deprivation of sleep can cause irritability, lack of concentration, possibly disorientation, and other problems. Rest facilitates rejuvenation and allows the body to recuperate and receive strength. Many, including me, have gone to the doctors with ailments such as the flu and have been told to drink a lot of fluids and to rest.

When one is rested, one is generally able to better approach a task, perhaps with more vigor, enthusiasm, or just a better capacity to think through an issue. We are, as the reader may observe, attempting to get the body in a condition to be able to fully experience the Merry Heart theory by the practice of the Spiritual Euphoric Therapy. Rest is one of those steps that need to be practiced in the march toward that end.

T is for trust in divine power, the eighth law of health. To begin the practice of trusting in the divine power, you need to recognize that you cannot save yourself from the evils that are in the world. Your best protective and sophisticated equipment cannot prevent someone from harming you. Your life is fragile and can be taken away from you in an instant, and how will you answer to your Maker for the life you lived? You need to know that you will be safe now and when you die. Remember: NEW STARTS. N = Nutrition; E = Exercise; W = Water; S = Sunlight; T = Temperance; A = Air; R = Rest; T = Trust in Divine Power; and S = Selfless Giving (to God and others).

After you have recognized your need for something to fill the void that you have in your life, you need to seek help from a higher power (God). How do you do that? You can get down on your knees and say, "God, I am a sinner, and I need salvation and help. I want to know you. Please come into my life and save me." You will be amazed at the difference that will make in your life. Believe what you read and begin to practice it. Start attending a church that believes, teaches, and practices Bible principles. Life will take on a new meaning for you, and others will see the difference. You will gain victory over some habits that you never thought you could break. You will begin to think more positive thoughts. Some things that bothered you before will become insignificant. Your attitude will change. You will be a better employee and a more amiable neighbor. You will gain more credibility. It will get you through the dark days and help motivate you to practice the other seven laws of health. You will be a new person.

When Jesus comes into your life, you have recourse for the ills that befall you. You have consolation and sustenance from the source of power. And even in the most difficult situations where you may experience constant excruciating pain, if death comes knocking at your door, you have this assurance that you will live again after you die (John 11:23-25). How will this take place? Paul the apostle says that "the Lord himself shall descend from heaven with a shout, with the voice of the archangel, and with the trump of God: and the dead in Christ shall rise first" (1 Thessalonians 4:16). He further states: "Behold, I show you a mystery; we shall not all sleep [die], but we shall all be changed, in a moment, in the twinkling of an eye at the last trump" (1 Corinthians 15:51-52).

This fact, I suggest, has caused Satan and his imps much frustrations, depression, anger (Revelation 12:17), and fear. A reflection of that fear was manifested when Jesus went to the country of the Gadarenes, and two demoniacs met him. The demons in these two people "cried out, saying, what have we to do with thee, Jesus, thou Son of God? Art thou come hither to torment us before the time?" (Matthew 8:29). That means they are not being tormented now in "hell" but are on earth and are fearful of that awful time when they will be tormented in hellfire (Revelation 20:10).

Satan wants to deny us the privilege of going to heaven (the place from which he was expelled and to which he cannot return). He knows what heaven is like and hates to be missing out on the joys and pleasures that are there. Thus he orchestrates false teachings and false religions so people will be distracted and lose their souls. That's why it is not enough for a person to just choose a religion. One needs to choose the religion that provides the solution to the problem of sin, evil, and death. Christianity is the one that offers this solution because Jesus demonstrated that he can heal the sick and raise the dead and that he himself died and rose again. It is in his teachings that the Merry Heart theory rests and upon which the Spiritual Euphoric Therapy (SET) is founded. Trust in divine power, the eighth law of health, and it will lift you out of the doldrums of hopelessness and despair. It is indeed a path to hope and happiness because through this mechanism, fear can be effectively neutralized.

The ninth principle that should be practiced if a person desires to have a merry heart that is therapeutic to the whole person is the idea of helping others—giving of yourself and your means to others as well as to God. There is satisfaction in knowing that you have done something that benefits humanity. This is especially true when you are able to see the smile of gratitude on someone's face or the eyes of appreciation from the receiver. True living lies in selfless giving, and there is no better model for humans than the one found in the Bible—a manual for successful living. It seems logical then we would consult this manual that had been provided for our guide to daily living. It really does make sense.

Reading the Manual and Applying Its Principles

When a person begins to study the Bible—the Word of God—with sincerity of heart, that is, want to know what's right and having a desire to do what God requires, the Holy Spirit enlightens the mind and changes the heart so that his lifestyle begins to mirror that of Christ's. Those who accept Jesus as LORD and Savior clue to the preaching of the gospel or through some other source, see the Bible as a must-read book. The acceptance of Jesus as Savior and Lord begins the process of sanctification (holy living). Sanctification is the process that leads to perfection. Therefore, for them, the Bible becomes the manual or handbook for day-to-day survival.

Sanctification is the day-by-day growth in the Lord. Studying the Bible is the day-by-day struggle against sin. Growing up in Christ is the work of a lifetime. But the fear of not making it to heaven will be gone for those who believe God and trust his Word, which says that he will perform what he has promised, giving us eternal life. If the Christian sincerely takes hold on God's Word, the ordinary man's fears, that is, the man without Christ, are not a problem to him anymore. He is assured that if he stays in contact with the Divine One, everything will be all right.

Communicate Daily with the Source

To experience real power as a disciple of Jesus, a person most have daily communication with him. One might ask how that is possible. The answer is simple: ask those who have had the experience or just try it for yourself.

Secondly, Jesus Christ, the Son of God and Redeemer of humankind, is the only being who claims to have power over sin. He was killed in the presence of many people. He was buried in a tomb that was sealed by the government and watched night and day. He rose from the dead and came out of the tomb, and none of the guards could stop him. He appeared to many people at different times. He ate and talked with his friends and gave them instructions about what to do when he was gone. He went up to heaven in the presence of many individuals (Luke 24:50-52)—not in a spaceship or an airplane or with helium strapped onto him. He just took off in bodily form and went right up to heaven.

Furthermore, before his death, Jesus personally placed his hand on dead people or called to them, and they came back from the dead. Through him only can we obtain relief from our care and partake of all the things that God wants to bestow on us. There is no power that is equal to or higher than Jesus. He is the only one we can rely on for support, defense, and salvation.

Such is the basis for our constant contact with Jesus. The Apostle Paul exhorted the Thesalonians to pray without ceasing (1 Thessalonians 5:17). This is also applicable to us because "whatsoever was written aforetime was written for our learning and admonition that we through patience and comfort of the scriptures might have hope" (Romans 15:4). Daily contact with this source of life is our only means of survival in a world where almost everyone is looking out for himself. The existing fear in our society is a reminder of our need to engage in constant prayer and communion with God.

To ensure that we and our families are in daily contact with God, morning and evening devotions should be a priority: These must include the study of God's Word, the Bible. We are to use every opportunity during the day to say a prayer. Perhaps it's in the field or office when we are alone. Whenever and wherever the circumstances dictate it, we should pray.

The family devotion, however, is a time that brings the family together in a different way. It provides time for group communication with God. It provides solidarity within the home. It cements the family relationship and gives the opportunity to publicly express praise and thanksgiving and to share problems and issues that fascinate or terrify us. It should he the capstone to all family-time moments. Of course, it does not replace personal time with God, but corporate devotion helps to protect the family in many ways. By so doing, our hearts will not fail us for fear and for looking after the things that are coming upon the earth (Luke 21:26). He who is above all and over all is our shield and defense. Using this approach, fear can be effectively neutralized, and the fear trap can be avoided.

Daily communication with God is practiced not to make sure that he does not forget us; rather, it is to make sure that we do not forget him. It is to maintain our relationship with him. It is to keep us in the path of righteousness or right doing. It is to help mold our character so that we begin to act like Jesus and think the way he wants us to think. We are sinful, and as such, we act sinful; yet we must have a change of character, to if eye are to be found worthy to enter his kingdom when he returns for his people.

Prepare to Relocate

Scientists have informed us that they believe there are more than one billion galaxies in the universe. Does that mean that once you get to the last galaxy, when you look over the edge or out there somewhere, there is nothing? Or, do you see what St. Paul in scripture calls the third heaven (2 Corinthians 12:2) where God dwells? Or, would they conclude that heaven is one of those galaxies—perhaps the farthest one where no humans can on their own, reach? Whatever answer a scientist would give to those questions is not so much my point. Bear in mind that science deals with observation and experimentation to obtain facts, not conjectures.

When scientists say we "believe or think ..." that becomes a faith-based assumption or concept, not verified fact. So, my point is that if scientists, in the context of our discussion, can believe what they do not see and have not proven—that there are more than one billion galaxies and that they are 20,000 to 25,000 light years apart from each other (and many of them believe in the possibility that there are other planets with conditions conducive to life and that there may be extraterrestrial beings), surely, any scientist or ordinary individual, whether they are agnostic, atheist, or none of the above, can, without the fear of ostracism, exercise that same faith in believing that there is a literal place out there in space or beyond that is called heaven. This is a justifiable belief because many people saw Jesus ascend in bodily form into the clouds out of their sight, without any mechanical engine attached to him to provide power. That was a scientific fact because it was observed and verified by many. They touched him and spoke to him before he physically demonstrated his superiority over gravity.

Before Jesus left this earth, he told his disciples that he was going away to prepare a place for them and those who put their trust in him (John 14:1-3, Mark 13:27). Ever since, Christians have looked with great anticipation for his second advent. It is what Titus calls "that blessed hope, and the glorious appearing of the great God and our Savior Jesus Christ" (Titus 2:13).

Many people who today enjoy financial and social satisfaction may be reluctant to part with such luxurious lifestyles. While some are content, many of them will admit that they are not truly happy. The bizarre things that such lifestyles require of them are sometimes depressing. Some desperately desire a way of escape. I have listened to wealthy, famous, socially accepted people express their misery and frustration with life. Yet some people are tempted to exclaim, "If I had their money, I'd be as happy and free as a lark!" Little do these people know of the pressures that accompany some of these affluent celebrities.

Mind you, some have accumulated wealth, are proud of how they achieved it, and are very happy and contented materially. Yet most of them still suffer from the shortcomings of the spiritual aspects of their lives. The majority of them are unwilling to cast their lot with Jesus to make themselves ready for his return.

Unfortunately, most people who are not preparing for his second coming are the millions of middle-class individuals who are burdened down with heavy taxes, debt, and the pressures of everyday life. Sadder still is the fact that the poor—those who have not and are struggling to be in a position to have are likewise passing up the opportunity to accept Jesus and prepare for his second advent. Many have given up hope.

Both the haves and the have-nots will benefit from the second advent of Jesus. The rich will find protection and safety from those who would destroy them and take their wealth; the middle class will find relief from taxation and the thankless grind at the mill every day; the poor will leave behind the slum and the cycle of poverty. Jesus's return is a great opportunity for debt relief as well as death relief. Would you be willing to trade your wealth, status, position, middle-class life, or poverty—even your present address—for this moment? That is the question that all must answer.

At that time, there will be eternal peace on this earth. Things will be as God intended them to be when he made Adam and Eve. Revelation 21 describes the holy city that will descend to this earth and conditions that will exist. There will be no more heartache, no more sorrow, no more pain, and no more death. The inhabitants of the city will never say, "I am sick" (Isaiah 33:24). Fear will not only be neutralized, it will be banished forever.

What could prevent you from accepting the invitation to accept the God of Creation as the true God and Jesus Christ his Son as your Lord and Savior? Why would anyone not seize the moment and prepare for relocation? We will be relocated to heaven and then come back to this earth in the New Jerusalem to live here forever. What an awesome thought! What a grand opportunity!

If you have already accepted Jesus and you learned new truths from God's Word through this book, why don't you ask him to help you begin living what you have read? Go ahead and do it now! If you do it, you will not have to fear the day of his appearing. You will be prepared for relocation, and the power of fear will have been effectively neutralized in your life.

CHAPTER 14

CONCLUSION

A s this book has demonstrated, fear is the absorption of negative thoughts by the mind, causing a transmittal of unwelcomed impulses to the body that result in behavior that otherwise would not have occurred. Without these negative thoughts, one would do just about anything one's mind is set on doing without regard for results. Expectations of negative results or of what may occur during an attempt at something bring deliberation before an act is committed.

The Physical versus the Abstract

As we have seen, neurotransmitters in the brain move messages from one cell to another, so an increase or decrease of vital substances in the brain changes its communication and results in different emotional responses. However, the Designer gave the ability to the brain to both generate thoughts and to be aware of the nature of those thoughts, allowing the brain to exercise a will to accept, reject, and act or not act upon those thoughts. That power is a dimension that no human study can fathom. Why: That ability is from the external, not internal. It was given to the brain, not produced by it. This quantum leap from the physical to an abstract dimension is of such interest that the scientific realm is vigorously engaged in artificial intelligence research.

Thoughts transcend moods. A person may be in a bad mood because of some chemical imbalance in the brain, but that person can decide to ignore the way he feels by deliberately choosing to invoke certain principles that enable him to be amiable to others despite the temptation to do otherwise. Thoughts can also create moods: bad thoughts produce bad moods, while good thoughts produce good moods. And thoughts can counteract one another. A good thought can not only override a bad mood but can also dispel or replace a bad thought. Hence, brain activity, though physical in nature, has an "abstract ability" to govern the result of those activities. Unless some significant and permanent physical damage prevents rational thinking, thoughts rule and not moods. The fears that individuals possess originate in the mind and are the result of negative thinking.

If no thoughts were generated by the brain, there would be no need for a brain and no need for the individual. This is not to say that people who are brain damaged should be annihilated. We are referring to the general construct of humankind. Although it is important to understand how your brain works and what its effects on you are, it is equally, if not more, important to understand that no matter your mental condition or deficiencies, you can control your thoughts and make life better.

Using the principles embedded in Spiritual Euphoric Therapy (SET), you can effectively neutralize fear and experience an emotive healing. You can start at any of the nine principles of SET (see chapter 13 for details). The goal is for you to have the merry-heart experience. The objective is for you to begin practicing those principles today. Especially if you have health risks, you should consult your physician before you begin certain SET applications (such as exercise or certain regimens). But starting where you are and gradually building up will eventually get you where you want to go.

Remember: eat nutritiously, exercise often, drink an adequate amount of water daily, get enough sunlight (or at least vitamin D with calcium), be temperate—avoid excesses and taking harmful substances—get fresh air and adequate rest, and trust God (divine power). The ninth principle is helping others through giving of yourself and your means. Those principles are truly the way to hope and happiness, and those around you will see and feel the difference.

We have also seen that fear is not all bad. A certain kind of fear is necessary. Humankind is admonished in the Bible to fear God by reverencing God as greater than all else. God's attributes and vastness are beyond human comprehension, and none can vie with him. Realization of God's strength proves it foolhardy to set oneself contrary to God's demands.

Fear of potential consequences of action, we have also discovered, can serve as an inhibitor of negative behavior but also as a motivator for bravery. Fear of an enemy overrunning a country, decimating the army, and occupying that territory in a dictatorial manner motivates troops to fight fierce battles and act heroically.

Individuals' Fears

We are aware of 581 actual fears or phobia descriptions (see appendix C). Every human being is impacted by at least one of them. A courageous person willing to die for a cause may actually be as fearful and cowardly as a cat being chased by a dog. How? The same way a person in a blazing building decides to jump from the thirtieth floor instead of being burned, certain responses are based on the "greater fear."

The religious fanatic who believes that his god will punish him if he does not murder, maim, or destroy others considers a perceived retribution more terrifying than the commission of a heinous act in which he also dies. Such suicides may look courageous to those who share the same belief but is called cowardice by the ones on whom such a crime is perpetrated.

Every person, great or small, suffers fear to some degree. A survey of 350 diverse respondents showed that over 99 percent have experienced fear. Many fears originate in childhood and young adulthood and emerge as we mature. We must recognize the existence of fear before we can adequately address it. Tracing the genealogy of a fear can help. Next, self-evaluation should take place. What happens when you experience fear? Are you sweaty, frozen, at a loss for words? If you probe the power that fear exerts over you, fear can be a less overwhelming experience.

To break the power of fear and enjoy' life, you can restrain and defeat your fears through Spiritual Euphoric Therapy (SET), which is based on biblical principles. Neutralization of your fears is the rejection of negative thoughts that control your mind; instead activate the promises found in God's Word. Dwell upon those promises. Repeat them as often as you can. Meet each negative thought with a positive one—especially one from the Scriptures. This way, your life can be one of happiness and triumph.

Corporate Fears

Corporate fear is nothing but an aggregate of the fears of many individuals who have come together and expressed those fears orally, in writing, or in their actions. Neutralizing corporate fear means instilling change in individuals, from the board of directors to managers and supervisors. However, a charismatic, autocratic, yet well-respected president or CEO can aggressively implement policies that counteract negativism and fear and even change the corporate culture. Industrial counseling based in the principles of Christianity can help to realign a corporation's paradigm to produce more positive interaction and higher productivity. Counseling can be done at the managerial, supervisory, and individual employee levels, and meetings and group activities can serve as pivotal fear-relieving points.

Societal Fears

Societies are driven both by political ideologies and religious belief systems. Some individuals and churches fear that their belief systems may be threatened or even made extinct by secular cultural systems of ideas that challenge those religious beliefs. Those fears lead to defensive and sometimes offensive measures. Societies around the world have enacted laws, established courts of justice, raised armies, and instituted policies to protect their ideologies and their citizenry from intrusion by those espousing ideas contrary to those systems.

This is especially true if those opposing views include violence and advocacy for overthrow of the existing governments. Economies are established based on political and religious or nonreligious systems. Therefore, if a given political system is overthrown, it could mean the establishment of a different economic system that impacts trade and commerce. This awareness has brought great concern, even fear, to many countries that consider themselves vulnerable. A new threat is cyber terrorism. Virtually all countries are potential victims to this threat.

While the United States is aggressively pursuing an active strategy to defeat terrorism in all its forms, it faces a different kind of national fear. People, especially politicians, athletes, media personnel, and others in the public's eye are very careful not to offend any social group (ethnic, gender, religion, and so on). Thus, fear of offending others causes people to make speeches that are politically correct. For example, some Christians use the Bible to preach against the acts of adultery (Mark 10:19), fornication, dishonesty, lying (Proverbs 12:22), and other vices. People do not seem to argue that these errant behaviors are genetic and therefore they cannot help being that way. They do not say that Christians are adulterer phobic, liar phobic, or dishonesty phobic (really no such terms).

However, if they use a text from that same Bible (i.e., Leviticus 18:22) to state that the homosexual person may be a wonderful individual, honest, trustworthy, and a productive citizen, but the homosexual act (not the individual) is condemned by God, they are called homophobic. Why is that?

Many people do not understand why Christian's are placed in this quandary with the fear of ostracism since it is not equivalent to being born with, for example, blue eyes when you prefer brown. Unless you get brown contact lenses, people will always see blue eyes. That is genetic, not a preference resulting from an urge or some conscious or subconscious issues. I believe sincere dialogue with sensitivity and openness to acceptance of the Word of God can produce better understanding and genuine change. It is not only in this area that understanding and change is needed. Our approach to solving racial issues needs to be continually refined to produce balanced reasoning and not stereotypical thinking. A person's race is genetic, but a person's thinking about another race is a choice.

There has been much improvement in race relations in the United States in recent years, but the integument of some underlying fear seems very thin, and work needs to be done on all sides to improve this situation. From the end of the 1960s to the present, I have resided on the East Coast and in the Southwest and have observed people's attitudes toward various races. Some were uncomfortable when faced with issues that called for collaboration with other races because they did not want to offend.

Societal fear is real. It is not a figment of imagination. We find fear even in government. U.S. presidents, legislators, and constituents debate how best to fix Social Security because they fear that the fund may go bankrupt and will not be there for succeeding generations. Some have even said that by increasing the federal deficit, we are mortgaging our children's future. There is fear that the country is getting cynical and losing confidence in Washington (lawmakers). Real fears exist in society, and SET has the answer to this dilemma. The SET principles must be applied one person at a time till society is permeated, saturated, and reoriented.

SET is so powerful because it relies on a higher power. Those who use this approach with their clients or patients consult their handbook—the Bible—for their diagnoses and treatment plan. While each person (client, counselee, patient) has different issues and needs a specific plan tailored for the individual situation, the biblical handbook provides a general diagnosis and prescription for humanity's mental illness.

The Designer, knowing the composition and condition of the mind (unlike the secular psychotherapist) states that the heart is deceitful and wicked and asks the question: who can know it? (Jeremiah 17:9). No one knows the answer to that question but God. The author of the handbook for the practitioner of spiritual psychotherapy tells us why. God says, "I ... made thee ... and formed thee from the womb" (Isaiah 44:2), and I know your thoughts even before you think them (Psalm 139:2). God can discern what you are thinking and what you intend to do (Hebrews 4:12). Furthermore, God's diagnosis of your mental condition is that your mind is carnal—sinful, messed up, in turmoil, and contrary to God's will (Romans 8:7). Therefore, no person—psychologists, psychiatrists, or any other mental health practitioner—can solve the problem, only God can.

The Bible says, If you come to me, "I will give you rest" (Matthew 11:28). God will reprogram your mind by giving you a new heart (Ezekiel 36:26). Trust God, who will give you the strength to cope with life (Isaiah 26:4). We have the assurance from Isaiah 49:15 that God will not forget us but will watch over us and protect us.

The power that is in the Word of God is enough to calm the soul, generate a positive mental outlook, and give courage to face any situation that might otherwise intimidate an individual. One should always remember that the Mighty God who created the heaven and the earth, whose word can be relied upon, said:

> But now thus saith the LORD that created thee, O Jacob, and he that formed thee, O Israel [those who trust in Him], Fear not: for I have redeemed thee, I have called thee by thy name; thou art mine. When thou passest through the waters, I will be with thee; and through the rivers, they shall not overflow thee: when thou walkest through the fire, thou shalt not be burned; neither shall the flame kindle upon thee.
>
> (Isaiah 43:1-2)

All those who trust in God hold onto that promise, which dispels all fears and provides courage to face the trials of life. When the path one has to tread seems fraught with dangers and seemingly insurmountable obstacles, when negative thoughts of failure approach, when paranoia taps at the door of your mind, grasp the hand of the omnipotent. Claim God's promises and he will see you through.

Negative thoughts may still arise because fear cannot be destroyed. Fear, however, Can be neutralized by using biblical principles such as the Merry Heart theory and SET. One never comes to the end of the neutralization process, but if the principles are followed continually; fear can have no dominion over you—it is effectively neutralized.

This book was written to encourage those who suffer from fear. The formula for addressing individual, organizational, and societal fears presented here is designed to show that fear's power can be neutralized through the acceptance and practice of God's Word. Finally this work seeks to convince you that if you call on Jesus when you are in trouble, believe in him, and .accept his Word, God will deliver you completely or support you in your challenges. A biblically based lifestyle can enable the perpetual neutralization of the power of all fears, offering enjoyment of a life of triumph, health, and wholeness. This is truly a path to hope and happiness.

The End of All Fears

One day, fears will be history. Some may refer to that time as a time of utopia. Others refer to it as a time when we will be in paradise. Regardless of how pleasant and beautiful you can describe it, it will be the ultimate dream, the ultimate hope, and the ultimate reality for the righteous and truehearted. Here is how John, in the Bible, describes that time:

> And I saw a new heaven and a new earth: for the first heaven and the first earth were passed away; and there was no more sea.... And I heard a great voice out of heaven saying, Behold, the tabernacle of God is with men, and he will dwell with them, and they shall be his people, and God himself shall be with them, and be their God. And God shall wipe away all tears from their eyes; and there shall be no more death, neither sorrow, nor crying, neither shall there be any more pain: for the former things are passed away.
>
> (Revelation 21:1-4

In that day, fears will not only he neutralized, it will be a thing of the past. Every citizen of this planet should take comfort that the chaos that exists in this world is only for a time. So I say to them that are of a fearful heart, be strong, fear not: behold your God will come ... he will come and save you. Then the eyes of the blind shall be opened, and the ears of the deaf shall be unstopped. Then shall the lame man [or woman} leap as an hart, and the tongue of the dumb sing: for in the wilderness shall waters break out, and streams in the desert (Isaiah 35:4-6).

In that day, there will be no more cancer, no more arthritis, no more high blood pressure, no more multiple sclerosis, no more Alzheimer's, and no more heart problems. There will be no more broken marriages, no more family disputes, no more disappointments, no more physical or emotional abuse; there will be nothing that will cause psychological or physical pain.

Oh, dear reader, you are now empowered to put aside your fears, even for a moment, and try to grasp the concept of a world with only joy, happiness, and love. If you have known only heartache all your life, it may be difficult for you to grasp that concept, but try anyhow. God has promised a future world of peace without the presence of fear. You can be a part of it if you allow yourself to take hold of what this book has tried to convey to you. It's now up to you. Your fears can be neutralized, and you can have hope and be happy if you make the principles of SET a reality in your life.

BIBLIOGRAPHY

Adizes, Ichak. Corporate Lift-Cycles. Englewood Cliffs, NJ: Prentice Hall, 1988.

Altshuler, Larry. Bottom Line's. Balanced Healing. Stamford, CT: Harbor Press, Inc., 2004.

Anderson, N. T. Helping Others Find Freedom in Christ. Ventura, CA: Regal Books, 1984.

Bernstein, Theodore. Bernstein Reverse Dictionary. and ed. NY: Random House, 1988.

Blake, R., and Mouton, J. S. The Managerial Grid III. Houston, TX: Gulf Publishing Company, 1985.

Bloch, Sydney. An introduction to the psychotherapies. Fourth Edition. New York: Oxford University Press, 2006.

Boeree, C. George. 2003. General Psychology: Erik Erikson. Adapted from my Erik Erikson Personality Theories page. http://webspace. ship.edu/cgboer/ genpsyerikson.html.

Brill, A.A. The Basic Writings of Sigmund Freud. New York: The Modern Library Edition 1938 (Translated and Edited, with an Introduction). 1965.

Clinton, Timothy, and Ohlschlager, George. Competent Christian Counseling. Colorado Springs, Colorado. Waterbrook Press. Vol. 1. 2002

Cloud, H. Changes that Heal. Grand Rapids, MI: Zonderman Publishing House. 1992.

Craighead, W. Edward. Nemeroff, Charles B. 2001. The Corsine Encyclopedia of Psychology and Behavioral Science. Psychology—Encyclopedias. Behavioral Sciences—Encyclopedias. New York. Wiley & Sons (US). http://www.netlibrar): com/Reader/

Dobson. James. Family News from Di: James Dobson. Colorado Springs: Focus on the Family. June 2000.

Drucker. P. F. Management, Tasks, Responsibilities, Practices. NY: Harper & Rowe. 1974.

Dziegielewski, Sophia F. DSM-IV-TR in Action. New York: Wiley & Sons. Inc. 2002.

Finley, Mark. Solid Ground. Hagerstown, MD: Review and Herald Publishing Association. 2004.

Forbes, B. C. The Forbes Leadership Library: Thoughts on Courage. Chicago, IL: Triumph Books. 1997.

Fuerst, W. Fundamentals of Nursing. Philadelphia, PA: J. B. Lippincott. 5th ed. 1974.

Gates, H. and C. West. The Future of the Race. NY: Alfred A. Knopf. 1996.

Gherman, E. M. The Psychobiology of Stress: Stress and the Bottom Line. AMACOM, American Management Associations, New York. 1981.

Glazer, Sarah. 2007. Prayer and Healing. Abstract. The CQ Researcher. January 14, 2005. 15: 2. http://library.cqpress.com/cgresearcher/ppv.php?id=cqresrre2005011400.

Gray, Alan. 2006. Scarborough Hypnotherapy Practice. A-Z of Phobias. http://mvw.scarborough-hypnotherapy.co.uk/html/ fearlist.htm.

Gray, J. Men Are from Mars, Women Are from Venus. New York: Harper Coffins. 1993.

Hall, C. S., and V. J. Nordby. A Primer of Jungian Psychology. NY: Meridian. 1999.

Hart, Archibald. D. The Anxiety Cure, Nashville: Word Publishing. 1999.

Hart, Achibald. D. 2000. "Power over Panic." Christian Counseling Today. American Association of Christian Counselors. Forest, Virginia. 8(4):14-15.

Hersey, P. & Blanchard, K. H. Management of Organizational Behavior, Utilizing Human Resources. Englewood Cliffs, NJ: Prentice Hall. 6th ed. 1993.

Hoopes, James. 2003. Management Consulting News. Meet the MasterMinds: James Hoopes Takes on the False Prophets of Management. http://www.managementconsultingnews.com/interviews/hoopes_interview.php.

Jung, C. G. The Basic lirritings of C G. Jung. NY: The Modern Library. 1954.

Jung, G. A. Understanding and Comparing Counseling Therapies. Southwest Bible College and Seminary Edition. Louisiana. 1997.

Kempling, Chris. 1999. The Faith-Health Connection. http:// www3. telus.net/chriskempling/pages/FaithHealth.html.

Kinnear, Karen L. Single Parents: a reference handbook. Contemporary World Issues. Santa Barbara, California. ABC-CLIO, Inc. 1999.

Koocher, Gerald P, Norcross, John C., Hill III, Sam S. Psychologists' Desk Reference. New York: Oxford University Press. Second Edition. 2005.

Koppel, Ted. October to, 2000. The Holy Land: Moment of Crisis Nightline Town Meeting from Jerusalem." Broadcast 10/10/2000. New York: ABC.

Kort, M. The Soviet Colossus, a History of USSR. NY: Charles

Scribner's Sons. 1985.

Lawson, D. M. Give to Live. La Jolla, CA: Alti. 1995.

Ludington, Aileen and Diehl, Hans. Health Power: Healthy by Choice, Not Chance. Hagerstown. MD: Review and Herald Publishing Association. 2002.

McGregor, D. Managing the Human Side of Enterprise. NY: Wiley. 1985.

McIlhaney Jr., Joe S. with Nethery, Susan. 1001 Health-Care Questions Women Ask. Grand Rapids, MI: Baker Books. 1998. MacKenzie, A. The Time Trap. NY: Anacom, a Division of the

American Management Association. 1991.

Meier, Paul. D., Frank B. Minirth, Frank B. Wichern, Donald E. Ratcliff, 1997. Introduction to Psychology and Counseling. 2d ed. Grand Rapids, MI: Baker Books. 1997.

Morgan, T. FDR: A Biography. NY: Simon & Schuster. 1985.

Mosbacher, G. It Takes Money, Honey. NY: Reagan Books. 1999.

Moyers, B. Healing on the Mind NY: Doubleday. 1993.

Nerum, Hilde, BSc(Midwifery), Lotta Halvorsen BSc(Midwifery), Tore Sorlie MDPhD, Pal Oian MDPhD (2006): Maternal Request for Cesarean Section due to Fear of Birth: Can it Be Changed Through Crisis-Oriented Counseling? Birth 33 (3), 221-228. http://www.blackwell-synergy.com/ doi/abs/10.1111/ j.1523-536X. 2006.00107.x?prevSearc.

Neuman, Frederic. Fighting Fear: An Eight-week Guide to Treating Your Own Phobias. NY: Macmillan. 1985.

News-Medical.Net, July 18, 2005. http://www.news-medical. net/?id= 11744. Olshan, N. H. Depression. NY: Franklin Watts. 1982.

Olshan, N. H. Depression. NY: Fanklin Watts. 1982.

Popenoe, David and 'Whitehead, Barbara Dafoe. NMP Annual Report 2002 V3. The National Marriage Project: The State of Our Unions. June 2002 http://marriage.rutgers.edu/Publications/ SOOU/SOOU2002.pdf

Priddle, Alisa. "Panic in Detroit: DaimlerChrysler's Jim Holden Pays the Price for Stuttgart's Jitters." Wards Auto World. 2000 (December): 42.

The Random Acts of Kindness Foundation http://www.actsofkindness. org/inspiration/health/detail.asp?id=1

Robbins, Stephen P. and Coulter, Mary,. 1999. Management. 6th ed. Upper Saddle River, NJ: Prentice Hall. 1999.

Roeske, Nancy A. 1972. Examination of the Personality. Philadelphia, PA: Lee & Febiger.

Ross, M. A., Triumph Over Fear. NY: Bantam Books. 1994.

Saisto, Terhi. 2001. British Journal of Obstetrics and Gynaecology 108:492-498.

Schefft, Jen. 2007. Better Single Than Sorry: A No-Regrets Guide to Loving Yourself and Never Settling. http://www.harpercollins. com/books/9780061228070/Better_Single_Than_Sorry/ index. aspx

Schimelfening, Nancy. Update May 29, 2006.About.com: Depression. "Vitamin for Depression?" http://depression.about.com/ cs/diet/a/ vitamin.htm.

Smith, Susan Male; McDonald, Arline; Natow, Annette; Heslin, Jo Ann. complete Book of Vitamins & Minerals. Lincolnwood, IL: Publications International, Inc. 1996.

Solomon, Jay. 2000, November 29. Indonesia Faces Crisis as Separatism Spreads with Nation's Turmoil. The Wall Street Journal.

Tada, Joni Eareckson. 2006. Joni and Friends: International Disability Center:

=http://www.joniandfriends.org/about joni.php.

U.S.-Canada Air Quality Agreement 1996 Progress Report. April 12, 2007.

Wagner, Lilya. "Going Beyond GWP: The Role of Fundraising in Your Organization." Beyond The Bottom Line Conference. Loma Linda University: San Diego, CA. March 11-12, 2002.

Waterman Jr., R. H. The Renewal Factor: How the Best Get and Keep the Competitive Edge. NY: Bantam. 1987.

White, E.G. Ministry of Healing. Boise, ID: Pacific Press Publishing Association. 1942.

Winckler, Suzanne. 2000. University of California, Davis, Groundwater Cooperative Extension Program: "Healthy Living: Drinking Water, from 'Martha Stewart's Living,' June 2000, p.122-125."

APPENDICES

Appendix A

Resource for Comfort and Aid in Neutralizing Fear

Following is a list of scriptures for comfort and neutralization of fears and times when needed. The promises of the Scripture are for God's people in all ages. Some of the promises have primary and secondary applications. Nevertheless, they are to be claimed by those who trust in the LORD God of Heaven. He will honor their faith according to his will and our needs. These scriptures are taken from the King James Version (KJV), Revised Standard Version (RSV) and the New International Version (NIV).

Anxiety

Psalm 27:14	Wait on the Lord: Be of good courage, and he shall strengthen thine heart: wait, I say, on the Lord. KJV
Psalm 30:5	For his anger endureth but a moment; in his favor is life: weeping may indure for a night, but joy cometh in the morning. KJV
Philippians 4:6	Have no anxiety about anything, but in everything by prayer and supplication with thanksgiving let your requests be made known unto God. RSV
Philippians 4:39	And my God will supply every need of yours according to his riches in glory in Christ Jesus. RSV

| Luke 21:26 | Men's hearts failing them for fear, and for looking after those things which are coming on the earth: for the powers of heaven shall be shaken. KJV |

Traveling

Psalm 121:7-8	The LORD will keep you from all evil; he will keep your life. The LORD will keep your going out and your coming in from this time forth and for evermore. RSV
Proverbs 16:9	A man's mind plans his way, but the LORD directs his steps. RSV
Psalm 32:8	I will instruct thee and teach thee in the way which thou shall go: I will guide thee with mine eye. KJV

Bereavement

Isaiah 60:20	Thy sun shall no more go down; neither shall thy moon withdraw itself: for the LORD shall be thine everlasting light, and the days of thy mourning shall be ended. KJV
Job 14:14-15	If a man die, shall he live again? All the days of my appointed time will I wait, till my change come. Thou shall call, and I will answer thee. KJV
Psalm 71:2o	Thou ... shall quicken me again, and shall bring me up again from the depths of the earth. KJV
Isaiah 26:19	Thy dead men shall live, together with my dead body shall they arise. KJV
1 Thessalonians 4:16	For the Lord himself shall descend from heaven with a shout, with the voice of the archangel, and with the trump of God: and the dead in Christ shall rise first. KJV

Revelation 21:4	And God shall wipe away all tears from their eyes; and there shall be no more death, neither sorrow, nor crying, neither shall there be any more pain: for the former things are passed away. KJV

Sickness

Jeremiah 30:17	For I will restore health unto thee, and I will heal thee of thy wounds, saith the LORD. KJV
Psalm 103:2-3	Bless the LORD, O my soul ... who forgives all your iniquity, who heals all your diseases. RSV
Mark 14:36	And he said, "Abba, Father, all things are possible to thee; remove this cup from me; yet not what I will, but what thou wilt." RSV
Hebrews 13:5	For he Math said, I will never leave thee, nor forsake thee. KJV

When Enemies Attack

Psalm 46:1-2	God is our refuge and strength, a very present help in trouble. Therefore will we not fear. KJV
Psalm 27:1-14	The LORD is my light and my salvation; whom shall I fear? When evildoers assail me ... they shall stumble and fall. RSV
Isaiah 54:17	No weapon that is formed against thee shall prosper. KJV
Psalm 91:1-16	He that dwelled in the secret place of the Most High, shall abide under the shadow of the Almighty. KJV

When Success Eludes

Deuteronomy 28:1, 3 If thou shall hearken diligently unto the voice of the LORD thy God, to observe and to do all his commandments ... Blessed shall thou be in the city, and blessed shall thou lie in the field. KJV

Proverbs 10:22	The blessing of the Lord, it maketh rich, and in addeth no sorrow with it. KJV
Jeremiah 10:23	It is not in man that walketh to direct his steps. KJV
James 1:5	If any of you lacks wisdom, let him ask God, who gives to all men generously mid without reproaching, and it will be given him. RSV
Proverbs 22:4	By humility and the fear of the Lord are riches, and honor, and life.
John 4:13-14	Jesus answered and said unto her, Whosoever drinketh of this water shall thirst again. But whosoever drinketh of the water that I shall give him shall never thirst; but the water that I shall give him shall be in him a well of water springing up into everlasting life. KJV

When in Despair

Psalm 31:24	Be of good courage, and he shall strengthen your heart, all ye that hope in the Lotto. KJV
2 Kings 6:16	Fear not: for they that he with us are more than they that he with them. KJV
Psalm 50:15	And call upon me in the day of trouble: I will deliver thee and thou shall glorify me. KJV
Hebrews 13:5	I will never leave thee, nor forsake thee. KJV

Contemplating Marriage

Genesis 2:22-24 And the rib, which the LORD God had taken from man, made he a woman, and brought her unto the man. Therefore shall a man leave his father and his mother, and shall cleave unto his wife: and they shall be one flesh. KJV

1 Corinthians 7:9	But if they cannot exercise self-control, let them marry. For it is better to marry than to be aflame with passion. RSV

Hebrews 13:4	Marriage should be honored by all, and the marriage bed kept pure, for God will judge the adulterer and the sexually immoral. NIV
Proverbs 31:10-12	A good wife who can find? She is far more precious than jewels. The heart of her husband trusts in her.... She does him good, and not harm, all the days of her life. RSV

Discord in the Family

1 John 4:11	Beloved, if God so loved us, we ought also to love one another. KJV
Romans 12:9—10	Let love be genuine; hate what is evil, hold fast to what is good; love one another with brotherly affection; outdo one another in showing honor. RSV
Ephesians 6:1-4	Children, obey your parents in the LORD: for this is right ... And ye fathers, provoke not your children to wrath: but bring them up in the nurture and admonition of the LORD. KJV
Ephesians 5:21-25	Submitting yourselves one to another in the fear of God. Wives submit yourselves unto your own husbands as unto the LORD.... Husbands, love your wives, even as Christ also loved the church, and gave himself for it. KJV

Loneliness

Hebrews 13:5	I will never leave thee, nor forsake thee. KJV Isaiah 43:2 When you pass through the waters I will be with you; and through the rivers, they shall not overwhelm you; when you walk through the fire you shall not be burned, and the flame shall not consume you. RSV

Fearful

Psalm 91:1   He that dwelleth in the secret place of the Most High, shall abide under the shadow of the Almighty. KJV (Note: Read all of Psalm 91.) Hebrews 13:6 so we may boldly say, The LORD is my helper, and I will not fear what man shall do unto me. KJV

Guilt

1 John 1:9   If we confess our sins, he is faithful and just to forgive us our sins, and to cleanse us from all unrighteousness. KJV

2 Chronicles 30:9   For the LORD your God is gracious and merciful, and will not turn away his face from you, if ye return unto him. KJV

Psalm 103:12   As far as the east is from the west, so far hath he removed our transgressions from us. KJV

Micah 7:19   And thou wilt cast all their sins into the depths of the sea. KJV

Hebrews 8:12   And their sins and their iniquities will T remember no more. KJV

2 Corinthians 5:17   Therefore, if anyone is in Christ, he is a new creation; the old has passed away, behold the new has come. RSV

Appendix B

Maintaining Mental Strength and Vigor

Read the Bible daily and seek to share at least one aspect of God's goodness to you with someone else. Engage the mind in contemplation of the various fascinating aspects of nature. Read books that bring fresh knowledge and that cause the mind to think critically and evaluate them in the light of God's Word.

Sing songs of hope and assurance to reinforce your positive mental attitude and pray as often as you can. Believe that the God of Creation loves and cares about you and will hear and answer you when you call on him. Then watch God work in your behalf. You are already a success.

Appendix C1

List of 581 Phobia Descriptions Including Dr. Alan Gray's 576 (with permission)

List of Fears by Alphabet   **Phobias**

A	
Abuse: sexual	Contreltophobia
Accidents D	Dystychiphobia
Acknowledging the presence of fear in one's life	Acknowlophobia
Air	Anemophobia
Air swallowing	Acrophobia
Airborne noxious substances	Acrophobia
Airsickness	Aeronausiphobia
Alcohol	Methyphobia or potophobia
Alone, being or	Autophobia or monophobia
Alone, being or solitude	Isolophobia
Amnesia	Amnesiphobia
Anger	Cholerophobia
Angina	Anginophobia
Animals Z	Zoophobia
Animals, skins of or fur	Doraphobia
Animals, wild	Agrizoophobia
Ants	Myrmecophobia
Anything new	Neophobia
Asymmetrical things	Asymmetriphobia
Atomic explosions	Atomosoobt Atomosophobia
Automobile, being in a moving	Ochophobia
Automobiles	Motorphobia

List of Fears by Alphabet	Phobias
B	
Bacteria	Bacteriophobia
Bald people	Peladophobia
Bald, becoming	Phalacrophobia
Bathing	Ablutophobia
Beards	Pogonophobia
Beaten by a rod or instrument of punishment, or of being severely criticized	Rhabdophobia
Beautiful women	Caligynephobia
Beds or going to bed	Clinophobia
Bees	Apiphobia or Melissophobia
Bicycles	Cyclophobia
Birds	Ornithophobia
Black	Melanophobia
Blindness in a visual field	Scotom aph obi a
Blood	Hemophobia, hemaphobia, or Hcmatophobia
Blushing or the color red	Erythrophobia, Erytophobia, or Ercuthophobia
Body odors	Osmophobia or Osphresiophobia
Body, things to the left side of the body	Levophobia
Body, things to the right side of the body	Dextrophobia
Bogeyman or Bogies	Bogyphobia
Bolsheviks	Bolshephobia
Books	Bibliophobia
Bound or tied up	Merinthophobia
Bowel movements: painful	Defecalocsiophobia
Brain disease	Meningitophobia
Bridges or of crossing them	Gephyrophobia
Buildings: being close to high buildings	Batophobia
Bullets	Ballistophobia
Bulls	Taurophobia
Bunts or beggars	1-1 obophobi a
Burglars, or being harmed by wicked persons	Scelerophobia

List of Fears by Alphabet   Phobias

Buried alive, being or cemeteries	Taphephobia or Taphophobia
C	
Cancer	Cancerophobia, carcinophobia
Car or vehicle, riding in	Amaxophobia
Cats	Aclurophobia, ailurophobia, dlurophobia, telinophobia, galeophobia, or gatophobia
Celestial spaces	Astrophobia
Cemeteries	Coimetrophobia
Cemeteries or being buried alive	Taphephobia or taphophobia
Ceremonies, religious	Teleophobia
Changes, making; moving	Tropophobia or metathesiophobia
Chickens	Alektorophobia
Child, bearing a deformed; deformed people	Teratophobia
Childbirth	Maleusiophobia, tocophobia, parturiphobia, or lockiophobia
Children	Pedophobia
Chinese or Chinese culture	Sinophobia
Chins	Geniophobia
Choking or being smothered	Pnigophobia or pnigerophobia
Choking	Anginophobia
Cholera	Chorophobia
Church	Ecclesiophobia
Clocks	Chronomentrophobia
Clocks or time	Chronophobia
Clothing	Vestiphobia
Clouds	Nephophobia
Clowns	Coulrophobia
Coitus	Coitophobia
Cold or cold things	Frigophobia
Cold: extreme, ice or frost	Cryophobia
Cold	Cheimaphobia, cheimatophobia, psychrophobia, or psychropophobia
Color purple	Porphyrophobia

List of Fears by Alphabet   **Phobias**

Color red or blushing	Erythrophobia, ervtophobia, or ereuthophobia
Color yellow	Xanthophobia
Color white	Leukophobia
Colors	Chromophobia or chromatophobia
Comets	Cometophobia
Computers or working on computers	Cyberphobia
Confined spaces	Claustrophobia
Constipation	Coprastasophobia
Contamination, dirt or infection	Molysmophobia or molysomophobia
Contamination with dirt or germs	Misophobia or mvsophobia
Cooking	Mageirocophobia
Corpses	Necrophobia
Cosmic phenomenon	Kosmikophobia
Creepy, crawly things	lierpetophobia
Criticized severely, or beaten by rod or instrument of punishment	Rhabdophobia
Criticism	Enissophobia
Crosses, or the crucifix	Stauropliobia
Crossing streets	Agyrophobia or dromophobia
Crowded public places like markets	Agoraphobia
Crowds or mobs	Enochlophobia, demophobia, or ochlophobia
Crucifix, the or crosses	Staurophobia
Crystals or glass	Crystallohobia
D	
Dampness, moisture or liquids	Hygrophobia
Dancing	Chorophobia
Dark or night	Nyctophobia
Dark place, being in	Lygophobia
Darkness	Achluophobia or myctophobia, or scotophobia
Dawn or daylight	Eosophobia
Daylight or sunshine	Phengophobia
Death or dying	Thanatophobia

List of Fears by Alphabet   **Phobias**

Death or dead things	Necrophohia
Decaying matter	Seplophobia
Decisions: making decisions	Decidophobia
Defeat	Kakorrhaphiophobia
Deformed people or bearing a deformed child	Teratophobia
Deformity or unattractive body image	Dysmorphophobia
Demons	Demonophobia or Daemonophobia
Dental surgery	Odontophobia
Dentists	Dentophobia
Dependence on others	Soteriophobia
Depth	Bathophobia
Diabetes	Diabetophobia
Dining or dinner conservations	Delpnophobia
Dirt, contamination or infection	Molysmophobia or molysomophobia
Dirt or germs, being contaminated with	Misophobia or mysophobia
Dirt on u filth	Rhypophobia or rupophobia
Dirty, being dirty or personal filth	Automysophobia
Disease	Nosophobia, nosemaphobia, or Pathophobia
Disease and suffering	Pa n thoph obi a
Disease, a definite	Monopathophobia
Disease, brain	Meningitophobia
Disease, kidney	Albumi nurophobia
Disease, rectal	Rectophobia
Dizziness or vertigo when looking down	Illyngophobia
Dizziness or whirlpools	Dinophobia
Doctor, going to the	I atrophob ia
Doctrine, challenges to or radical deviation from official	Heresyphobia or hereiophobia
Dogs or rabies	Cynophobia
Dolls	Pediophobia
Double vision	Diplophobia
Drafts	Acrophobia or anemophobia
Dreams, wet	Oneirogmophobia
Dreams	Oneirophobia

List of Fears by Alphabet   **Phobias**

Drinking	Dipsophobia
Drugs, new	Neopharmaphobia
Drugs or taking medicine	Pharmacophobia
Dryness	Xerophobia
Dust	Amathophobia or koniophobia
Duty or responsibility, neglecting	Paralipophobia
Dying or death	Thanatophobia
E	
Eating or swallowing	Phagophobia
Eating or tbod	Sitophobia or sitiophobia
Eating or swallowing or of being eaten	Phagophobia
Eight, the number	Octophobia
Electricity	Electrophobia
Englishness	Anglophobia
Erect penis	Medorthophobia
Erection, losing an	Medomalacuphobia
Everything	Panophobia, panphobia, pamphobia, or pantophobia
Eyes	Ommetaphobia or ommatophobia
Eyes, opening one's	Optophobia
F	
Fabrics, certain	Textophohia
Failure	Atychiphobia or kakorrhaphiophobia
Fainting	Asthenophobia
Fatigue	Kopophobia
Fearful situations: being preferred by a phobic	Counterphobia
Feathers or being tickled by feathers	Pteronophobia
Fecal matter, feces	Coprophobia or scatophobia
Female genitals	Kolpophobia
Female genitalia	Eurotophobia
Fever	Febriphobia, fibriphobia, fidriophobia, or pyrexiophobia
Filth or dirt	Rhypophobia
Fire	Arsonphohia or pyrophobia
Firearms	Hoplophobia

List of Fears by Alphabet   **Phobias**

Fish	Ichthyophobia
Flogging or punishment	Mastigophobia
Floods	Antlophobia
Flowers	Anthrophobia or anthophobia
Flutes	Aulophobia
Flying	Aviophobia, aviatophobia, or pteromerhanophobia
Fog	Homichlophobia or nebulaphobia
Food or eating	Sitophobia or sitiophobia
Food	Cibophobia
Foreigners or strangers	Xenophobia
Forests or wooden objects	Xylophobia
Forests	Hylophobia
Forests, dark wooded area, of at night	Nyctohylophobia
Forgetting or being forgotten	Athazagoraphobia
France or French culture	Francophobia, gallophobia, or galiphobia
Freedom	Eleutherophobia
Friday the thirteenth	Paraskavedekatriaphobia
Frogs	Batrachophobia
Frost, ice or extreme cold	Cryophobia
Frost or ice	Pagophobia
Functioning or work: surgeon's fear of operating	Ergasiophobia
Fur or skins of animals	Doraphobia
Future	Futurophobia
G	
Gaiety	Cherophobia
Garlic	Alliumphobia
Genitals, particularly female	Kolpophobia
Genitalia, female	Eurotophobia
Germans or German culture	Germanophobia or teutophobia
Germs or dirt, being contaminated with	Misophobia or mysophobia
Germs	Verminophobia
Ghosts or specters	Spectrophobia

List of Fears by Alphabet   **Phobias**

Ghosts	Phasmophobia
Girls, young or virgins	Parthenophobia
Giving permission or allowing one's self to explore one's fears	Alliophobia
Giving permission to others or allowing one's self to explore one's life for fears	Alleophobia
Glass or crystals	Crystallophobia
Glass	Hyelophobia, hyalophobia, or nelophobia
Gloomy place, being in	Lygophobi a
God or gods	Zeusophobia
Gods or religion	Theophobia
Gold	Aurophobia
Good news, hearing good newe	Euphobia
Gravity	Barophobia
Greek or Greek culture	Hellophobia
Greek terms	Hellenologophobia
Giving one's self or others permission to explore one's fears	Alliophobia
H	
Hair	Chaetophobia, trichopathophobia, trichophobia, or hypertrichophobia
Halloween	Samhainophobia
Handwriting	Graphophobia
Harmed by wicked persons; bad men or burglars	Scelerophobia Cardiophobi;
Heart	
Heat	Thermophobia
Heaven	Ouranophohia or uranophobia
Heights	Acrophobia, altopllobia, batophobia, hypsiphohia, or hyposophobia
Hell	Hadephobia, stygiophobia, or stigiophobia
Heredity	Patroiophobia
Holy things	Hagiophobia
Home	Ecophohia

List of Fears by Alphabet	Phobias
Home surroundings or a house	Oikophobia
Home, returning	Nostophobia
Home surroundings	Eicophohia
Homosexuality or of becoming homosexual	Homophobia
Horses	Equinophohia or hippophobia
Hospitals	Nosocomephohia
House or home surroundings	Oikophobia
Houses or being in a house	Domatophobia
Hurricanes and tornadoes	Lilapsophobia
Hypnotized, being or of sleep	Hypnophobia
Heaven	Ouranophohia or uranophobia
Heights	Acrophobia, altophobia, batophobia, hypsiphobia, or hyposophobia
Hell	Hadephobia, stygiophobia, or stigiophobia
Heredity	Patroiophobia
Holy things	Hagiophobia
Homeome	Ecophobia
Home surroundings or a house	Oikophobia
Home, returning	Nostophobia
Home surroundings	Eicophobia
Homosexuality or of becoming homosexual	Homophobia
Horses	Equinophobia or hippopbobia
Hospitals	Nosocomephobia
House or home surroundings	Oikophobia
Houses or being in a house	Domatophobia
Hurricanes and tornadoes	Lilapsophobia
Hypnotized, being or of sleep	Hypnophobia
I	
Ice or frost	Pagophobia
Ice, frost or extreme cold	Cryophobia
Ideas	Ideophobia
Ignored, being	Athazagoraphobia Atelophobia
Imperfection	

List of Fears by Alphabet   **Phobias**

Inability to stand	Basiphobia or basophobia
Infection, contamination or dirt	Molysmophobia or molvsomophobia
Infinity	Apeirophobia
Injections	Trypanophobia
Injury	Traumatophobia
Insanity, dealing with	Lyssophobia
Insanity	Dementophobia or maniaphobia
Insects	Acarophobia, entomophobia, or insectophobia
Insects that eat wood	Isoptcrophobia
Insects that cause itching	Acarophobia
Itching	Acarophobia
J	
Japanese or Japanese culture	Japanophobia
Jealousy	Zelophobia
Jews	Judeophobia
Joint immobility	Ankylophobia
Jumping from high and low places	Catapedaphobia
Justice	Dikephobia
K	
Kidney disease	Albuminurophobia
Kissing	Philemaphobia or philematophobia
Knees	Genuphobia
Knowledge	Gnosiophobia or epistemophobia
L	
Lakes	Limnophobia
Large things	Megalophobia
Laughter	Geliophobia
Lawsuits	Liticaphobia
Learning	Sophophobia
Left-handed; objects at the left side of the body	Sinistrophobia
Leprosy	Leprophobia or lepraphobia
Lice	Pediculophobia or phthiriophobia

List of Fears by Alphabet   **Phobias**

List of Fears by Alphabet	Phobias
Light	Photophobia
Light flashes	Selaphobia
Lightning and thunder	Brontophobia or karaunophobia
Lights, glaring	Photoaugliaphobia
Liquids, dampness or moisture	Hygrophobia
Locked in an enclosed place	Cleithrophobia, cleisiophobia, or elithrophobia
Lockjaw or tetanus	Tetanophobia
Loneliness or of being oneself	Eremophobia or eremiphobia
Looking up	Anablephobia or anablepophobia
Loud noises	Ligyrophobia
Love, sexual love	Erotophobia
Love play	Malaxophobia or sarmassophobia
Love, falling or being in	Philophobia
M	
Machines	Mechanophobia
Mad, becoming	Lyssophobia
Many things	Polyphobia
Marriage	Gamophobia
Materialism	Hylephobia
Matter, decaying	Seplophobia
Meat	Carnophobia
Medicine, taking; or drugs	Pharmacophobia
Medicines, mercurial	Hydrargyophobia
Memories	Mnemophobia
Men, bad or burglars or being harmed by wicked persons	Scelerophobia
Men	Androphobia, arrhenphobia, or hominophobia
Menstruation	ivlenophobia
Mercurial medicines	Hydrargyophobia
Metal	Metallophobia
Meteors	Meteorophobia
Mice	Musophobia, murophobia, or suriphobia

List of Fears by Alphabet   **Phobias**

Microbes	Bacillophobia or microbiophobia
Mind	Psychophobia
Mirrors or seeing oneself in a Mirror	Eisoptrophobia
Mirrors	Catoptrophobia
Missiles	Ballistophobia
Mistakes	Imperfectophobi a
Mobs or crowds	Demophobia, enochlophobia, or ochlophobia
Moisture, dampness or liquids	Hygrophobia
Money.	Chrometophobia or chrematophobia
Moon	Selenophobia
Mother-in-law	Pentheraphobia
Moths	A lottephobia
Motion or movement	Kinetophobia or kinesophobia
Moving or making changes	Tropophobia
Moving automobile or vehicle, being in	Ochophobia
Muscular incoordination (ataxia)	Ataxiophobia
Mushrooms	Mycophobia
Music	Melophobia
Myths or stories or false statements	Mythophobia
N	
Names or hearing a certain name	Onomatophobia
Names	Nomatophobia
Narrow things or places	Stenophobia
N	
Names or hearing a certain name	Onomatophobia
Names	Nomatophobia
Narrow things or places	Stenophobia
N	
Names or hearing a certain name	Onomatophobia
Names	Nomatophobia
Narrow things or places	Stenophobia
Narrowness	Anginophobi a
Needles	Aichmophobia or helonephobia

List of Fears by Alphabet   **Phobias**

New, anything or novel	Kainophobia, kainolophobia, cenophobia, centophobia, or neophobia
Newness	Cainophobia, cenophohia, centophobia, or cainotophobia
News: hearing good news	Euphohia
Night or dark	Nyctophobia
Night	Noctiphobia
Noise	Acousticophobia
Noises, loud	Ligyrophobia
Noises or voices, speaking aloud, or telephones	Phonophobia
Northern lights	Auroraphobia
Nosebleeds	Epistaxiophobia
Novelty or anything new	Kainophobia or kainolophobia
Novelty	Cainophobia or cainotophobia
Nuclear weapons	Nucleomituphobia
Nudity	Gyrnnophobia or nudophobia
Number 8	Octophobia
Number 13	Triskadekaphobia
Numbers	Arithmophobia or numerophobia
O	
Objects, small	Tapinophobia
Ocean or sea	Thalassophobia
Odor, personal	Bromidrosiphobia, bromidrophobia, osmophohia, or osphresiophobia
Odor, that one has a vile odor	Autodysomophobia
Odors or smells	Olfactophobia
Official doctrine, challenges to or radical deviation from	Heresyphobia or hereiophobia
Old people	Gerontophobia
Old, growing	Gerascophobia or gerontophobia
Open spaces	Agoraphobia
Open high places	Aeroacrophobia
Operation, surgical	Tomophobia

List of Fears by Alphabet **Phobias**

Opinions	Allodoxaphobia
Others, dependence on	Soteriophobia
Otters	Lutraphobia
Outer space	Spacephobia
P	
Pain	odynophobia, or odynephobia
Paper	Papyrophobia
Parasites	Parasitophobia
Parents-in-law	Soceraphobia
Peanut butter sticking to the roof of the mouth	Arachibutyrophobia
Pellagra	Pellagrophobia
Penis, erect	Medorthophobia
Penis, especially erect	Phallophobia
Penis, erect: seeing, thinking about or having	Ithyphallophobia
Penis, losing an erection	Medomalacuphobia
People	Anthropophobia
People in general or society	Sociophobia
People, deformed or bearing a deformed child	Teratophobia
Permission to self or others to explore one's fears	Alliophobia
Permission to self or others to explore one's life for fears	Alleophobia
Philosophy	Philsosphobia
Phobias	Phohophobia
Phobic preferring fearful situations	Counterphobia
Pins and needles	Belonephobia
Pins	Enetophobia
Place: locked in an enclosed place	Cleithrophobia, cleisiophobia, or clithrophobia
Place, being in a dark or gloomy	Lygopliobia
Places, certain	Topophobia
Places, crowded public	Agoraphobia
Places, open high	Aeroacrophobia

List of Fears by Alphabet	Phobias
Places or things, narrow	Stenophobia
Plants	Botonophohia
Pleasure, feeling	Hedonophobia
Poetry	Metrophobia
Pointed objects	Aichmophobia
Poison	lophobia
Poisoned, being	Toxiphobia, toxophobia, or toxicophobia
Poliomyelitis, contracting	Poliosophobia
Politicians	Politicophobia
Pope	Papaphobia
Poverty	Peniaphobia
Precipices	Cremnophobia
Priests or sacred things	Hierophobia
Progress	Prosophobia
Property	Orthophobia
Prostitutes or venereal disease	Cypridophobia, cypriphobia, cyprianophobia, or cyprinophobia
Punishment or flogging	Ailastigophobia
Punishment by a rod or other instrument, or of being severely criticized	Rhabdophobia
Punishment	Poinephobia
Puppets	Pupaphobia
Purple, color	Porphyrophohia
R	
Rabies	Cynophobia, hydrophobobophobia, hydrophobia, kynophobia, or lyssophohia
Radiation or X-rays	Radiophohia
Railroads or train travel	Siderodromophobia
Rain	Ombrophobia or pluviophohia
Rape	Virginitiphobia
Rat, great mole	Zemmiphobia
Relatives	Syngenesophohia

List of Fears by Alphabet	Phobias
Religion or gods	Theophobia
Religious ceremonies	Teleophohia
Reptiles	Herpetophobia
Responsibility or duty, neglecting	Paralipophobia
Responsibility	Hypengyophobia or hypegiaphobia
Ridiculed, being	Catagelophobia or katagelophobia
Rivers	Potamphobia or potamophobia
Road travel or travel	Hodophobia
Robbers or being robbed	Harpaxophobia
Rooms, empty	Cenophobia or centophobia
Rooms	Koinoniphobia
Ruin	Atephobia
Running water	Potamophobia
Russians	Russophobia
S	
Sacred things or priests	I licrophohia
Satan	Satanophobia
Scabies	Scahiophohia
School, going to school	Didaskaleinophobia
School	Scolionophobia
Scientific terminology, complex	Hellenologophobia
Scratches or being scratched	Amychophohia
Sea or ocean	Thalassophobia
Self, seeing oneself in a mirror	Eisoptrophobia
Self, personal odor	Bromidrosiphobia or bromidrophobia
Self, being alone	Autophobia, eremophobia, eremiphobia, or isolophohia
Self, being dirty	Automysophobia
Self, being oneself	Autophobia
Self, being seen or looked at	Scopophobia or scoptophobia
Self, being touched	Aphenphosmophobia
Self, that one has a vile odor	Autodysomophobia
Semen	Spermatophobia or spermophohia
Sermons	Homilophobia
Sex	Genophobia

List of Fears by Alphabet	Phobias
Sex, opposite	Heterophobia or sexophobia
Sexual abuse	Agraphobia or contreltophobia
Sexual intercourse	Coitophobia
Sexual love or sexual questions	Erotophobia
Sexual perversion	Paraphobia
Shadows	Sciophobia or sciaphobia
Shellfish	Ostraconophobia
Shock	Hormephobia
Sin or of having committed an unpardonable sin	Enosiophobia or enissophobia
Sin	Hamartophobia
Single: staying single	Anuptaphobia
Sinning	Peccatophobia
Sitting down	Kathisophobia
Sitting	Cathisophobia or thaasophobia
Situations, certain	Topophobia
Skin disease	Dermatophobia
Skin of animals, fur	Doraphobia
Sleep	Somniphobia
Sleep or being hypnotized	Hypnophobia
Slime	Blennophobia or myxophobia
Small things	Microphobia, mycrophobia, or tapinophobia
Smells or odors	Olfactophobia
Smothered, being or choking	Pnigophobia or pnigerophobia
Snakes	Ophidiophobia or snakephobia
Snow	Chionophobia
Social (fear of being evaluated negatively in social situations)	Social Phobia
Society or people in general	Anthropophobia or sociophobia
Solitude	Monophobia
Sounds	Acousticophobia
Sourness	Acerophobia
Space, closed or locked in an enclosed space	Cleithrophobia, cleisiophobia, clithrophobia

List of Fears by Alphabet   **Phobias**

Space, outer	Spacephobia
Spaces, confined	Claustrophobia
Spaces, empty	Cenophobia, centophobia, or kenophobia
Spaces, open	Agoraphobia
Speak, trying to	Glossophobia
Speaking	Laliophobia or lalophobia
Speaking aloud, voices or noises, or telephones	Phonophobia
Speaking in public	Glossophobia
Specters or ghosts	Spectrophobia
Speed	Tachophobia
Spiders	Arachnephobia or arachnophobia
Spirits	Pneumatiphobia
Stage fright	Topophobia
Stairs or climbing stairs	Climacophobia
Stand, inability to	Basiphobia or basophobia
Standing upright	Basistasiphobia or Basostasophobia
Standing up	Stasiphobia
Standing up and walking	Stasibasiphobia
Stared at, being	Ophthalmophobia
Stars	Siderophobia or astrophobia
Statements, false or myths or stories	Mythophobia
Staying single	Anuptaphobia
Stealing	Cleptophobia or kleptophobia
Stepfather	Vitricophobia
Stepmother	Novercaphobia
Stings	Cnidophobia or linonophobia
Stooping	Kyphophobia
Strangers or foreigners	Xenophobia
Streets, crossing streets	Dromophobia
Streets	Agyrophobia
String	Linonophobia
Storm, thunder	Brontophobia
Swallowing or eating	Phagophobia

List of Fears by Alphabet   **Phobias**

List of Fears by Alphabet	Phobias
Symbolism	Symbolophobia
Syphillis (lues)	Luiphobia or syphilophobia
T	
Tapeworms	Taeniophobia
Taste	Geumaphobia or geumophobia
Technology	Technophobia
Teeth	Odon tophobi a
Termites	Isopterophobia
Tests, taking	Testophobia
Tetanus or lockjaw	Tetanophobia
Theaters	Theatrophobia
Theology	Theologicophobia
Things, many	Polyphobia
Things, large	Megalophobia
Things or places, narrow	Stenophobia
Things, small	Microphobia or mvcrophobia
Thinking	Phronemophobia
Thunder	Ceraunophobia
Thunder and lightning	Astraphobia, astrapophobia, brontophobia, or keraunophobia
Tuberculosis	Phthisiophobia or tuberculophobia
Tyrants	Tyrannophobia
U	
Ugliness	Cacophobia
Undressing in front of someone	Dishabillophobia
Urine or urinating	Urophobia
V	
Vaccination	Vaccinophobia
Vegetables	Lachanophobia
Venereal disease or prostitutes	Cypridophobia, cypriphobia, cyprianophobia, or cyprinophobia
Ventriloquist's dummy	Automatonophobia
Vision: double vision	Diplophobia
Voices or noises, speaking aloud or telephones	Phonophobia

List of Fears by Alphabet   **Phobias**

Voids or empty spaces	Kenophobia
Vomiting secondary to airsickness	Aeronausiphobia
Vomiting	Emetophobia
W	
Waits, long	Macrophobia
Walking	Ambulophobia, basistasiphobia, or basostasophobia
Washing	Abultophobia
Wasps	Spheksophobia
Water	Hydrophobia
Waves or wavelike motions	Cymophobia or kymophobia
Wax statues	Automatonophobia
Weakness	Asthenophobia
Wealth	Plutophobia
Weapons, nuclear	Nucleomituphobia
Weight, gaining	Obesophobia or pocrescophobia
Wind	Ancraophobia or anemophobia
Wine	Oenophobia
Witches and witchcraft	Wiccaphobia
Women	Gvnephobia or gvnophobia
Wooden objects or forests	Xvlophobia
Words	Logophobia or verbophobia
Words, long	Hippopotomonstrosesquippedaliophobia or sesquipedalophobia
Work	Ergophobia or ponophobia
Worms	Scoleciphobia
Worms, being infested with	Helminthophobia
Wrinkles, getting	Rhytiphobia
Writing	Graphophobia
Writing in public	Scriptophobia
X	
X-rays or radiation	Radiophobia
Y	
Yellow color	Xanthophobia

Appendix C2

List of 581 Phobia Descriptions Including Dr. Alan Gray's 576 (with permission)

List of Phobias by Alphabet   **Fears**

A	
Ablutophobia	Bathing
Abultophobia	Washing
Acarophobia	Insects that cause itching
Acarophobia	Itching
Acarophobia, entomophobia, or inscctophobia	Insects
Acerophobia	Sourness
Achluophobia, myctophobia, or scotophobia	Darkness
Acknowlophobia	acknowledging the presence of fear in one's life
Aclurophobia, ailurophobia, elurophobia, felinophobia, galeophobia, or gatophobia	Cats
Acousticophobia	Noise
Acousticophobia	Sounds
Acrophobia, altophobia, batophobia, hypsiphobia, or hyposophobia	Heights
Aeroacrophobia	Open high places
Aeroacrophobia	Places, open high
Aeronausiphobia	Airsickness
Aeronausiphobia	Vomiting secondary to airsickness
Acrophobia	Air swallowing
Acrophobia	Airborne noxious substances
Acrophobia or ancmophobia	Drafts
Agoraphobia	Places, crowded public
Agoraphobia	Crowded public places like markets
Agoraphobia	Open spaces
Agoraphobia	Spaces, open
Agraphobia or contreltophobia	Sexual abuse
Agrizoophobia	Animals, wild
Agyropllobia	Streets

List of Phobias by Alphabet   **Fears**

Agyrophobia or dromophobia	Crossing streets
Aichmophobia	Pointed objects
Aichmophobia or belonephobia	Needles
Albuminurophobia	Disease: kidney
Albuminurophobia	Kidney disease
Alektorophobia	Chickens
Algiophobia, ponophobia, odynophobia, or odynephobia	Pain
Alliumphobia	Garlic
Allodoxaphobia	Opinions
Alliophobia	Giving permission or allowing one's self to explore one's fears
Alleophobia	Permission to self or others to explore one's life for fears
Amathophobia or koniophobia	Dust
Amaxophobia	Car or vehicle, riding in
Ambulophobia, basistasiphobia,or basostasophobia	Walking
Amnesiphobia	Amnesia
Amychophobia	Scratches or being scratched
Anablephobia or anablepophobia	Looking up
Ancraophobia or anemophobia	Wind
Androphobia, arrhenphobia, or hominophobia	Men
Anemophobia	Air
Anginophohia	Angina
Anginophohia	Choking
Anginophobia	Narrowness
Anglophobia	Englishness
Ankylophobia	Joint immobility
Anthrophobia or anthophobia	Flowers
Anthropophobia	People
Anthropophobia or sociophobia	Society or people in general
Antlophobia	Floods
Anuptaphobia	Single: staying single

List of Phobias by Alphabet   Fears

Anuptaphobia	Staying single
Apeirophobia	Infinity
Aphenphosmophobia	Self, being touched
Aphenphosmophobia, haphephobia, haptephobia, or chiraptophobia	Touched, being touched
Apiphohia or melissophobia	Bees
Arachibutyrophobia	Peanut butter sticking to the roof of the mouth
Arachnephobia or arachnophobia	Spiders
Arithmophobia or numerophobia	Numbers
Arsonphobia or pyrophobia	Fire
Asthenophobia	Fainting
Asthenophohia	Weakness
Astraphobia, astrapophobia, brontophobia, or keraunophobia	Thunder and lightning
Astrophobia	Celestial spaces
Asymmetriphobia	Asymmetrical things
A taxiophobia	Muscular incoordination (ataxia)
Atelophobi a	Imperfection
Atephobia	Ruin
Athazagoraphobia	Forgetting or being forgotten
Athazagoraphobia	Ignored, being
Atomosophobia	Atomic explosions
Atychiphobia or kakorrhaphiophobia	Failure
Aulophobia	Flutes
Aurophobia	Gold
Auroraphobia	Northern lights
Autodysomophobia	Odor, that one has a vile odor
Autodvsomophobia	Self, that one has a vile odor
Automatonophobia	Ventriloquist's dummy
Automatonophobia	Wax statues
Automvsophobia	Dirty, being dirty or personal filth
Automysophobia	Self, being dirty
Autophobia	Self, being oneself
Autophobia or monophobia	Alone, being

List of Phobias by Alphabet — **Fears**

List of Phobias by Alphabet	Fears
Autophobia, eremophobia, eremiphobia, or isolophobia	Self, being alone
Aviophobia, aviatophobia, or Pteromerhanophobia	Flying
B	
Bacillophobia or microbiophobia	Microbes
Bacteriophobia	Bacteria
Ballistophobia	Bullets
Ballistophobia	Missiles
Barophobia	Gravity
Basiphobia or basophobia	Inability to stand
Basiphobia or basophobia	Stand, inability to
Basistasiphobia or basostasophobia	Standing upright
Bathophobia	Depth
Batophobia	Buildings: being close to high buildings
Batrachophobia	Frogs
Belonephobia	Pins and needles
Bibliophobia	Books
Blennophobia or myxophobia	Slime
Bogyphobia	Bogeyman or bogies
Bolshephobia	Bolsheviks
Botonophobia	Plants
Bromidrosiphobia or bromidrophobia	Self, personal odor
Bromidrosiphobia, bromidrophobia, osmophobia, or osphresiophobia	Odor, personal
Brontophobia	Storm, thunder
Brontophobia or karaunophobia	Lightning and thunder
Bufonophobia	Toads
C	
Cacophobia	Ugliness
Cainophobia or cainotophobia	Novelty
Cainophobia, cenophobia, centophobia, or cainotophobia	Newness
Caligynephobia	Beautiful women
Caneerophobia or carcinophobia	Cancer

List of Phobias by Alphabet   **Fears**

Cardiophobia	Heart
Carnophobia	Meat
Catagelophobia or katagelophobia	Ridiculed, being
Catapedaphobia	jumping from high and low places
Cathisophobia or thaasophobia	Sitting
Catoptrophobia	Mirrors
Cenophobia or centophobia	Rooms, empty
Cenophobia, centophobia, or kenophobia	Spaces, empty
Ceratmophobia	Thunder
Chaetophobia, trichopathophobia, trichophobia, or hypertrichophobia	Hair
Cheimaphobia, cheimatophohia, psychrophobia, or psvchropophobia	Cold
Cherophohia	Gaiety
Chionophobia	Snow
Cholerophobia	Anger
Chorophobia	Cholera
Chorophobia	Dancing
Chrometophobia or chrematophobia	Money
Chromophohia or chromatophobia	Colors
Chronomentrophobia	Clocks
Chronophobia	Clocks or time
Cibophobia	Food
Claustrophobia	Confined spaces
Claustrophobia	Spaces, confined
Clcithrophobia, cleisiophobia, or Clithrophobia	Space, closed or locked in an enclosed space
Clcithrophobia, cleisiophobia, or clithrophobia	Locked in an enclosed place
Clcithrophobia, cleisiophobia, or clithrophobia	Place: locked in an enclosed place
Cleptophobia or kleptophobia	Stealing
Climacophohia	Stairs or climbing stairs
Clinophobia	Beds or going to bed
Cnidophobia or linonophohia	Stings

List of Phobias by Alphabet — Fears

List of Phobias by Alphabet	Fears
Coimetrophobia	Cemeteries
Coitophobia	Coitus
Coitophobia	Sexual intercourse
Cometophobia	Comets
Contreltophobia	Abuse: sexual
Coprastasophobia	Constipation
Coprophobia or scatophobia	Fecal matter, feces
Coulrophobia	Clowns
Counterphobia	Fearful situations: being preferred by a phobic
Counterphobia	Phobic preferring fearful situations
Cremnophobia	Precipices
Cryophobia	Cold: extreme, ice or frost
Cryophobia	Frost, ice or extreme cold
Cryophobia	Ice, frost or extreme cold
Crystallohobia	Crystals or glass
Crystallophobia	Glass or crystals
Cyberphobia	Computers or working on computers
Cyclophobia	Bicycles
Cymophobia or kymophobia	Waves or wavelike motions
Cynophobia	Dogs or rabies
Cynophobia, hydrophobophobia, hydrophobia, kynophobia, or lyssophobia	Rabies
Cypridophobia, cypriphobia, cyprianophobia, or cyprinophobia	Prostitutes or venereal disease
Cypridophobia, cypriphobia, cyprianophobia, or cyprinophobia	Venereal disease or prostitutes
D	
Decidophobia	Decisions: making decisions
Defecaloesiophobia	Bowel movements: painful
Delpnophobia	Dining or dinner conservations
Deinentophobia or maniaphobia	Insanity
Demonophobia or Daemonophobia	Demons
Demophobia, enochlophobia, or ochlophobia	Mobs or crowds

240

List of Phobias by Alphabet   **Fears**

Dendrophobia	Trees
Dentophobia	Dentists
Dermatophobia	Skin lesions
Dermatosiophobia	Skin disease
Dextrophobia	Body, things to the right side of the body
of the body	
Diabetophobia	Diabetes
Didaskaleinophobia	School, going to school
Dikephobia	Justice
Dinophobia	Dizziness or whirlpools
Diplophobia	Double vision
Diplophobia	Vision: double vision,
Di psophobia	Drinking
Dishabillophobia	Undressing in front of someone
Domatophobia	Houses or being in a house
Doraphobia	Animals, skins of or fur
Doraphobia	Fur or skins of animals
Doraphobia	Skin of animals, fur
Dromophobia	Streets, crossing streets
Dysmorphophobia	Deformity or unattractive body image
Dystychiphobia	Accidents
E	
Ecclesiophobia	Church
Ecophobia	Home
Eicophobia	Home surroundings
Eisoptrophobia	Mirrors or seeing oneself in a mirror
Eisoptrophobia	Self, seeing oneself in a mirror
Electrophobia	Electricity
Elcuthcrophobia	Freedom
Emetophobia	Vomiting
Enetophobia	Pins
Enissophobia	Criticism
Enochlophobia, demophobia, or ochlophobia	Crowds or mobs

List of Phobias by Alphabet   **Fears**

Enosiophobia or enissophobia	Sin or of having committed an unpardonable sin
Eosophobia	Dawn or daylight
Epistaxiophobia	Nosebleeds
Equinophobia or hippophobia	Horses
Eremophobia or eremiphobia	Loneliness or of being oneself
Ergasiophobia	Functioning or work: surgeon's fear of operating
Ergophobia or ponophobia	Work
Erotophobia	Love, sexual love
Erotophobia	Sexual love or sexual questions
Erythrophobia, erytophobia, or ereuthophobia	Blushing or the color red
Erythrophobia, erytophobia, or ereuthophobia	Color red or blushing
Euphobia	Good news, hearing good news
Euphobia	News: hearing good news
Eurotophobia	Female genitalia
Eurotophobia	Genitalia, female
F	
Febriphobia, fibriphobia, fidriophobia, or pyrexiophobia	Fever
Francophobia, gallophobia, or galiphobia	France or French culture
Frigophobia	Cold or cold things
Futurophobia	Future
G	
Gamophobia	Marriage
Gcliophobia	Laughter
Gcniophobia	Chins
Gcnophobia	Sex
Genuphobia	Knees
Gephyrophobia	Bridges or of crossing them
Gerascophobia or gerontophobia	Old, growing
Germanophobia or teutophobia	Germans or German culture
Gerontophobia	Old people

List of Phobias by Alphabet   **Fears**

List of Phobias by Alphabet	Fears
Geumaphobia or geumophobia	Taste
Glossophobia	Speak, trying to
Glossophobia	Speaking in public
Gnosiophobia or epistemophobi	Knowledge
Graphophobia	Handwriting
Graphophobia	Writing
Gymnophobia or nudophobia	Nudity
Gynephobia or gynophobia	Women
H	
Hadephobia, stygiophobia, or stigiophobia	Hell
Hagiophobia	Holy things
Hamartophobia	Sin
Harpaxophobia	Robbers or being robbed
Hedonophobia	Pleasure, feeling
Heliophobia	Sun or sunlight
I lellenologophobia	Greek terms
Hellenologophobia	Scientific terminology, complex
Hellophobia	Greek or Greek culture
Helminthophobia	Worms, being infested with
Hemophobia, hemaphobia, or hematophobia	Blood
Heresyphobia or hereiophobia	Doctrine, challenges to or radical deviation from official
Heresyphobia or hereiophobia	Official doctrine, challenges to or radical deviation from
Herpetophobia	Creepy, crawly things
Herpetophobia	Reptiles
Heterophobia or sexophobia	Sex, opposite
Hierophobia	Priests or sacred things
Hierophobia	Sacred things or priests
H ippopotomonstrosesqui- ppedaliophobia or sesquipedalophobia	Words, long
Hobophobia	Bums or beggars
Hodophobia	Road travel or travel
Hodophobia	Travel or road travel

List of Phobias by Alphabet   **Fears**

List of Phobias by Alphabet	Fears
Homichlophobia or nebulaphobia	Fog
Homilophobia	Sermons
Homophobia	Homosexuality or of becoming homosexual
Hoplophobia	Firearms
Hormephobia	Shock
Hydrargyophobia	Medicines, mercurial
Hydrargyophobia	Mercurial medicines
Hydrophobia	Water
Hyelophobia, hyalophobia, or nelophobia	Glass
Hygrophobia	Dampness, moisture or liquids
Hygrophobia	Liquids, dampness or moisture
Hygrophobia	Moisture, dampness or liquids
Hylephobia	Materialism
Hylophobia	Forests
Hypengyophobia or hypegiaphobia	Responsibility
Hypnophobia	Hypnotized, being or of sleep
Hypnophobia	Sleep or being hypnotized
I	
Iatrophobia	Doctor, going to the
Ichthyophobia	Fish
Imperfectophobia	Mistakes
Ideophobia	Ideas
Illyngophobia	Dizziness or vertigo when looking down
Iophobia	Poison
Isolophobia	Alone, being or solitude
Isopterophobia	Insects that eat wood
Isopterophobia	Termites
Ithyphallophobia	Penis, erect: seeing, thinking about or having
J	
Japanophobia	Japanese or Japanese culture
Judeophobia	Jews
K	
Kainophobia or kainolophobia	Novelty or anything new

List of Phobias by Alphabet

List of Phobias by Alphabet	Fears
Kainophobia, kainolophobia, cenophobia, centophobia, or neophobia	New, anything or novel
Kakorrhaphiophobia	Defeat
Kathisophobia	Sitting down
Kenophobia	Voids or empty spaces
Kinetophobia or kinesophobia	Motion or movement
Koinoniphobia	Rooms
Kolpophobia	Female genitals
Kolpophobia	Genitals, particularly female
Kopophobia	Fatigue
Kosmikophobia	Cosmic phenomenon
Kyphophobia	Stooping
L	
Lachanophobia	Vegetables
Laliophobia or lalophobia	Speaking
Leprophobia or lepraphobia	Leprosy
Leukophobia	Color white
Levophobia	Body, things to the left side of the body
Ligyrophobia	Loud noises
Ligyrophobia	Noises, loud
Lilapsophobia	Hurricanes and tornadoes
Lilapsophobia	Tornadoes and hurricanes
Limnophobia	Lakes
Linonophobia	String
Liticaphobia	Lawsuits
Logophobia or verbophobia	Words
Luiphobia or syphilophobia	Syphillis (lees)
Lutraphobia	Otters
Lygophobia	Dark place, being in
Lygophobia	Gloomy place, being in
Lygophobia	Place, being in a dark or gloomy
Lyssophobia	Insanity, dealing with
Lyssophobia	Mad, becoming
M	
Macrophobia	Waits, long

List of Phobias by Alphabet	Fears
Maleusiophobia, tocophobia, parturiphobia, or lockiophobia	Childbirth
Mastigophobia	Flogging or punishment
Mastigophobia	Punishment or flogging
Mechanophobia	Machines
Medomalacuphobia	Erection, losing an
Medomalacuphobia	Penis, losing an erection
Medorthophobia	Erect penis
Medorthophobia	Penis, erect
Megalophobia	Large things
Megalophobia	Things, large
Melanophobia	Black
Melophohia	Music
Meningitophobia	Brain disease
Meningitophobia	Disease, brain
Menophobia	Menstruation
Merinthophobia	Bound or tied up
Metallophobia	Metal
Meteorophobia	Meteors
Methyphobia or potophobia	Alcohol
Metrophobia	Poetry
Microphobia or mycrophobia	Things, small
Microphobia, mycrophobia, or tapinophobia	Small things
Misophobia or mysophobia	Contamination with dirt or germs
Misophobia or mysophobia	Dirt or germs, being contaminated with
Misophobia or mysophobia	Germs or dirt, being
Mnemophobia	Memories
Molysmophobia or molysomophobia	Contamination, dirt or infection
Nlolysinophobia or molysomophobia	Dirt, contamination or
Nlolysinophobia or molysomophobia	Dirt, contamination or infection
Molysmophohia or molysomophobia	Infection, contamination or dirt
Monopathophobia	Disease, a definite
Monophobia	Solitude
Motorphobia	Automobiles
Mottephobia	Moths

List of Phobias by Alphabet   **Fears**

List of Phobias by Alphabet	Fears
Musophobia, murophobia, or suriphobia	Mice
Mycophobia	Mushrooms
Myrmecophobia	Ants
Mythophobia	Myths or stories or false statements
Mythophobia	Statements, false or myths or Stories
N	
Necrophobia	Corpses
Necrophobia	Death or dead things
Neopharmaphobia	Drugs, new
Neophobia	Anything new
Nephophobia	Clouds
Nlageirocophobia	Cooking
NIalaxophobia or sari assophobia	Love play
Noctiphobia	Night
Nomatophobia	Names
Nosocomephobia	Hospitals
Nosophohia, nosemaphobia, or pathophohia	Disease
Nostophobia	Home, returning
Nou'crcaphobia	Stepmother
Nucleomituphohia	Nuclear weapons
Nucleomituphohia	Weapons, nuclear
Nyctohylophobia	Forests, dark wooded area, of at night.
Nyctophobia	Dark or night
Nyctophobia	Night or dark
O	
Obesophobia or pocrescophobia	Weight, gaining
Ochophobia	Automobile, being in a moving
Ochophobia being in	Moving automobile or vehicle, being in
Octophobia	Eight, the number
Octophobia	Number 8
Odontophobia	Dental surgery
Odontophobia	Teeth
Oenophobia	Wine
Oikophobia	Home surroundings or a house

List of Phobias by Alphabet   **Fears**

Oikophobia	House or home surroundings
Olfactophobia	Odors or smells
Olfactophobia	Smells or odors
Ombrophobia or pluviophobia	Rain
Ommetaphobia or ommatophobia	Eyes
Oneirogmophobia	Dreams, wet
Oneirophobia	Dreams
Onomatophobia	Names or hearing a certain name
Ophidiophobia or snakephobia	Snakes
Ophthalmophobia	Stared at, being
Optophobia	Eyes, opening one's
Ornithophobia	Birds
Orthophobia	Property
Osmophobia or osphresiophobia	Body odors
Ostraconophobia	Shellfish
Ouranophobia or uranophobia	Heaven
P	
Pagophobia	Frost or ice
Pagophobia	Ice or frost
Panophobia, panphobia, pamphobia, or pantophobia	Everything
Panthophobia	Disease and suffering
Papaphobia	Pope
Papyrophobia	Paper
Paralipophobia	Duty or responsibility, neglecting
Paralipophobia	Responsibility or duty, neglecting
neglecting	
Paraphobia	Sexual perversion
Parasitophobia	Parasites
Paraskavedekatriaphobia	Friday the 13th
Parthenophobia	Girls, young or virgins
Patroiophobia	Heredity
Peccatophobia	Sinning
Pediculophobia or phthiriophobia	Lice
Pediophobia	Dolls

List of Phobias by Alphabet

List of Phobias by Alphabet	Fears
Pedophobia	Children
Peladophobia	Bald people
Pellagrophobia	Pellagra
Peniaphobia	Poverty
Pentheraphobia	Mother-in-law
Phagophobia	Eating or swallowing
Phagophobia	Eating or swallowing or of being eaten
Phagophobia	Swallowing or eating
Phalacrophobia	Bald, becoming
Phallophobia	Penis, especially erect
Pharmacophobia	Drugs or taking medicine
Pharmacophobia	Medicine, taking; or drugs
Phasmophobia	Ghosts
Phengophobia	Daylight or sunshine
Phengophobia	Sunshine or daylight
Philemaphobia or philematophobia	Kissing
Philophobia	Love, falling or being in
Philsosphobia	Philosophy
Phobophobia	Phobias
Phonophobia	Noises or voices, speaking aloud, or telephones
Phonophobia	Speaking aloud, voices or noises, or telephones
Phonophobia	Voices or noises, speaking aloud or telephones
Photoaugliaphobia	Lights, glaring
Photophobia	Light
Phroncmophobia	Thinking
Phthisiophobia or tuberculophobia	Tuberculosis
Placophobia	Tombstones
Plutophobia	Wealth
Pneumatiphobia	Spirits
Pnigophobia or pnigerophobia	Choking or being smothered
Pnigophobia or pnigerophobia	Smothered, being or choking
Pogonophobia	Beards

List of Phobias by Alphabet	Fears
Poinephobia	Punishment
Poliosophobia	Contracting Poliomyelitis
Politicophobia	Politicians
Polyphobia	Many things
Polyphobia	Things, many
Porphyrophobia	Color purple
Porphyrophobia	Purple, color
Potamophobia	Running water
Potainphobia or potamophobia	Rivers
Prosophobia	Progress
Psellistnophobia	Stuttering
Psvchophobia	Mind
Pteronophobia	Feathers or being tickled by feathers
Pupaphobia	Puppets
R	
Radiophobia	Radiation or X-rays
Radiophobia	X-rays or radiation
Rectophobia	Disease, rectal
Rhabdophobia	Beaten by a rod or instrument of punishment, or of being severely criticized
Rhabdophobia	Criticized severely, or beaten by rod or instrument of punishment
Rhabdophobia	Punishment by a rod or other instrument, or of being severely criticized
Rhypophobia	Filth or dirt
Rhypophobia or rupophobia	Dirt or filth
Rhytiphobia	Wrinkles, getting
Russophobia	Russians
S	
Samhainophobia	Halloween
Satanophobia	Satan
Scabiophobia	Scabies
Scelerophobia	Burglars, or being harmed by wicked persons

List of Phobias by Alphabet   **Fears**

Scelerophobia	Harmed by wicked persons; bad men or burglars
Scelerophobia	Men, bad or burglars or being harmed by wicked persons
Sciophobia or sciaphobia	Shadows
Scoleciphobia	Worms
Scolionophobia	School
Scopophobia or scoptophobia	Self, being seen or looked at
Scotomaphobia	Blindness in a visual field
Scriptophobia	Writing in public
Selaphobia	Light flashes
Selenophobia	Moon
Seplophobia	Decaying matter
Seplophobia	Matter, decaying
Siderodromophobia	Railroads or train travel
Siderodromophobia	Trains, railroads or train travel
Siderophobia or astrophobia	Stars
Sinistrophobia	Left-handed; objects at the left side of the body
Sinophobia	Chinese or Chinese culture
Sitophobia or sitiophobia	Eating or food
Sitophobia or sitiophobia	Food or eating
Soceraphobia	Parents-in-law
Social Phobia	Social (fear of being evaluated negatively in social situations)
Sociophobia	People in general or society
Somniphobia	Sleep
Sophophobia	Learning
Soteriophobia	Dependence on others
Soteriophobia	Others, dependence on
Spacephobia	Outer space
Spacephobia	Space, outer
Spectrophobia	Ghosts or specters
Spectrophobia	Specters or ghosts
Spermatophobia or spermophobia	Semen

List of Phobias by Alphabet   **Fears**

Spheksophobia	Wasps
Stasibasiphobia	Standing up and walking
Stasiphobia	Standing up
Staurophobia	Crosses or the crucifix
Staurophobia	Crucifix, the or crosses
Stenophobia	Narrow things or places
Stenophobia	Places or things, narrow
Stenophobia	Things or places, narrow
Symbolophobia	Symbolism
Svngenesophobia	Relatives
T	
Tachophobia	Speed
Taeniophobia	Tapeworms
Taphephobia or taphophobia	Buried alive, being or cemeteries
Taphephobia or taphophobia	Cemeteries or being buried alive
Tapinophobia	Objects, small
Taurophobia	Bulls
Technophobia	Technology
Teleophobia	Ceremonies, religious
Teleophobia	Religious ceremonies
Teratophobia	Child, bearing a deformed; deformed people
Teratophobia	Deformed people or bearing a deformed child
Teratophobia	People, deformed or bearing a deformed child
Testophobia	Tests, taking
Tetanophobia	Lockjaw or tetanus
Tetanophobia	Tetanus or lockjaw
Textophobia	Fabrics, certain
Thalassophobia	Ocean or sea
Thalassophobia	Sea or ocean
Thanatophobia	Death or dying
Thanatophobia	Dying or death
Theatrophobia	Theaters

List of Phobias by Alphabet | **Fears**

List of Phobias by Alphabet	Fears
Theologicophobia	Theology,
Theophobia	Gods or religion
Theophobia	Religion or gods
Thermophobia	
Tomophobia	Operation, surgical
'comophobia	Surgical operations
Topophobia	Places, certain
Topophobia	Situations, certain
Topophobia	Stage fright
Toxiphobia, toxophobia, or toxicophobia	Poisoned, being
Traumatophobia	Injury
Trichinophobia	Trichinosis
Triskadekaphobia	Number r3
Tropophobia	Moving or making changes
Tropophobia or metathesiophobia	Changes, making; moving
Trypanophobia	Injections
Ttremophobia	Trembling
Tyrannophobia	Tyrants
U	
Urophobia	Urine or urinating
V	
Vaccinophobia	Vaccination
Verminophobia	Germs
Vestiphobia	Clothing
Virginitiphobia	Rape
Vitricophobia	Stepfather
W	
Wiccaphobia	Witches and witchcraft
X	
Xanthophobia	Color yellow
Xanthophobia	Yellow color
Xenophobia	Foreigners or strangers
Xenophobia	Strangers or foreigners
Xenophobia	Dryness

List of Phobias by Alphabet   Fears

Xylophobia	Forests or wooden objects
Xylophobia	Wooden objects or forests
Z	
Zelophobia	Jealousy
Zemmiphobia	Rat, great mole
Zeusophobia	God or gods
Zoophobia	Animals

INDEX

Index Notes
fig. following a page number
indicates a figure or diagram
The abbreviation SET refers to
Spiritual Euphoric Therapy

described, 34, 44, 106, 114, 128, 136, 142, 175, 185
in the workplace, 75, 84, 88
life maintenance wheel, 117, 118, 185
NEW START program, 185, 186, 191
principles,17, 19, 22, 29, 30, 38-40, 44, 55, 69, 71, 75, 81, 93, 97, 115, 117, 122, 123, 126, 129, 130, 132, 135, 142, 150, 154, 156-158, 162, 174, 176, 178, 181, 183-185, 191, 193, 198-201, 203, 204
time-frame release capsule, 117, 122, 153
spiritual psychotherapy, 29, 202
Stalin, Joseph, 148-149
Stein, Marvin, 40
Strategic Defense Initiative (SDI), 150
Swinburne, Algernon C., 37
syndromatic stress, 40
Tadajoni E., 181
temperance, 170, 189, 190, 191
therapies, traditional, 115, 126, 131, 96, 120
Adlerian, 129, 130
avoidance, 24, 26,123, 124, 131
behavior, 125, 126
existential, 130
Gestalt, 131
head-on, 124, 125
Jungian, 129
person-centered, 130
psychoanalytic, 128
rational emotive, 125, 126
re-design, 126
reality, 125

transactional, 131
time-frame release capsule, 117, 122, 153
See also Spiritual Euphoric
Therapy (SET), 29, 97,113, 115, 118, 138, 142, 153, 170, 185, 187, 190-192, 198, 199
Time Trap, 176
transactional analysis, 131
traveling, fear of, 48, 61, 178, 179
Trotsky, Leon, 148
trust, 19, 46, 62, 78, 84, 89, 90, 94, 95, 100, 102, 103-105, 116, 118, 130, 145, 162, 168, 174, 177, 179, 181, 183, 184, 191-193, 195, 198, 201, 202
Understanding and Comparing
Counseling Therapies, 126
unfaithfulness, 172, 179
vitamin D, 188, 189, 198
Wagner, Lilya, 140
Waterman, Robert, Jr., 134
White, Ellen, 118
Whitehead, Barbara D., 95, 96
Winckler, Suzanne, 188
women, 18, 26, 62, 81, 84, 94-107, 109-111, 171
and intimacy, 62, 105, 107, 108, 131
workplace, 22, 75, 84, 88
corporate culture, 133, 200
World War II fears, 148-150
worry, 25, 30, 37, 40, 41, 57, 68, 123, 137, 175, 179

www.ingramcontent.com/pod-product-compliance
Lightning Source LLC
Chambersburg PA
CBHW022046020426
42335CB00012B/575